Spd Rdng
The Speed Reading Bible

37 Techniques, Tips and Strategies For Ultra Fast Reading (including Study Skills, Memory and Accelerated Learning)
by
SUSAN NORMAN & JAN CISEK

The Speed Reading Bible: easy speed-reading skills with proven results for you to apply immediately to any reading material (books, reports, journals, manuals, textbooks, online texts, ebooks, etc) so you can **read more, more quickly,** more effectively, whether you are a **professional**, an entrepreneur, a **student** or **teacher**, a home educator, or simply interested in your own learning and **personal development**, in any subject (including business, medicine, law, IT, acting and **languages**), by showing you, among other things, how to use your eyes more efficiently, **remember more**, access your learning intelligence, take meaning from the minimum of input, **focus** on your **purpose**, find the hot spots of information you need, and put it all into practice, with the result that you **free up time** and **save money** as you **become more successful** in business and in life.

Saffire PRES

First published as an ebook October 2010
This edition published 2013 (Version 3.3)
by
Saffire Press,
Loufenway, East Lane, Wheathampstead, Herts AL4 9BP, UK
information@saffirepress.co.uk
www.saffirepress.co.uk

Contact authors
Susan Norman susan@spdrdng.com
Jan Cisek jan@spdrdng.com
www.spdrdng.com

ISBN 978-1-90156-412-9

Printed on paper with a certificate from the Forest Stewardship Council (FSC).

**This book is dedicated to you
– the Spd Rdr**

TABLE OF CONTENTS

PRACTICE TEXTS 118

MORE ABOUT READING 140

GLOSSARY/INDEX 156

EXPERT TIP

While you're learning, use well-written books you can understand easily – it will give you confidence in your new approach to reading. Once you've mastered all the techniques, you will be able to apply them to any written material – including books, journals, reports and articles, both on- and off-line.

INTRODUCTION
AND HOW TO USE THIS BOOK

Welcome to Spd Rdng – a collection of techniques we know will both speed up your reading and allow you to process material 10 times faster, or even more.

If you read the book in order, you will effectively be following our two-day workshop, but many of the techniques, insights and suggestions are self-standing so feel free to read them in the order which makes most sense to you (there's a lot of cross-referencing in case you need to check out something which has been presented earlier). But however you approach the book, we strongly suggest that you actually try things out as you go. As we say in the book, reading is just the first step; it's only useful if you put the information into practice.

If you haven't got time to read the whole book at the moment, then the techniques which will make the biggest immediate difference to your reading are:
#1 Apply skills you already have
#2 Preview
#3 Don't think 'reading', think 'finding information'
#4 Have a clear purpose for reading
#5 Apply the 80/20 rule to your reading
#6 Read the message not the words
#14 Get in a good state for reading
#17 Take notes with mindmaps and rhizomaps
#18 Have 20-minute work sessions
Plus the Underlining technique (p 12)

We've tried to make it as easy as possible for you to pick up and review the ideas:
1) the titles of the techniques are self-explanatory
2) each of the techniques is summarised at the beginning of its section
3) there is an extensive and helpful glossary/index
4) we give examples of people's actual experience – including our own
5) there are 'expert tips' throughout which will give you extra help

Enough for now. But if you feel you'd like to get in touch with us at any point, feel free to contact us through our website: www.spdrdng.com

Enjoy!
Susan and Jan

What do you want from your improved reading?

Most people say that they want to 'read faster' – and you will learn ways of doing that in this book. However, what they also mean is that they want to 'save time' and 'get through many more books'. And when they think about it, they also want other things.

DO IT NOW **Highlight/tick which of the following you would like from this book. Add other reading skills you want too.**

- ☐ reading faster
- ☐ saving time by using more effective strategies
- ☐ finding information I need quickly
- ☐ getting the gist of what a book is about
- ☐ getting the detail as well as the gist
- ☐ reading more efficiently and effectively
- ☐ synthesizing information from a variety of sources
- ☐ understanding what I read
- ☐ organising the information so I can apply it
- ☐ retaining/remembering/being able to recall the information
- ☐ articulating the information (speaking or writing about it)
- ☐ building up my expertise in a subject quickly
- ☐ improving my concentration
- ☐ keeping motivated while I'm reading
- ☐ feeling confident in my reading ability
- ☐ reading critically – not just accepting everything I read
- ☐ ignoring information I don't need
- ☐ applying all of this online
- ☐ increasing my vocabulary
- ☐ passing tests
- ☐ enjoying the process

- ☐ ....

- ☐ ....

- ☐ ....

- ☐ ....

- ☐ ....

You'll get it all – and more – with spd rdng!

What is your current reading speed?

If you'd like to find out your current reading speed, or judge how much more quickly you're reading after implementing the spd rdng techniques, then do the following test before you start reading.

You need:
- an accurate timer/alarm clock
- a book you haven't read (and won't read until you've finished Spd Rdng) – with mostly continuous text
- possibly a calculator and post-it notes

FIRST TEST / Before
Make a note of the title ....

Choose a place to start reading, eg the start of any chapter, and mark it (eg with a post-it note).
Set your timer to five minutes.
Start reading at your normal pace, making sure that you understand what you are reading.
Stop reading when the timer goes off and mark your stopping place.

Starting page .... Finishing page ....
Number of pages/words/lines read ....

Calculate your reading speed (before//after) as follows:
- Number of pages read ....//............................
  (this figure is enough for most people, but if you want to be more accurate, continue with the following calculations)
- Average number of lines on a page ....//................
  (count the number of lines on a typical page)
- Average number of words on a line ....//................
  (choose three full lines, count the number of words in each, add them together and divide by three)
- Number of words read in five minutes ....//...............
  (multiply together the three previous calculations – pages x lines x words)
- Reading speed in words per minute (wpm)
  ....//...............
  (divide by five the number of words read in five minutes)
OR
If you are using the Spd Rdng texts in this book, note the number of words read and divide by 5.

By the way ...

You can use the 'Practice texts' or 'More about reading' section at the back of the book to check your reading speed. We have already counted the words for you.

SECOND TEST / After

Do the test again after you've worked with the spd rdng techniques in this book. For an accurate result, make sure you have actually tried out the techniques in this book, not just read about them.

Prepare to repeat the test again. Use the same book, but start in a different place.

Before you begin, make sure you:

- speed up your brain by super-duper-reading 10 or more pages from your test book (#13)
- open your peripheral vision by focusing on your concentration point (#10)
- get into a good state by taking a deep breath and smiling

Do the test (but, for test accuracy, do not test yourself on pages you have super-duper-read).

Starting page ………… Finishing page …………
Number of pages/words/lines read ………………

Afterwards, note how much more quickly you are reading: ………

Additionally, as you will know by now, spd rdng is much more than just reading more quickly – so note down at least three other techniques which will save you time:

1 ……………………………………………………………………………………

2 ……………………………………………………………………………………

3 ……………………………………………………………………………………

By the way …

When testing your reading speed and whenever you're working with books, always go at your best comprehension speed – as fast as you can while being able to understand what you're reading.

QUICK TEST

Many of the individual techniques in this book can dramatically increase your reading speed. Where we recommend that you test yourself, do so by reading at a comfortable speed with comprehension for **one minute** with a timer before you try the technique – and compare it with a one-minute read (still with comprehension) using the technique.

Checklist – what sort of reader are you now?

Before you start reading the techniques in this book, you might like to think about the sort of reader you consider yourself to be right now. Tick/highlight the statements in both lists that describe you as a reader. Just go with your first reaction. There are no right or wrong answers – what matters is your opinion of yourself. You will learn things about yourself that will help you to become a much more effective reader.

List 1
- ☐ I am a poor reader.
- ☐ Reading is a chore. I put it off as long as possible.
- ☐ I often feel overwhelmed by the amount I've got to read.
- ☐ I read really slowly.
- ☐ I don't like to mark or write in my books.
- ☐ I feel I might miss something if I don't read from cover to cover.
- ☐ I always read in the same way, no matter what I'm reading.
- ☐ I worry that I won't remember what I've read.
- ☐ I get bogged down in detail before I've understood the big picture.
- ☐ I think I am or may be dyslexic.

If any of the statements in List 1 describes you, this book will help.

List 2
- ☐ I love reading.
- ☐ I read a lot.
- ☐ I can find key information quickly.
- ☐ I use a variety of techniques for different material.
- ☐ I'm familiar with the 80/20 rule, and with thin slicing, and I apply these concepts to reading.
- ☐ I happily ignore information that is not relevant or that I already know.
- ☐ I can usually decide quickly how useful a book is to me.
- ☐ I have strategies which mean I usually remember what is important to me.
- ☐ I always know why I am reading before I start.
- ☐ I want to improve the way I read.

If you answered yes to 8 or more of the statements in List 2, you may already be a natural spd rdr. You may also be surprised to find that this book can give you new insights into how to read and learn even more effectively.

Once you have read and started applying the techniques in this book, you might like to return to this page and tick/highlight (or untick/unhighlight) some of the statements!

Double your reading speed – right now

If the only thing you want is to double your reading speed, then learn the underlining technique here. It takes about five minutes.

For learning purposes, choose a book with extended lengths of uninterrupted text. Alternatively use the 'Practice texts' or the 'More about reading' section at the back of the book.

Compare your 'before' and 'after' reading speed by doing the **QUICK TEST** (p 9).

To learn the underlining technique

1   Place your finger below the first line of text. Read five or six lines of text with comprehension at your normal speed, underlining the words with your finger as you do so. (This is to make sure you are reading the words and not looking at your finger.)

2   On the next page, still using your finger as a marker, start reading about one centimetre into each line and stop reading about one centimetre before the end of the line. This means that you're not underlining or looking consciously at the words in the first centimetre or last of each line, but realise that you can still understand the text (you can pick up the words at either end of the line in your peripheral vision). Read in this way, with comprehension at your normal speed, to the end of the page.

3   Still starting and ending one centimetre into the line (ie underlining and reading just the centre words in each line), use your finger to set the pace – and the pace is one second per line. 'Read' to the bottom of the page at this speed, looking at the words above your finger. Don't worry about understanding the text. You shouldn't. The aim here is simply to speed up your eyes and brain. Just keep up the pace.

4   Continue at the pace of one second per line for about 10 or 12 pages. After four or five pages, begin to notice words and phrases as you skim past them. Your aim is not to understand at this pace so keep going quickly – do not slow down.

5   If you are testing your before and after speed, you are about to do your second test, so mark your starting point from where you have just stopped. Set your timer. Smile. Start reading at your best comprehension speed. Underline as much of the line as necessary and read at a speed which allows you to comprehend what you are reading.

Most people find that they have at least doubled their reading speed just with this one technique.

Underlining is one of the speed reading patterns – there are several more (#15). But although it is very useful to be able to read quickly, reading faster is only part of the picture. If you put the other techniques in the book into practice, not only can you further increase your reading speed, but you should also be able to process textual material about 10 times more efficiently, while also retaining and using what you have read much more effectively.

Remember, it doesn't matter how much faster you get if you're going in the wrong direction to start with. You might be the fastest driver, but a slightly slower driver who knows the shortcuts will get to the destination first. Why not take a look at the other spd rdng strategies and see how quickly you can reach your destination?

THE 37 SPD RDNG TECHNIQUES

Apply skills you already have

SUMMARY *You can immediately read more effectively simply by applying skills you already have:*
* *get a book's message by reading it like a newspaper*
* *get specific information by using the book like a dictionary*

Use books, don't let books use you.

Remember, you are not starting from nothing. You already have skills which you apply to reading. You already know how to extract information quickly and easily from newspapers, dictionaries, emails, etc. Start thinking about how you can use your existing skills more effectively by applying them to books.

Do you read each of these in the same way? If not (hopefully not), then think about what you do with them; how you actually read them. Compare your insights with our suggestions.

* **Newspapers**
* **Dictionaries**
* **Poems and novels**
* **Emails**
* **Factual books**

Newspapers
People rarely pick up a newspaper and read it from the first page to the last without skipping anything. Typically they go quickly through the paper looking at headlines and picture captions. They choose one or two articles or sections which interest them to read in more detail. They might go directly to a section that interest them. They do not hesitate to omit sections which are irrelevant to them, nor to stop reading if they are no longer getting the information they want. And they throw it away – even if they haven't read everything. To find out what a book is about, read it as if it's a newspaper.

Dictionaries
When you use a dictionary (or any other reference book), you look up a word and then close the book. If you simply want to find specific information in a book, you do not have to read the whole thing. Use the index or contents page, or flick through the book looking at chapter headings, etc, to find it. When you have found the information you need, close the book and put it back on the shelf until you need it again.

> **99** *Although we usually refer to getting information from books, the spd rdng techniques work on all kinds of reading materials: reports, online reading, ebooks, journals, etc. Check out also 'reading for pleasure' and 'digital and online reading' in the end section: 'More about reading'.*

EXPERT TIP

If you want to understand a book's message, read it in the same way as you read newspapers.

EXPERT TIP

Look up specific information you need from a book as if it were a dictionary.

Poems and novels

Poems and novels are usually read for pleasure (in leisure time). It is likely therefore that you will be happy to read them slowly, particularly if you want to savour the language, or get engrossed in the story. You may even wish to read poetry aloud to enjoy the sound of the words. So when reading for pleasure or leisure purposes, read in any way you like and as quickly or slowly as you please. (When *studying* poems and novels, use the techniques in this book.)

Emails

You are probably already confident about sorting through emails quickly, deleting the spam, scanning through for relevant information, filing, and acting on those which are urgent or which can be dealt with very quickly. This approach is particularly relevant to looking quickly through reports, legal summaries, contracts, etc, to find out first what is important. If necessary, you can look at relevant details afterwards.

EXPERT TIP

Do not try to read for leisure and for information at the same time. Pleasure always wins.

The techniques in this book also work for **online/digital texts**, but most people are already applying many of these techniques to digital reading. It's usually a case of transferring digital skills to books, journals, reports, etc.

Factual books

The spd rdng techniques are largely designed to help you get the information you need from factual books which you do not particularly want to read for pleasure. If you are enjoying the content, then you can read it slowly as leisure reading. However, if you want to retain the information, you need to apply the other spd rdng techniques. You'll find there's a different sort of pleasure – pleasurable satisfaction – to be had from being in control of your reading and getting information quickly and easily from books.

EXPERT TIP

Transfer the skills you already use for reading emails and online to other materials.

By the way ...

In addition to these specific strategies, remember that you are already in the habit of reading different things differently. We encourage you to do more of it more consciously. If you're not convinced, just think how you read the following: a thriller, a love letter, a 'keep off the grass' sign a recipe, a journal relevant to your job, a text from a friend, a letter from your bank about your overdraft, a letter from your bank about their new accounts, a religious book (eg the Bible, the Koran), a train timetable, a magazine in the dentist's waiting room ... the list is endless. The key is to read at the **appropriate** speed.

Preview before you start reading

02

SUMMARY *Spend 2 to 5 minutes looking through the book, finding out what it's about before you start reading. Just this one technique can save you hours of time and money (by identifying books you don't have to read or buy).*

It's amazing how many people decide to buy or read a book based simply on its title, cover or subject matter. They buy it without even opening it. Then once they've started reading, they somehow feel obliged (to whom?) to continue reading to the end.

You no longer need to waste time like that. Just because a book's on your subject, it doesn't mean it's a good book. Previewing helps you recognise the difference between good and bad books before you've spent time reading them all the way through.

The purpose of previewing is to find out in general what the book is about and to enable you to decide:
- whether or not to buy/borrow/read it
- what useful information you can get from it (your purpose)
- how long it's worth spending on it (or whether it's a book of reference that you'll want to go back to several times)

HOW TO preview
- open the book and **flick backwards and forwards** through it two or three times to get a feel for it, noticing the **layout**, size of font, any graphs, pictures, illustrations, captions, etc
- quickly read the **cover blurb** front and back (but be aware that this is written by the publishers to try to sell the book and it is not always accurate)
- check the **date** of publication (this is crucial for subjects which go out of date quickly, such as computing or quantum physics)
- read the **contents list**, and look through the book at chapter **titles** and **headings**
- look through the **index** for key terms and ideas which are relevant to you (notice how many entries there are for relevant terms – check this book to see which techniques we think are most important)
- **search** for something you know should be covered about this subject
- evaluate the **credibility** of the author and the dependability of the information – and, if relevant, the people who recommended it to you
- check the **bibliography** for credibility and for possible sources of further information

99 *You can't judge a book by its cover."*

- check for chapter **summaries** (a quick source of key information) – in particular check the first and last chapters and the begninings and ends of chapters
- open the book at random and **read a couple of paragraphs** to judge the style of writing

Not all books have all these parts (eg summaries, index), but look for them, and look through them if appropriate.

As you preview, you can be ...
- thinking what you anticipate learning from this book. Why spend time on it? What do you want out of it?
- deciding how easy it's going to be to access the information you want
- thinking how much you already know of what's in the book
- noticing What's missing? What do you need that isn't in this book?
- deciding whether to buy/borrow/read the book, or not.

At any stage, if you discover you've got the wrong book for what you need, put it down and find another. If you decide to go ahead, you will already have gained a good overview of what the book's about and what information it contains.

Previewing digitally and online The previewing procedure for digital books or online texts is basically the same as for hard copy material. Remember to check online reviews. As soon as you've identified key terms, use your search facility to find things more quickly, and you can use your scroll function to look quickly through text.

Purpose If you've decided to go ahead, then decide (as part of your previewing time)
- What is your purpose? (#4) Why are you going to read this book? What information do you want from it? What will you **do** with the information you get?
- How much time is it worth spending on this book?

Preview a study reading list
Sometimes books are prescribed (eg for a course of study), so you have no option about which ones to read. However, as a student, spend a couple of days before your course previewing all the books on your reading list. You'll be amazed at how much you learn about your subject and about where to find information when you need it – and it's an excellent way of getting an overview (#25) of a new subject.

Getting through the book pile!
The more books you preview, the easier it becomes to decide how useful or valuable they are to you. Most of us have got a

---

Jan's experience

Jan regularly spends an hour or two in a bookshop just previewing 15 to 25 books – after which he might buy one or two. The only books he regrets buying are the ones he buys online without having previewed them.

pile of books we feel we need to get through. So why not start by previewing all the books or journals on your bookshelves (and bedside table)? It's a great way to discover where to find information you might need at a future date and to help you feel comfortable about all the material you've got to read. A lot of information will also be going into your non-conscious mind and long-term memory (see #29).

Thin slicing

The aim when you're reading a book for factual information is to get as much information as possible by reading as few words as possible. (What Malcolm Gladwell calls 'thin-slicing' in his book 'Blink'.) Previewing is an excellent start to this whole process.

How would you cut a cake in order to find out what it's like? Obviously you'd cut a thin slice vertically (hence thin-slicing). But for many people, the way they read a book (chapter by chapter) is like eating a cake one horizontal layer at a time. You have to eat almost the whole thing in order to be sure what the cake is like. Not very efficient – and you don't really even get the full experience of the cake!

DO IT NOW

Practise your previewing skills on this Spd Rdng book. You've got a maximum of five minutes, starting now.

Don't think 'reading', think 'finding information'

SUMMARY *Change your mindset from 'how many books I've read' (quantity) to 'how much information I've got' (quality). If you think about using books to look for information, you will approach them differently.*

When you are reading factual books (rather than reading for leisure), it is important to realise that what you are doing is 'looking for information'. You are in the same business as Google, and it is not necessary or desirable to 'read' in the traditional way in order to access information. Once you decide that what you are really doing is looking for information, it can be easier to put many of the other techniques in this book into practice.

Consider these two statements:
> *'I read 20 books.'*
> *'I got all the information I needed to complete the task really quickly.'*

Reading a lot of books (the first statement) sounds quite good initially, but then you might question, 'Were they the right books?' 'How much of the information they contained was relevant?' 'What did I do with all the information I read?' 'How much do I remember?' 'Was the amount of time and effort worth the result?' Getting the information you need is what helps you achieve your goals.

Change your thinking
from the **quantity** of reading
to the **quality** of information.

Additionally, when you start thinking about what you're going to **do** with the information you get, your reading will become more productive. It doesn't matter how many books you read about swimming, you can't swim until you get in the water.

Consider getting the information elsewhere
Remember there may be other sources or ways for getting the information you want. Does a summary exist? Maybe there's a simpler (or more detailed) or better-written book more suited to your purpose. Or maybe you can get information online? Or from a mentor? Is it worth giving this book shelf-space? Is it worth committing time and money to it?

Have a clear purpose for reading

SUMMARY *Know what you want to get from a book before you start reading. Are you reading for pleasure (doing what pleases you) or for information? If you're reading for information, set your purpose, which will either be*
a) *to find specific information, or*
b) *to discover its message, what it's about.*

Although it may seem obvious, it is important to know **why** you are reading a book. What is your purpose? What information do you want? What do you want to do with that information? You wouldn't call a meeting without having an agenda. Reading a book without a purpose is like calling a meeting to discuss whatever anyone thinks is useful.

Information or leisure?
The first distinction is to note whether you are reading for information or reading as a leisure pursuit. Don't try to do both at the same time. Pleasure will always win. Besides, using the spd rdng techniques to get on top of your reading brings a different sort of pleasure or satisfaction. (See 'Reading for pleasure' p 142)

Reading purpose or life goal?
Do not confuse your purpose for reading the book with your bigger goals in life:
- pass an exam = *life goal*
- get info to write essay = *reading purpose*
- get rich = *life goal*
- find six principles for investing = *reading purpose*
- find six ways I can money = *reading purpose*
- find six ways I can save money = *reading purpose*

Message or specific information?
Once you have established that you are reading for information, there are two basic purposes for working with a text:
- looking for **specific information** which you know (or hope) you will find in the book – this is called **scanning** or the **dictionary** approach
- finding out a book's message, what it is about – **skimming**, or the **newspaper** approach. Once you know what the book is about, any subsequent purpose with the book will be looking for information (scanning) – it becomes a book of reference.

Note that 'skimming' and 'scanning' are terms which refer to purpose rather than ways of reading. Skimming requires that you approach a book as you would a newspaper. Scanning requires

> **"** *If you're not sure why you're doing something, you can never do enough of it."*
> *David Allen*
> *'Getting Things Done'.*

that you approach the book as you would a dictionary or a book of reference. What you actually do with both skimming and scanning will be very similar, eg use the contents and index, look quickly down a page for key information, etc.

Have a SMART purpose
In business, people are often told to set a 'SMART' purpose. This applies to reading too.

SMART stands for: **S**pecific
Measurable
Achievable
Real
Timed

Evaluating your purpose
Having decided that you want to read a book, you set a purpose. You then check your purpose against the SMART criteria – in reverse order:

Timed We recommend that you work with a book in blocks of 20 minutes (#18) – so set your time limit at 20 minutes and stick to time (#23). If you are working with several books in a syntopic processing session (#22) your time limit will be 75 minutes.

T can also stand for **Timely.** A purpose is always stronger when you have an immediate need for information. Read what you need. However we also encourage reading as much as possible in order to build up a good 'background knowledge' of relevant subjects (This is your 'schema' – how much you know about a subject or the world. The more you know, the easier is to absorb new information.)

Real Don't make up a reason for reading a book which isn't real. Make sure you're reading because you need something from the book. If in doubt, ask yourself 'What's in it for me?' (WIIFM?) What do I want to do with the information? How will this help me? In what circumstances? When?

R could also stand for **Relevant**. Is this information relevant to me now? Ask yourself, 'In what context will I use this information?'

R is sometimes said to stand for 'realistic'. We think 'realistic' is too close in meaning to 'achievable' and not particularly helpful. Only when your purpose is real are you going to achieve best results from your reading.

EXPERT TIP

When you are given 'comprehension questions' to check your understanding of a text, always read the questions first and treat them as your purpose. Read the text only to answer the questions.

Achievable You want to get as much information as possible in the time, but your purpose must be achievable/realistic. Don't be tempted to look for more than one thing at a time; it will slow you down. What you can achieve in a fixed time frame depends on such things as how well you already know the subject, how well the material is presented, etc. With practice you will realise just how much you can achieve in a short space of time, which will enable you to adjust your purpose to fit the time.

Measurable If something is not measurable, it is very hard to know whether or not you have achieved it. If possible ask for a specific number, eg 'six time-management techniques which I can immediately put into practice at work'. Going for a specific number of techniques also encourages you to keep to a time limit and to keep moving on to look for more information. Six techniques or ideas is a good number for a 20-minute session.

Specific The clearer and more tightly-defined your purpose, the more information you are likely to get from the material. The more general your purpose, or having more than one purpose, the less information you are likely to get. Strangely, you'll find with experience that less really is more.

Clearly define the **context** in which you will use the information – it makes it easier for your brain to recognise what you need. 'I want to be a better actor' is too general. 'I want to learn six techniques for making this specific character [give name] more believable in this play [give name]' is specific and therefore achievable. You absorb the information more readily when it is in context, here relating to a specific character. (You learn techniques for different sorts of characters as and when you need to portray them – and gradually you build up your repertoire with experience.)

If you want to know things about 'people', then set your purpose to discover information first about yourself – then about a specific person you know. It's easier to understand information in relation to one specific person, situation or context than in the abstract. It gives your mind something to hold on to and it's more memorable.

If in doubt, ask yourself, 'What will I **do** with the information?'

99 *The man who chases two rabbits catches neither."*
Chinese proverb

BAD PURPOSE vs GOOD PURPOSE

Consider the difference between bad and good purposes for reading books (you'll find more examples in the section on syntopic processing (#22):

X Bad purpose   To learn about decision making (vague)
V Good purpose   To identify six strategies that will enable me to make good decisions at work

X Bad purpose   To pass my exam (general goal)
V Good purpose   To mindmap the information to write this essay (give title)

X Bad purpose   To improve my understanding of this computer software program (too vague)
V Good purpose   To identify and use the sequence of commands to complete one specific job using this program (preferably while working at the computer)

X Bad purpose   To learn Spanish (vague; this is a goal)
V Good purpose   To identify six similarities and six differences between English and Spanish; or to identify 10 new Spanish verbs and how they're used

X Bad purpose   Because my teacher told me to
V Good purpose   (If possible find out why your teacher wants you to know this information, but if you can't then make your best guess ...) To write down six important bits of information from this book/chapter

X The worst purpose   To know everything in this book ('everything' is not an efficient filter for your brain)
V Good purpose   To write down the key message of this book and six other important points

V Good purpose   To read this book slowly in bed to help me switch off before I go to sleep

One of the most common mistakes beginners make when stating their purpose is to start listing all the things they want to find from their reading. Although this isn't a bad thing (they're just pre-empting the 20-minute session), it's not necessary. Your purpose is, for example, 'to find six things ... (whatever they may be)'. You do not have to list in advance of your 20-minute session what those six things will be.

YES BUT ...

What if I start working with the book and discover that I've got the wrong purpose?

You can change your purpose at any time if you discover that the book doesn't contain what you expected – or you can stop reading the book and find one that does fulfil your purpose.

I can't identify a purpose

If you can't immediately think of a good purpose for reading the book, ask yourself the following questions until you can identify your purpose:

- Why am I reading this book? (eg for information, for leisure purposes)
- What information do I need from it?
- What do I want to do with the information? How will I put it into practice? In what context? (eg write a report, prepare for an exam question, manage my time better at work)
- Do I really want to spend my time reading this book? Is there something better I could be doing or a better book I could be reading?
- Do I need all the information in this book, or will it be enough (at this stage) just to do a five-minute preview, or just to get some of the information?
- If my purpose is to 'find out what is in this book' (so that I can have a more specific purpose) or even 'to define my purpose', what's the minimum amount of information I need in order to achieve that?
- Default purpose: to find six interesting things in this book that I can tell x [name person]

Priming your non-conscious mind

Having a clear purpose is like giving your brain a filter for the information. As you read, your brain can notice that 'this is important' or 'this is not relevant'. Otherwise all the information seems to be of equal value – and it's more difficult to find things to take note of and remember. Your purpose acts like a magnifying glass for the important information.

Have you ever noticed how something you've never heard of before comes to your attention, and within the next week or so you hear about it in two or three other contexts? Or how you buy a car and every other car on the road seems to be the same as yours? This is because you've signalled to your non-conscious mind (your learning mind) that you're interested in something, you've primed your brain, and whenever it notices that thing over the next period of time, it brings it to your conscious awareness. Presumably those things were there anyway, but previously you might not have noticed them consciously.

Martin's BIGGEST learning

"That it's a good idea to know WHY I'm reading something. (I can't believe now that I didn't know that!)" It took me quite a while to understand what a 'good purpose' is, but now, whenever I pick up a book, I automatically think about my purpose. 'What do I want?' Sometimes my purpose is just to find out whether a book has anything in it that I might need – but knowing that is enough to stop me spending unnecessary time reading books I don't need! And if I only want one bit of information from a book, then I only spend the time it takes to get that one bit of information.

If you prime your non-conscious mind with your purpose for reading a book, then it will help you notice things relevant to that purpose. Strangely, you also notice a lot of other things too – because your mind is evaluating everything to sort information into 'relevant' and 'non-relevant' categories. ('Relevant' and 'not relevant' are also useful ways of consciously categorising information as you read.)

With practice you will probably be able to achieve several purposes at one time, but when you first start you will notice many more benefits if you set one very precise purpose each time you work with a book. This is only a purpose for a 20-minute session – after which you can always set another work session. How do you eat an elephant? One bite a time. How do you get a large amount of information? In manageable chunks.

Bertrand Russell was amusing but wrong when he said, *'There are two reasons for reading a book –*
one, so you can enjoy it,
two, so you can boast about it.'

The two main reasons are actually
one, for enjoyment
two, for information.
Don't try to do both at the same time.

Apply the 80/20 rule to your purpose

SUMMARY *When you apply the 80/20 rule to reading, you realise that*
a) *in general, 80% of the meaning of a book is contained in about 20% of the words, and*
b) *if you are satisfied with achieving 80% of your purpose, then you can achieve five times as much in the time available (ie you can achieve four other purposes to 80% in the time you save).*

The 80/20 rule (in *'Living the 80/20 way'* by Richard Koch) states that approximately 20% of the effort we expend produces 80% of the results we can expect. In order to produce the remaining 20% to reach '100% perfection', we have to spend a disproportionate amount of time (four times more).

In reading, we can easily get 80% of a book's message relatively quickly. Why not spend the 'remaining' time reading another four books?

Similarly, if we want to achieve a particular purpose, being content with achieving 80% of that purpose will leave lots of time to achieve four other purposes to that level. After all, 80% is more than enough to get you a first class honours degree in most subjects at Oxford University! How much more do you need?

Overcoming perfectionism
The main purpose of this approach is for you to let go of your desire for perfection. You can still go for perfection in your life goal – but realise that you can achieve that perfection more quickly by getting information five times faster, simply by applying the 80/20 rule. Be content that you have enough.

The least helpful saying for would-be perfectionists is 'if a job's worth doing, it's worth doing well'. If a job's worth doing, it's worth doing. How well it's worth doing it depends on the circumstances. You can quickly tidy a room without needing to spring clean, and if you haven't got time to spring clean it will probably still be worth tidying the room. There are many books which really do not warrant you spending much time on them, or which do not warrant spending time on them now. Conversely even if you've only got five minutes before a meeting, you can get a lot of information by reading quickly through relevant papers before the meeting starts.

> 99 *Celebrate any progress. Don't wait to get perfect."*
> Ann McGee Cooper

"The 80/20 rule. That I don't have to do everything perfectly or completely."

I now live my life by the 80/20 rule – work stuff, personal stuff, everything. I feel so much clearer and I get so much more done. And my reading's improved too.

YES BUT ...

We want our airline pilots and brain surgeons to be perfectionists. What happens if we need ALL the information in the book?

1 You don't need it all on the first reading – and you cannot expect to be an expert after reading one book. Start with the preview (#2). Then get an overview of the subject (#25). If necessary divide the task into numerous smaller tasks and be content with achieving 80% of your purpose with each of these tasks – focusing on the things which are most usual and which you are going to need most often. Then look up the final details as you need them.

2 Most things in life (jobs, subjects) consist of 80% of things which happen most of the time and 20% of things which happen occasionally. Learn the 80% of usual things first. Even brain surgeons do special preparation for uncommon procedures.

3 Remember that any one book is not the only source of information – and learning is not just from books. You can read all you like about swimming, but it's the practice of staying afloat and moving through the water that makes you a swimmer. Intersperse your reading with practical experience – then read more as you identify what you most need to know.

If you're still not completely convinced, then accept 80% of your purpose, and use rapid reading from cover to cover (#24) to quickly glean any remaining information. And by the way, in most books the message is carried by even less than 20% of the words. The key is to find the words that carry the bulk of the meaning (hot spots #11).

The 80/20 rule

The 80/20 rule was named the 'Pareto principle' by business management thinker Joseph M Juran. The Italian economist Vilfredo Pareto observed in his garden that 80% of his peas were produced by 20% of peapods, which led him to notice that 80% of Italy's income went to 20% of the population.

A rule of thumb in business is that 80% of sales come from 20% of customers, while the remaining 80% of customers only generate 20% of income. The rule applies in many other aspects of life too:

- 80% of Hollywood films contain 30% of actors
- 80% of crime is committed by 20% of criminals
- 80% of decisions are made in 20% of the meeting time
- 80% of weblinks point to 15% of web pages
- 80% of a book's message is, in most cases, contained in less than 20% of the words

Read the message, not the words

06

SUMMARY *When you concentrate on the message and the meaning, it is not necessary to read every word in order to understand what the writer is saying.*

Reading is only partially to do with how your eyes work – it is much more to do with how your brain works. And what is important is that you understand the message, not that you have focused on every word that makes up that message.

It is rarely necessary to read every letter in a word, or every word in a sentence, in order to understand the message. There is a lot of predictability in language, so we can often guess what comes next – you've probably had the experience of turning over a page and knowing in advance what word comes next. Also our brains are designed to decipher messages – even when the information is incomplete. If you go for meaning rather than the form (words and letters), you will assimilate information more quickly.

This is what makes the difference between a well-written text and a badly-written text: in a well-written text you can easily predict what comes next, except when the author wants to surprise you! If you find you're reading word for word, ask yourself if it's the book's fault, not yours.

Today, with text messaging, many more people are used to making sense of non-standard text, so they are already predisposed to applying the same technique to reading standard text more quickly.

Notice how easy it is to understand the following example – and then think about how this might affect how you read 'normally'.

> **99** *I am not a speed reader. I am a speed understander."*
>
> *Isaac Asimov*

Cambridge

Aoccdrnig to rscheearch at Cmabrigde Uinervtisy, it deosn't mttaer in waht oredr the ltteers in a wrod are, the olny iprmoetnt tihng is taht the frist and lsat ltteer be at the rghit pclae. The rset can be a total mses and you can sitll raed it wouthit porbelm. Tihs is bcuseae the huamn mnid deos not raed ervey lteter by istlef, but the wrod as a wlohe. And you touhhgt taht spellnig was iprmoatnt!

If you read the 'Cambridge' text again as quickly as possible, you'll notice that the quicker you read it, the easier it is to get the meaning. This is because it's easier to understand the meaning of individual words (and sentences) when they are in the context of an idea – even with the additional challenge of misspelled words. Speeding up your reading will help with your comprehension.

Dyslexic?

By the way, if you think you are or might be 'dyslexic', the Cambridge example should reassure you that you can still become an excellent reader. You've already worked out your own strategies for reading – and you may well find that this book validates some of the things you have been doing anyway.

Reading word by word

Reading word by word in order to get the message is very inefficient. Not only does it mean that you are reading slowly, it is also more difficult to understand the meaning. **If – you – don't – believe – us – try – reading – this – section – aloud – slowly – one – word – at – a – time – and – see – how – much – more – difficult – it – is – to – get – a – clear – understanding – of – the – message.**

The habit of reading word by word is left over from the early days of learning to read when you were still working out how the letters built up to form words. Unfortunately, further reading skills are not routinely taught in schools, which means that you either have to work them out for yourself – some people come up with their own 'quicker reading system' – or master them from a course or a book like this.

Reading and writing share many common features and they are taught as if they're opposite sides of the same system. But writing is about setting down your thoughts, letter by letter, word by word. Although reading sometimes involves deciphering text word by word (eg complex ideas) or letter by letter (complex words), reading is primarily about recognising the message, which is best done by taking in large chunks of text at one time (see patterns #15).

Chunking for meaning

Many speed reading books and computer programs encourage you to build up your reading speed by reading several words at one time – two words, then three words, four, five, etc. However, chunking the text according to the number of words is completely arbitrary. Intelligent spd rdrs chunk according to meaning – which is how the brain makes sense of text. Notice the difference using this paragraph as an example:

Chunking every three words – difficult to understand:
Many speed reading
books and computer
programs encourage you
to build up
your reading speed
by reading several
words at one
time – two words,
then three words,
four, five, etc.

Chunking according to meaning – easy to understand:
Many speed reading books
and computer programs
encourage you
to build up your reading speed
by reading several words
at one time –
two words, then three words, four, five, etc.

Questioning

One way to encourage yourself to look for meaning is to ask yourself questions about the text. Question what you think it will be about in advance of reading, and the importance of different paragraphs and ideas. Having an alert, questioning mind is an optimal state (#14) for taking in new information.

DO IT NOW   Prediction

Do you notice how often when you're reading and turn a page that you know what the next word is going to be? If you were reading any of the following and they stopped at this point at the end of a page, could you predict the word at the beginning of the next page?
1. As they say, too many cooks spoil …
2. I've read every book Dickens …
3. She hated her nose so she had cosmetic …
4. And they all lived happily …
5. I know the question, but what's the …
6. He had blond, curly …
7. You'll never guess who I …
Even if you guess wrongly, the fact is you've made a guess. If your guess is correct, you speed up your reading. If you guess wrongly, you notice all the more strongly what the correct word is.

Answers 1 the broth 2 wrote 3 surgery 4 ever after 5 answer? 6 hair 7 saw /met /
bumped into (they all mean approximately the same thing)

> **99** *We see largely with the mind, and only partly with the eyes."*
> Dr W Bates

Smile – enjoy what you're reading

SUMMARY *Being in a happy, positive frame of mind makes it easier to take in information. Even faking a smile can have a similar effect.*

Your state can strongly affect how well you read at any given moment – and therefore there are several techniques designed to get you into the best state for reading. The first is simply to smile. And even when you relax your face, keep the smile in your eyes. Feel your inner smile.

Research has shown that people understand better and take in more information when they're happy. So the happier you are, the better reader you become.

Further research has shown that the physical effect of smiling can affect our mood positively (it releases endorphins, the happy hormones) and make us feel even more like smiling. So if you don't initially feel like smiling, 'fake it till you make it!'

And yet more research indicated that seeing someone else smile, or even just looking at the picture of a smile, can cause you to smile.

DO IT NOW   Smile

Take fewer 'stops' per line

SUMMARY *Deliberately fix your eyes on only four, three or two points in a line as you read – and then do it more quickly. You take in the words on either side of your 'fixation' using peripheral vision.*

Your **foveal vision** (or macular vision) encompasses what you can see directly in front of you which is in focus. All the other things you can see around you without looking at them directly (and which will be out of focus to a greater or lesser degree) are taken in through **peripheral vision**. You notice this most particularly in films when the camera focuses first on something close and then on something behind it. Try it by looking at something on the other side of the room and then becoming aware of how other things you can see to the sides of you are slightly blurred. But notice too how easy it is to make sense of what you're seeing even when it isn't clearly in focus.

Slow readers stop to read every word. Fast readers take fewer 'stops' and use peripheral vision to make sense of the words on either side. Very fast readers focus their eyes in the centre of the page and pick up the information on either side using peripheral vision (super-reading #15). They frequently also take in two or three lines at a time too – bearing in mind that the purpose is to understand the meaning, not to notice words.

When you read, your eyes do not move smoothly along the line, they jump along and focus at different points. (Test this by lightly touching the closed eyelid of one eye while you read with the other. You'll feel the closed eye jumping to match the movements of the other.) These jumps are called saccades.

When slow readers stop on every word, they are using foveal vision so each word is clearly in focus. This is appropriate when learning to read initially, when trying to decipher difficult handwriting, or occasionally when struggling with difficult words or difficult concepts. However, it is not necessary to see every word clearly in order to understand the message. In reading, your brain is more important than your eyes. People who read quickly stop fewer times along the line and rely on their peripheral vision to take in the information to either side of the word they are focusing on. (See chunking for meaning #6)

Take fewer stops
The first step in reading more quickly, then, is to take in more information each time your eyes come to rest. With lines of a short

width (eg in magazine columns), just look at the middle of the line and move your eyes continuously downwards (super-reading #15).

With normal pages, try drawing four light pencil lines down the page and use them as a guide to where to focus your eyes and take in the information to either side. (It will take about two minutes' practice to learn how to move your eyes in this way while also taking in the information.) It's even easier if you open your peripheral vision first (#9).

Move quickly on from using four lines, to three lines, to two lines. With practice you will be able to read whole pages by just looking down the middle of the page (super-reading #15).

Avoid subvocalising
An additional benefit of taking fewer stops per line is that it is less easy to sub-vocalise (say the words to yourself as you read). This in itself may also help you read more quickly – and in turn, the faster you read, the less easy it is to sub-vocalise. (See also Subvocalising/vocalising #19)

Open your peripheral vision

SUMMARY *Look straight ahead, relax your eyes and be aware of as much as you can see to both sides of you at the same time. Then pick up the book and start reading.*

If you open your peripheral vision, you can take in more information each time your eyes come to rest on a word (take fewer stops per line #8).

HOW TO do it

To open your peripheral vision, look straight ahead and focus on the far wall. Put your hands, palms together, in front of your eyes, and gradually move them outwards and then backwards, towards your ears, all the while continuing to focus on the far wall, and keeping your eyes relaxed. Stop moving your hands just at the point where you are still aware of them if you wiggle your fingers. Smile and feel your eyes relax. Notice how much more you can see on both sides at the same time.

Research by Taylor Schmitz of the University of Toronto suggests that simply being in a good state helps people to have better peripheral vision.

Next time you read: open your peripheral vision, pause and plan what you're about to do, take a deep breath in, smile, relax as you breathe out and start reading. You do not have to consciously think about your peripheral vision as you read – this state lasts for at least 20 minutes if it is not interrupted.

10 Take your awareness to your concentration point

SUMMARY *Focus on a point about 15 cms above and slightly behind the top of your head (your concentration point) – take a deep breath in and relax your eyes as you breathe out. Then start reading.*

Many people can increase their reading speed simply by taking their attention to the concentration point about 15 cms above and slightly behind the top of the head. Many notice a different quality to their reading, saying the text is 'clearer' and 'easier to understand'. Their ability to concentrate is also enhanced.

TEST YOURSELF ...

... before and after doing this technique to see the difference it makes to you – see QUICK TEST (p 9).

HOW TO do it

Close your eyes. Take your attention to (ie simply become aware of) a point about 15 cms above and slightly behind the top of your head. Even with your eyes closed, feel your eyes softening as your peripheral vision opens. Pause and plan what you are going to do once you start your reading session. Take a deep breath in, smile and open your eyes as you exhale. Start reading.

You do not need to keep concentrating on the point as you read. If you find your concentration wandering after a time, take a short break to move and breathe and then re-focus on the concentration point before you start reading again.

Additional help

The more you take your concentration to this point, the easier it gets, but if initially you need some help, try whichever of the following works best for you. (You might like to try them all before deciding.)

- Touch the top of your head and move your hand back and up to the concentration point. Move your attention to the point, and keep it there when you remove your hand.
- Imagine placing an orange on that point (initially it can be easier to focus on something concrete rather than a space)
- Instead of an orange, try a melon ...
- ... or a balloon or a balloon
- Relax and focus on your left foot; then take your attention to your right knee; then to your left hip, right palm, left elbow,

right shoulder – and then to the concentration point above and behind your head.

Opening your peripheral vision
Focusing on the concentration point automatically opens your peripheral vision (#9).

Do it before you start driving (you're much more aware of other road users), when you're walking at night (it's easier to avoid trouble), just before you start an exam paper (you get into a good state for remembering information) – or whenever you feel you would benefit from greater powers of (effortless) concentration.

How do we know about this point?
First think about this question: What do the following have in common?
• dunce   • wizard   • saint   • yogi

Answer? All (originally) knew the importance of focusing on a point above and behind the crown of the head in order to enhance their ability to concentrate and be fully aware.

This point has been well known for many years. It is depicted as a halo in many pictures of Christian saints, yogis know it as the 8th chakra (which gives access to universal wisdom), and witches and wizards wore a hat which reminded them to focus on this point in order to enhance their magic powers.

In the 13th century, a Franciscan monk and philosopher, John Duns Scotus, developed a 'duns cap' to be worn by children who needed something to help them focus. Detractors of Scotus made fun of the cap. Over time the 'dunce's cap' came to be associated with 'stupid' children, and was eventually misunderstood and used to stigmatise and make fun of such children.

More recently, when Ron Davis was working with children diagnosed as dyslexic, he discovered that asking the children to concentrate on this point was enough to allow many of them to start reading (see his book 'The Gift of Dyslexia'). When Paul Scheele was developing his PhotoReading system, he thought that concentrating on this point might also help everyone read better. And it does make a difference for most people.

11 Focus on 'hot spots' of key information

SUMMARY *Not all the words on a page contain the same amount of information. Focus on the hot spots – the words and phrases that contain the book's message and/or that fulfil your purpose – and skim quickly past the rest.*

According to Dr Russell Stauffer (author of *'Teaching Reading As A Thinking Process'* 1969), in most books the meaning is actually carried by 4-11% of the words – so if you only read the key words, phrases and sections which contain the new information you need, you will understand the author's message and/or achieve your purpose (#4). The trick, therefore, is to concentrate on the 4-11% and learn to gloss over the other 89-96%.

> **99** *The art of being wise is knowing what to overlook."*
> William James

How do I recognise a hot spot?
Pick up any factual book and read a page. As you go, underline or higlight any words, phrases, sentences or paragraphs which are essential to understanding the author's message. 'Key words' will probably be nouns (and verbs) – words expressing concepts, eg:
whales, largest mammal, cetaceans, dolphins
The sorts of words you can often overlook without losing the meaning are 'grammar words', such as:
a, the, is, were, very, there are, actually, not
So to get the key message from the first paragraph in this section, you would need to read:
meaning carried (by) 4-11% words
The rest of the paragraph is **grammar** (*the, is, actually, by, of the*), **explanation** (repetition, saying the same thing in different words), **credibility** or **proof** (*according to Dr Stauffer*, etc). And in other books you might get lots of **stories** or **examples** and in most texts you also get a lot of **repetition**.

Read uncritically!
How many times do you need to read something in order to understand? Once. For a difficult concept, or one you haven't met before, examples can be helpful, but again one example is often enough. However authors use these examples and repetition in order to put their idea forcefully, to help the reader understand, and to try to convince the reader to take a particular point of view.

People read more quickly when they agree with what is being proposed. Therefore, you can speed up your reading by accepting as true whatever the author says. Read uncritically until you have understood the author's point, and only then bring your critical

EXPERT TIP

Always check titles, subheadings, picture captions, bold text, summaries and quotations for key messages.

faculties to bear to decide whether you actually agree with the author or not.

Note – we're not saying you accept everything uncritically, only that 'suspending your disbelief' until you have fully understood the author's point will speed up your reading. When you do, you only need to get it once to get it, and you can move quickly past the repeated passages and examples. Paradoxically, you will also have a clear understanding of the author's position, which makes it easier for you to give more balanced criticism.

Most frequent words

Some speed reading books recommend that you learn the '100 most common words in English' to improve your comprehension and speed. However, the words used most frequently are words such as 'the, of, to, and, a, in, is, it' – not high content words. Notice how little you understand by concentrating on these words:

The man **was** standing **on the** corner **of the** street.

Compare that with how fully you comprehend the meaning by ignoring those words and concentrating on nouns and verbs:

The **man** was **standing** on the **corner** of the **street.**

You can pretty much use the 'most frequent words' lists as an indicator of the words you can safely overlook.

Words to look (out) for

While you're looking at **nouns, verbs, names** and **numbers** in order to understand the text's message, make sure that you also notice the **'WATCH OUT' WORDS.** Beware of words such as **'not, but, although, on the other hand, however'** that might indicate an opposite or different point of view. Slow down and check which point of view the author is putting forward.

To help you decide how much attention you need to give to different parts of the text, you might also look out for words or phrases which indicate their purpose, such as:

- opinion rather than fact *(in my view, in my opinion, I think)*
- explanation *(in other words, to put it another way, similarly)*
- examples, stories, case studies *(in the case of …, to illustrate this point)*
- lists *(firstly, in the first place)*
- importance *(crucially, a key factor)*

Look for the message

After a little practice with reading more quickly, you will find that you are focusing less and less on individual words, and rather understanding the meaning of chunks of text (#6).

DO IT NOW Hot spots

Identify hot spots using the article 'The Extended Mind'. (p 118)

99 *Like parachutes, minds work better when open."*

EXPERT TIP

The index is a good place to search for key words initially. As you read text, you can identify new key words – which you can then check in the index.

Sophie's BIGGEST learning

"**That I can read a book in the same way that I read a newspaper.**" It was a great revelation to realise that I already had many of the skills I needed. I just had to apply them to books. The newspaper thing helped me most when it came to finding hot spots of information. I do it all the time with newspapers. I get an idea of what an article is about. I read the information that I need or that interests me. I happily ignore things I don't need. And I'm confident when I put it down that I've got everything I needed without reading from cover to cover. Now I can do that with books too. I always thought there was something special about books, but they're just another source of information.

YES BUT ...
How do I read only the hot spots without reading all the other words?

1 In the same way that you can already read a newspaper (#1) – you glance through it, read bits to get a flavour and move on when you've 'got it'. You already know how to do it.

2 Read for sameness and difference (#12) – read more quickly (without concentrating on every word) when it's something you understand (same, what you already know), when information is repeated (same) or when numerous examples are given, and read more slowly when it's something new and different.

3 Read more slowly initially as you get your head around the style and what is being said. Then speed up and look for new information.

4 Use different patterns (#15) to scan the page.

Read for sameness and difference

12

SUMMARY *Ideas which are different and new give you new learning, things which are the same (known) confirm what you already know or give you greater depth of understanding. Noticing one or both keeps your brain alert and helps you take in information.*

When you're reading, consciously look for things which you know (same) and things which you don't know (different). It keeps your brain engaged by giving it a filter through which to judge what you're reading.

Sameness (known) Read for sameness as confirmation of what you already know or to deepen your understanding. It's what you're likely to notice first – and it makes you feel comfortable. Read for sameness when you are looking for something agreed by a number of people. Notice sameness when it is repetition – so that you can ignore it once you know the point being made.

Difference (unknown) Read for difference to learn something new. Read for difference when you want to know how authors view things uniquely.

Spd rdng is driven by difference
The spd rdng approach is largely driven by difference:
- people are different and take in and process information in different ways,
- books/texts are different and need different approaches,
- purposes for reading are different, you need to read different books at different speeds, etc –

which is why Spd Rdng advocates a variety of techniques and strategies which offer a flexible approach.

Other patterns
Besides sameness and difference, you can also keep an eye open for other patterns, such as:
- **Repetition** What ideas does the author keep repeating? (They are probably important.)
- **Exaggeration** The author might try to shock you into taking more notice of particular points. (Design features such as bold text, underlining, etc, might also come into this category.)
- **Change** Look out for changes of fact or opinion over time or from one book to another to see how thinking is evolving.
- **Omissions** As you read, ask yourself, 'What's missing? What aren't they telling me? What else do I need to know? (And where might I find the missing information?)'

Speed up your brain with 'super-duper-reading'

SUMMARY *Look quickly (1-4 seconds) down the middle of the page using your finger to guide you for about 10 pages or until you begin to make sense of some of the words. Then continue reading with comprehension – but you'll be reading more quickly because your brain is reacting more quickly.*

Have you ever come off a motorway into a 30 mph zone and found it really difficult to drive 'slowly' after having been driving at 70 mph? Your brain has adapted to reacting at the faster speed and then has difficulty in slowing down.

You can use this fact to speed up your reading. You 'speed up your eyes and your brain' by using the super-duper-reading technique before you settle down to whatever you really want to read. Having gone much faster than you can easily comprehend, when you read 'normally' at your best comprehension speed, you'll still be reading faster than if you'd just started reading without this preparation.

TEST YOURSELF ...

... before and after doing this technique to see the difference it makes to you – see QUICK TEST (p 9). Look for differences both in speed (quantity) and understanding/clarity of text (quality).

HOW TO super-duper-read

- Take a deep breath in, smile and as you exhale, focus on your concentration point to open your peripheral vision (#9 & #10). Pause and plan what you're about to do.
- Place your finger just under the centre word in the top line of the page (or column in a magazine).
- Focus your eyes on the words just above your finger.
- Run your finger smoothly down the page, keeping your eyes focused on the words just above it – at the rate of about four seconds per page.
- Although initially you are unlikely to be able to 'read' any words, after about six or seven pages, you might start to notice words and phrases. Once you start to notice words, and after a minimum of 10 pages, you are ready to start reading 'normally' (only faster than normal).
- Go back to the beginning of the section and start reading at your best comprehension speed.

Get in a good state for reading

SUMMARY *Having a relaxed, alert, questioning, purposeful mind is the ideal state for reading if you want to understand and remember information. Many of the other spd rdng techniques are also designed to get your mind and body in an optimal state for reading.*

The optimal state for understanding and taking in information is to be alert, relaxed, positive, purposeful and questioning and many of the techniques in this book are about getting into a good state for reading:
- check that physical factors are in your favour (#33) – in particular, sip water

Make sure you are:
- physically alert – take regular breaks (#27) and do some exercises which get your energy flowing and allow you to relax
- mentally alert – have a clear purpose (#4), talk to yourself (#19), take notes (#17)

Every time you start to read, get into the habit of:
- taking a deep breath in – and consciously relaxing your body as you breathe out
- smiling (#7) – and maintaining your inner smile even when you relax your face
- focusing on your concentration point (#10) to open your peripheral vision
- pausing and planning what you're about to do.

Triune brain theory

According to Paul McClean's triune brain theory, your brain cannot concentrate on higher thinking (eg reading) if you are physically uncomfortable (eg hungry, tired, needing the loo) or emotionally unbalanced (either sad or over-excited). Sort those things out before you start your work session.

Stress

80% of learning difficulties are caused by stress! Any stress will interfere to some extent with your reading ability. It therefore makes sense to make a habit of getting into a good state before you start reading. Always get into a good state before you read – and before you start driving, as you walk into the office, before you walk through your front door. Notice how the quality of your everyday life improves. And once this becomes a state you regularly get into, you'll find that you can use it consciously whenever you are in a potentially stressful situation, such as an exam, a job interview, or dealing with screaming children! And smile more...

EXPERT TIP

You'll take in information more easily if you keep guessing and anticipating what you think is coming next.

YES BUT ...

What if I've done all that and I'm just not in a good state?

Then do something else. Go for a walk. Get something else done. Think about something nice. Do something to make you feel good. And then go back to your reading. And the more you follow the simple formula 'breathe, smile, focus', the easier you will find it to get into a good state at will.

Use speed-reading patterns

SUMMARY *Use regular patterns to look down the page for hot spots of information. 'Super-read' (straight down the middle of the page), 'skitter' (randomly, or using patterns such as zigzag) or use other patterns such as 'underlining', 'first and last' or the 'capital-I shape'.*

You do not have to read sequentially, word by word, in order to get the information you need from a page. Use these speed-reading patterns to look around the page to find hot spots of key information (#11) – which will either be specific information you know is there, or to get an idea of what the page is about.

Why use speed-reading patterns?
The main purpose of these 'patterns' is to help you find hot spots of relevant information. Initially, the reason for following a pattern is to break you of the habit of reading every word sequentially. Later, you will not have to follow any one pattern slavishly, but while you are learning, we suggest that you try out each of them exactly as suggested here.

HOW TO do it
With each speed-reading pattern, the aim is to take in as much information as possible each time your eyes come to rest on the words on the page. When words make little or no sense, or when you come across concepts which you already know about, then move quickly on to another area.

Dipping
Having read quickly to find 'hot spots' (the areas with important information), then you can 'dip' into the material and read the relevant bits more slowly. Once you have understood the point, then speed up again and start looking for other hot spots. Do not get seduced into staying in 'slow reading' mode. This is a dip, not a bath!

Dipping might involve looking back to earlier information in order to make sense of the hot spot you've identified. This is quite acceptable and not the same as going back over and over the same piece of text because you haven't been concentrating – a habit which slows down many untrained readers.

Pacer
With each pattern, you use your finger – or a (capped) pen – as a pacer. Point your pacer at particular places on the page

> **"** *Reading furnishes the mind only with materials for knowledge; it is thinking that makes what we read ours."*
> *John Locke*

(underlining, running down the middle of the page, etc) and read the words just above it. Practise each pattern slowly initially to make sure you are looking at the words and not at your pacer.

Headings

Whichever pattern you are using, remember also to look specifically at any titles, headings, sub-headings or bold type which might give you clues as to the content. Picture captions, quotations and 'boxed' sections can help too.

Five Speed-Reading Patterns:
1 **Underlining**
2 **Super-reading**
3 **Skittering**
4 **Capital I-shape**
5 **First and last**

---

1 Underlining

Underlining is described at the beginning of the book as a way to double your reading speed. If you haven't already had a go, do so now – after first opening your peripheral vision (#9) or focusing on your concentration point (#10).

Underlining in brief:
- Read several lines at 'normal' speed while underlining the words with your finger.
- Continue reading in the same way but do not underline or consciously read the words in the first or last centimetre of each line.
- Continue in the same way but at the rate of about one second per line – too fast to understand what you're reading (this is to speed up your brain – just as with super-duper-reading #13).
- After two or three pages you should start comprehending occasional words at this high speed, at which point you can move to the next step.
- Go back to where you started underlining very fast and read at our best comprehension speed while continuing to underline as before.

Focus particularly on verbs and nouns (eg the **man** was **standing** on the **corner** of the **street**) since they contain most of the meaning in a sentence.

Underlining is the easiest pattern to master as it most nearly replicates traditional reading. However, as you get quicker, you'll realise that you're 'wasting' time going back to the beginning of the line each time, so you can go back along alternate lines in the opposite direction – effectively reading backwards on every alternate line. (**Forwards and backwards** could be considered a pattern in its own right.) It works better the faster you go, so it may be one to come back to once you've speeded up your reading using some of the other patterns. Try it first on magazine columns rather than full book pages.

Lorem ipsum dolor sit amet, consectetuer adipiscing elit. Nam cursus. Morbi ut mi. Nullam enim leo, egestas id, condimentum at, laoreet mattis, massa. Sed eleifend nonummy diam. Praesent mauris ante, elementum et, bibendum at, posuere sit amet, nibh. Duis tincidunt lectus quis dui viverra vestibulum. Suspendisse vulputate aliquam dui. Nulla elementum dui ut augue. Aliquam vehicula mi at mauris. Maecenas placerat, nisl at consequat rhoncus, sem nunc gravida justo, quis eleifend arcu velit quis lacus. Morbi magna magna, tincidunt a, mattis non, imperdiet vitae, tellus. Sed odio est, auctor ac, sollicitudin in, consequat vitae, orci. Fusce id felis. Vivamus sollicitudin metus eget eros.

Pellentesque habitant morbi tristique senectus et netus et malesuada fames ac turpis egestas. In posuere felis nec tortor. Pellentesque faucibus. Ut accumsan ultricies elit. Maecenas at justo id velit placerat molestie. Donec dictum lectus non odio. Cras a ante vitae enim iaculis aliquam. Mauris nunc quam, venenatis nec, euismod sit amet, egestas placerat, est. Pellentesque habitant morbi tristique senectus et netus et malesuada fames ac turpis egestas. Cras id elit. Integer quis urna. Ut ante enim, dapibus malesuada, fringilla eu, condimentum quis, tellus. Aenean porttitor eros vel dolor. Donec convallis pede venenatis nibh. Duis quam. Nam eget lacus. Aliquam erat volutpat. Quisque dignissim congue leo.

Mauris vel lacus vitae felis vestibulum volutpat. Etiam est nunc, venenatis in, tristique eu, imperdiet ac, nisl. Cum sociis natoque penatibus et magnis dis parturient montes, nascetur ridiculus mus. In iaculis facilisis massa. Etiam eu urna. Sed porta. Suspendisse quam leo, molestie sed, luctus quis, feugiat in, pede. Fusce tellus. Sed metus augue, convallis et, vehicula ut, pulvinar eu, ante. Integer orci tellus, tristique vitae, consequat nec, porta vel, lectus. Nulla sit amet diam. Duis non nunc. Nulla rhoncus dictum metus. Curabitur tristique mi condimentum orci. Phasellus pellentesque aliquam enim. Proin dui lectus, cursus eu, mattis laoreet, viverra at, quam. Curabitur vel dolor ultrices ipsum dictum tristique. Praesent vitae lacus. Ut velit enim, vestibulum non, fermentum nec, hendrerit quis, leo. Pellentesque rutrum malesuada neque.

Nunc tempus felis vitae urna. Vivamus porttitor, neque at volutpat rutrum, purus nisi eleifend libero, a tempus libero lectus feugiat felis. Morbi diam mauris, viverra in, gravida eu, mattis in, ante. Morbi eget arcu. Morbi porta, libero id ullamcorper nonummy, nibh ligula pulvinar metus, eget consectetuer augue nisi quis lacus. Ut ac mi quis lacus mollis aliquam. Curabitur iaculis tempus eros. Curabitur vel mi sit amet magna malesuada ultrices. Ut nisi erat, fermentum vel, congue id, euismod in, elit. Fusce ultricies, orci ac feugiat suscipit, leo massa sodales velit, et scelerisque mi tortor at ipsum. Proin orci odio, commodo ac, gravida non, tristique vel, tellus. Pellentesque nibh libero, ultricies eu, sagittis non, mollis sed, justo. Praesent metus ipsum, pulvinar pulvinar, porta id, fringilla at, est.

Phasellus felis dolor, scelerisque a, tempus eget, lobortis id, libero. Donec scelerisque leo ac risus. Praesent sit amet est. In dictum, dolor eu dictum porttitor, enim felis viverra mi, eget luctus massa purus quis odio. Etiam nulla massa, pharetra facilisis, volutpat in, imperdiet sit amet, sem. Aliquam nec erat at purus cursus interdum. Vestibulum ligula augue, bibendum accumsan, vestibulum ut, commodo a, mi. Morbi ornare gravida elit. Integer congue, augue et malesuada iaculis, ipsum dui aliquet felis, at cursus magna nisl nec elit. Donec iaculis diam a nisi accumsan viverra. Duis sed tellus et tortor vestibulum gravida. Praesent elementum elit at tellus. Curabitur metus ipsum, luctus eu, malesuada ut, tincidunt sed, diam. Donec quis mi sed magna hendrerit accumsan. Suspendisse risus nibh, ultricies eu, volutpat non, condimentum hendrerit, augue. Etiam eleifend, metus vitae adipiscing semper, mauris ipsum iaculis elit, congue gravida elit mi egestas orci. Curabitur pede.

Underlining
Underline the words with your pacer as you read them – and rely on your peripheral vision to pick up the meaning of the words at the beginning and end of each line.

2 Super-reading

Super-reading is exactly the same as super-duper-reading (#13) although it has a different purpose. You do super-duper-reading faster than you can comprehend the text in order to 'speed up your brain'. You super-read to look for hot spots of information

- Open your peripheral vision (#9) or focus on your concentration point (#10).
- Place your pacer (finger) just under the top line of the page (or column in a magazine) in the centre of the line (column).
- Focus your eyes on the words just above your pacer.
- Run your pacer smoothly down the page, keeping your eyes focused on the words just above it – and taking in the meaning of the whole line, trusting that you can pick up the words to either side through your peripheral vision.

Your aim initially is to super-read at the rate of about 10 seconds per page or column, and with practice you should get quicker. But if you find after about four pages that you're understanding absolutely nothing, then speed up your brain first with super-duper-reading (#13) and try again. If you're still getting nothing, allow yourself 20 seconds per page or column to start with and then gradually speed up.

Lorem ipsum dolor sit amet, consectetuer adipiscing elit. Nam cursus. Morbi ut mi. Nullam enim leo, egestas id, condimentum at, laoreet mattis, massa. Sed eleifend nonummy diam. Praesent mauris ante, elementum et, bibendum at, posuere sit amet, nibh. Duis tincidunt lectus quis dui viverra vestibulum. Suspendisse vulputate aliquam dui. Nulla elementum dui ut augue. Aliquam vehicula mi at mauris. Maecenas placerat, nisl at consequat rhoncus, sem nunc gravida justo, quis eleifend arcu velit quis lacus. Morbi magna magna, tincidunt a, mattis non, imperdiet vitae, tellus. Sed odio est, auctor ac, sollicitudin in, consequat vitae, orci. Fusce id felis. Vivamus sollicitudin metus eget eros.

Pellentesque habitant morbi tristique senectus et netus et malesuada fames ac turpis egestas. In posuere felis nec tortor. Pellentesque faucibus. Ut accumsan ultricies elit. Maecenas at justo id velit placerat molestie. Donec dictum lectus non odio. Cras a ante vitae enim iaculis aliquam. Mauris nunc quam, venenatis nec, euismod sit amet, egestas placerat, est. Pellentesque habitant morbi tristique senectus et netus et malesuada fames ac turpis egestas. Cras id elit. Integer quis urna. Ut ante enim, dapibus malesuada, fringilla eu, condimentum quis, tellus. Aenean porttitor eros vel dolor. Donec convallis pede venenatis nibh. Duis quam. Nam eget lacus. Aliquam erat volutpat. Quisque dignissim congue leo.

Mauris vel lacus vitae felis vestibulum volutpat. Etiam est nunc, venenatis in, tristique eu, imperdiet ac, nisl. Cum sociis natoque penatibus et magnis dis parturient montes, nascetur ridiculus mus. In iaculis facilisis massa. Etiam eu urna. Sed porta. Suspendisse quam leo, molestie sed, luctus quis, feugiat in, pede. Fusce tellus. Sed metus augue, convallis et, vehicula ut, pulvinar eu, ante. Integer orci tellus, tristique vitae, consequat nec, porta vel, lectus. Nulla sit amet diam. Duis non nunc. Nulla rhoncus dictum metus. Curabitur tristique mi condimentum orci. Phasellus pellentesque aliquam enim. Proin dui lectus, cursus eu, mattis laoreet, viverra sit amet, quam. Curabitur vel dolor ultrices ipsum dictum tristique. Praesent vitae lacus. Ut velit enim, vestibulum non, fermentum nec, hendrerit quis, leo. Pellentesque rutrum malesuada neque.

Nunc tempus felis vitae urna. Vivamus porttitor, neque at volutpat rutrum, purus nisi eleifend libero, a tempus libero lectus feugiat felis. Morbi diam mauris, viverra in, gravida eu, mattis in, ante. Morbi eget arcu. Morbi porta, libero id ullamcorper nonummy, nibh ligula pulvinar metus, eget consectetuer augue nisi quis lacus. Ut ac mi quis lacus mollis aliquam. Curabitur iaculis tempus eros. Curabitur vel mi sit amet magna malesuada ultrices. Ut nisi erat, fermentum vel, congue id, euismod in, elit. Fusce ultricies, orci ac feugiat suscipit, leo massa sodales velit, et scelerisque mi tortor at ipsum. Proin orci odio, commodo ac, gravida non, tristique vel, tellus. Pellentesque nibh libero, ultricies eu, sagittis non, mollis sed, justo. Praesent metus ipsum, pulvinar pulvinar, porta id, fringilla at, est.

Phasellus felis dolor, scelerisque a, tempus eget, lobortis id, libero. Donec scelerisque leo ac risus. Praesent sit amet est. In dictum, dolor eu dictum porttitor, enim felis viverra mi, eget luctus massa purus quis odio. Etiam nulla massa, pharetra facilisis, volutpat in, imperdiet sit amet, sem. Aliquam nec erat at purus cursus interdum. Vestibulum ligula augue, bibendum accumsan, vestibulum ut, commodo a, mi. Morbi ornare gravida elit. Integer congue, augue et malesuada iaculis, ipsum dui aliquet felis, at cursus magna nisl nec elit. Donec iaculis diam a nisi accumsan viverra. Duis sed tellus et tortor vestibulum gravida. Praesent elementum elit at tellus. Curabitur metus ipsum, luctus eu, malesuada ut, tincidunt sed, diam. Donec quis mi sed magna hendrerit accumsan. Suspendisse risus nibh, ultricies eu, volutpat non, condimentum hendrerit, augue. Etiam eleifend, metus vitae adipiscing semper, mauris ipsum iaculis elit, congue gravida elit mi egestas orci. Curabitur pede.

Maecenas aliquet velit vel turpis. Mauris neque metus, malesuada nec, ultricies sit amet, porttitor mattis, enim. In massa libero, interdum nec, interdum vel, blandit sed, nulla. In ullamcorper, est eget tempor cursus, neque mi consectetuer mi, a ultricies massa est sed nisl. Class aptent taciti sociosqu ad litora torquent per conubia nostra, per inceptos hymenaeos. Proin nulla arcu, nonummy luctus, dictum eget, fermentum et, lorem. Nunc porta convallis pede.

Super-reading

Go straight down the middle of the page or column.

Super-reading variations

- Since it can be more comfortable to read with more eye movement, follow a slightly wiggly line down the centre of the page rather than a straight one.
- Instead of placing your finger under the line, place your thumb above the line and look at the words below your thumb. This encourages you to keep moving and look forwards to what is coming rather than being tempted to look back at what you've already seen.
- Draw (or imagine) a line down the middle of the page/column as a guide for where to look.
- Keep your eyes moving down the centre of the page, but move your pacer down the (right or left) end of line you're on – you

pick up the movement in your peripheral vision, which keeps you moving and encourages you to keep your peripheral vision open.

- Instead of using one finger, use two fingers (your index finger and little finger) to define a central section of the line (rather than limiting your focus to one word). See picture.

Hint One way of developing your super-reading ability is to start with the underlining technique, then gradually (over a period of time or over the course of several pages) start and stop your pacer further into the line so that you are focusing consciously on a smaller and smaller strip in the centre of the page. Eventually you will simply be running your finger down the middle of the page, ie super-reading.

Learning super-reading
Move from the underlining pattern to super-reading by cutting off more words at the beginning and end of each line over a series of pages or over time.

3 Skittering

Skittering was named by Professor Michael Bennett from the University of Minnesota after the 'skitter bug' (US name for what in the UK is called a 'water boatman') – an insect which darts around on the surface of ponds.

The aim with skittering is to let your eyes jump around the page focusing on **hot spots** (#11) of information – or words which seem to give you the gist of what the text is about. As with any other pattern, when you find a hot spot, you can slow down and dip – read more slowly until you have understood the meaning of the text.

Zigzag
A common skittering pattern. The zigzags will be tighter or looser depending on how dense the information is on the page.

You can skitter in two ways:
- **randomly** – just let your eyes glance round the page
- by using **any pattern** of your choice – some people favour the shape of a question mark, or letting their eyes travel diagonally downwards across the page. Feel free to experiment. One of the most common patterns, though, is the **zigzag** – your eyes travel in big 'Z's going down the page. The Zs can either be large or narrow, depending on the density of the information.

Lorem ipsum dolor sit amet, consectetuer adipiscing elit. Nam cursus. Morbi ut mi. Nullam enim leo, egestas id, condimentum at, laoreet mattis, massa. Sed eleifend nonummy diam. Praesent mauris ante, elementum et, bibendum at, posuere sit amet, nibh. Duis tincidunt lectus quis dui viverra vestibulum. Suspendisse vulputate aliquam dui. Nulla elementum dui ut augue. Aliquam vehicula mi at mauris. Maecenas placerat, nisl at consequat rhoncus, sem nunc gravida justo, quis eleifend arcu velit quis lacus. Morbi magna magna, tincidunt a, mattis non, imperdiet vitae, tellus. Sed odio est, auctor ac, sollicitudin in, consequat vitae, orci. Fusce id felis. Vivamus sollicitudin metus eget eros.

Pellentesque habitant morbi tristique senectus et netus et malesuada fames ac turpis egestas. In posuere felis nec tortor. Pellentesque faucibus. Ut accumsan ultricies elit. Maecenas at justo id velit placerat molestie. Donec dictum lectus non odio. Cras a ante vitae enim iaculis aliquam. Mauris nunc quam, venenatis nec, euismod sit amet, egestas placerat, est. Pellentesque habitant morbi tristique senectus et netus et malesuada fames ac turpis egestas. Cras id elit. Integer quis urna. Ut ante enim, dapibus malesuada, fringilla eu, condimentum quis, tellus. Aenean porttitor eros vel dolor. Donec convallis pede venenatis nibh. Duis quam. Nam eget lacus. Aliquam erat volutpat. Quisque dignissim congue leo.

Mauris vel lacus vitae felis vestibulum volutpat. Etiam est nunc, venenatis in, tristique eu, imperdiet ac, nisl. Cum sociis natoque penatibus et magnis dis parturient montes, nascetur ridiculus mus. In iaculis facilisis massa. Etiam eu urna. Sed porta. Suspendisse quam leo, molestie sed, luctus quis, feugiat in, pede. Fusce tellus. Sed metus augue, convallis et, vehicula ut, pulvinar eu, ante. Integer orci tellus, tristique vitae, consequat nec, porta vel, lectus. Nulla sit amet diam. Duis non nunc. Nulla rhoncus dictum metus. Curabitur tristique mi condimentum orci. Phasellus pellentesque aliquam enim. Proin dui lectus, cursus eu, mattis laoreet, viverra sit amet, quam. Curabitur vel dolor ultrices ipsum dictum tristique. Praesent vitae lacus. Ut velit enim, vestibulum non, fermentum nec, hendrerit quis, leo. Pellentesque rutrum malesuada neque.

Nunc tempus felis vitae urna. Vivamus porttitor, neque at volutpat rutrum, purus nisi eleifend libero, a tempus libero lectus feugiat felis. Morbi diam mauris, viverra in, gravida eu, mattis in, ante. Morbi eget arcu. Morbi porta, libero id ullamcorper nonummy, nibh ligula pulvinar metus, eget consectetuer augue nisi quis lacus. Ut ac mi quis lacus mollis aliquam. Curabitur iaculis tempus eros. Curabitur vel mi sit amet magna malesuada ultrices. Ut nisi erat, fermentum vel, congue id, euismod in, elit. Fusce ultricies, orci ac feugiat suscipit, leo massa sodales velit, et scelerisque mi tortor at ipsum. Proin orci odio, commodo ac, gravida non, tristique vel, tellus. Pellentesque nibh libero, ultricies eu, sagittis non, mollis sed, justo. Praesent metus ipsum, pulvinar pulvinar, porta id, fringilla at, est.

Phasellus felis dolor, scelerisque a, tempus eget, lobortis id, libero. Donec scelerisque leo ac risus. Praesent sit amet est. In dictum, dolor eu dictum porttitor, enim felis viverra mi, eget luctus massa purus quis odio. Etiam nulla massa, pharetra facilisis, volutpat in, imperdiet sit amet, sem. Aliquam nec erat at purus cursus interdum. Vestibulum ligula augue, bibendum accumsan, vestibulum ut, commodo a, mi. Morbi ornare gravida elit. Integer congue, augue et malesuada iaculis, ipsum dui aliquet felis, at cursus magna nisl nec elit. Donec iaculis diam a nisi accumsan viverra. Duis sed tellus et tortor vestibulum gravida. Praesent elementum elit at tellus. Curabitur metus ipsum, luctus eu, malesuada ut, tincidunt sed, diam. Donec quis mi sed magna hendrerit accumsan. Suspendisse risus nibh, ultricies eu, volutpat non, condimentum hendrerit, augue. Etiam eleifend, metus vitae adipiscing semper, mauris ipsum iaculis elit, congue gravida elit mi egestas orci. Curabitur pede.

Maecenas aliquet velit vel turpis. Mauris neque metus, malesuada nec, ultricies sit amet, porttitor mattis, enim. In massa libero, interdum nec, interdum vel, blandit sed, nulla. In ullamcorper, est eget tempor cursus, neque mi consectetuer mi, a ultricies massa est sed nisl. Class aptent taciti sociosqu ad litora torquent per conubia nostra, per inceptos hymenaeos. Proin nulla arcu, nonummy luctus, dictum eget, fermentum et, lorem. Nunc porta convallis pede.

Lorem ipsum dolor sit amet, consectetuer adipiscing elit. Nam cursus. Morbi ut mi. Nullam enim leo, egestas id, condimentum at, laoreet mattis, massa. Sed eleifend nonummy diam. Praesent mauris ante, elementum et, bibendum at, posuere sit amet, nibh. Duis tincidunt lectus quis dui viverra vestibulum. Suspendisse vulputate aliquam dui. Nulla elementum dui ut augue. Aliquam vehicula mi at mauris. Maecenas placerat, nisl at consequat rhoncus, sem nunc gravida justo, quis eleifend arcu velit quis lacus. Morbi magna magna, tincidunt a, mattis non, imperdiet vitae, tellus. Sed odio est, auctor ac, sollicitudin in, consequat vitae, orci. Fusce id felis. Vivamus sollicitudin metus eget eros.

Pellentesque habitant morbi tristique senectus et netus et malesuada fames ac turpis egestas. In posuere felis nec tortor. Pellentesque faucibus. Ut accumsan ultricies elit. Maecenas at justo id velit placerat molestie. Donec dictum lectus non odio. Cras a ante vitae enim iaculis aliquam. Mauris nunc quam, venenatis nec, euismod sit amet, egestas placerat, est. Pellentesque habitant morbi tristique senectus et netus et malesuada fames ac turpis egestas. Cras id elit. Integer quis urna. Ut ante enim, dapibus malesuada, fringilla eu, condimentum quis, tellus. Aenean porttitor eros vel dolor. Donec convallis pede venenatis nibh. Duis quam. Nam eget lacus. Aliquam erat volutpat. Quisque dignissim congue leo.

Mauris vel lacus vitae felis vestibulum volutpat. Etiam est nunc, venenatis in, tristique eu, imperdiet ac, nisl. Cum sociis natoque penatibus et magnis dis parturient montes, nascetur ridiculus mus. In iaculis facilisis massa. Etiam eu urna. Sed porta. Suspendisse quam leo, molestie sed, luctus quis, feugiat in, pede. Fusce tellus. Sed metus augue, convallis et, vehicula ut, pulvinar eu, ante. Integer orci tellus, tristique vitae, consequat nec, porta vel, lectus. Nulla sit amet diam. Duis non nunc. Nulla rhoncus dictum metus. Curabitur tristique mi condimentum orci. Phasellus pellentesque aliquam enim. Proin dui lectus, cursus eu, mattis laoreet, viverra sit amet, quam. Curabitur vel dolor ultrices ipsum dictum tristique. Praesent vitae lacus. Ut velit enim, vestibulum non, fermentum nec, hendrerit quis, leo. Pellentesque rutrum malesuada neque.

Nunc tempus felis vitae urna. Vivamus porttitor, neque at volutpat rutrum, purus nisi eleifend libero, a tempus libero lectus feugiat felis. Morbi diam mauris, viverra in, gravida eu, mattis in, ante. Morbi eget arcu. Morbi porta, libero id ullamcorper nonummy, nibh ligula pulvinar metus, eget consectetuer augue nisi quis lacus. Ut ac mi quis lacus mollis aliquam. Curabitur iaculis tempus eros. Curabitur vel mi sit amet magna malesuada ultrices. Ut nisi erat, fermentum vel, congue id, euismod in, elit. Fusce ultricies, orci ac feugiat suscipit, leo massa sodales velit, et scelerisque mi tortor at ipsum. Proin orci odio, commodo ac, gravida non, tristique vel, tellus. Pellentesque nibh libero, ultricies eu, sagittis non, mollis sed, justo. Praesent metus ipsum, pulvinar pulvinar, porta id, fringilla at, est.

Phasellus felis dolor, scelerisque a, tempus eget, lobortis id, libero. Donec scelerisque leo ac risus. Praesent sit amet est. In dictum, dolor eu dictum porttitor, enim felis viverra mi, eget luctus massa purus quis odio. Etiam nulla massa, pharetra facilisis, volutpat in, imperdiet sit amet, sem. Aliquam nec erat at purus cursus interdum. Vestibulum ligula augue, bibendum accumsan, vestibulum ut, commodo a, mi. Morbi ornare gravida elit. Integer congue, augue et malesuada iaculis, ipsum dui aliquet felis, at cursus magna nisl nec elit. Donec iaculis diam a nisi accumsan viverra. Duis sed tellus et tortor vestibulum gravida. Praesent elementum elit at tellus. Curabitur metus ipsum, luctus eu, malesuada ut, tincidunt sed, diam. Donec quis mi sed magna hendrerit accumsan. Suspendisse risus nibh, ultricies eu, volutpat non, condimentum hendrerit, augue. Etiam eleifend, metus vitae adipiscing semper, mauris ipsum iaculis elit, congue gravida elit mi egestas orci. Curabitur pede.

Maecenas aliquet velit vel turpis. Mauris neque metus, malesuada nec, ultricies sit amet, porttitor mattis, enim. In massa libero, interdum nec, interdum vel, blandit sed, nulla. In ullamcorper, est eget tempor cursus, neque mi consectetuer mi, a ultricies massa est sed nisl. Class aptent taciti sociosqu ad litora torquent per conubia nostra, per inceptos hymenaeos. Proin nulla arcu, nonummy luctus, dictum eget, fermentum et, lorem. Nunc porta convallis pede.

4 Capital I-shape

The capital I-shape is formed by:

- Reading the first two or three lines on a page
- Super-reading down the middle of the page and then
- Reading the last two or three lines on the page

Many people find this combination of slower reading at the beginning and end of the page and a quick look down the middle of the page a reassuring first step towards super-reading alone.

Lorem ipsum dolor sit amet, consectetuer adipiscing elit. Nam cursus. Morbi ut mi. Nullam enim leo, egestas id, condimentum at, laoreet mattis, massa. Sed eleifend nonummy diam. Praesent mauris ante, elementum et, bibendum at, posuere sit amet, nibh. Duis tincidunt lectus quis dui viverra vestibulum. Suspendisse vulputate aliquam dui. Nulla elementum dui ut augue. Aliquam vehicula mi at mauris. Maecenas placerat, nisl at consequat rhoncus, sem nunc gravida justo, quis eleifend arcu velit quis lacus. Morbi magna magna, tincidunt a, mattis non, imperdiet vitae, tellus. Sed odio est, auctor ac, sollicitudin in, consequat vitae, orci. Fusce id felis. Vivamus sollicitudin netus eget eros.

Pellentesque habitant morbi tristique senectus et netus et malesuada fames ac turpis egestas. In posuere felis nec tortor. Pellentesque faucibus. Ut accumsan ultricies elit. Maecenas at justo id velit placerat molestie. Donec dictum lectus non odio. Cras a ante vitae enim iaculis aliquam. Mauris nunc quam, venenatis nec, euismod sit amet, egestas placerat, est. Pellentesque habitant morbi tristique senectus et netus et malesuada fames ac turpis egestas. Cras id elit. Integer quis urna. Ut ante enim, dapibus malesuada, fringilla eu, condimentum quis, tellus. Aenean porttitor eros vel dolor. Donec convallis pede venenatis nibh. Duis quam. Nam eget lacus. Aliquam erat volutpat. Quisque dignissim congue leo.

Mauris vel lacus vitae felis vestibulum volutpat. Etiam est nunc, venenatis in, tristique eu, imperdiet ac, nisl. Cum sociis natoque penatibus et magnis dis parturient montes, nascetur ridiculus mus. In iaculis facilisis massa. Etiam eu urna. Sed porta. Suspendisse quam leo, molestie sed, luctus quis, feugiat in, pede. Fusce tellus. Sed metus augue, convallis et, vehicula ut, pulvinar eu, ante. Integer orci tellus, tristique vitae, consequat nec, porta vel, lectus. Nulla sit amet diam. Duis non nunc. Nulla rhoncus dictum metus. Curabitur tristique mi condimentum orci. Phasellus pellentesque aliquam enim. Proin dui lectus, cursus eu, mattis laoreet, viverra sit amet, quam. Curabitur vel dolor ultrices ipsum dictum tristique. Praesent vitae lacus. Ut velit enim, vestibulum non, fermentum nec, hendrerit quis, leo. Pellentesque rutrum malesuada neque.

Nunc tempus felis vitae urna. Vivamus porttitor, neque at volutpat rutrum, purus nisi eleifend libero, a tempus libero lectus feugiat felis. Morbi diam mauris, viverra in, gravida eu, mattis in, ante. Morbi eget arcu. Morbi porta, libero id ullamcorper nonummy, nibh ligula pulvinar metus, eget consectetuer augue nisi quis lacus. Ut ac mi quis lacus mollis aliquam. Curabitur iaculis tempus eros. Curabitur vel mi sit amet magna malesuada ultrices. Ut nisi erat, fermentum vel, congue id, euismod in, elit. Fusce ultricies, orci ac feugiat suscipit, leo massa sodales velit, et scelerisque mi tortor at ipsum. Proin orci odio, commodo ac, gravida non, tristique vel, tellus. Pellentesque nibh libero, ultricies eu, sagittis non, mollis sed, justo. Praesent metus ipsum, pulvinar pulvinar, porta id, fringilla at, est.

Phasellus felis dolor, scelerisque a, tempus eget, lobortis id, libero. Donec scelerisque leo ac risus. Praesent sit amet est. In dictum, dolor eu dictum porttitor, enim felis viverra mi, eget luctus massa purus quis odio. Etiam nulla massa, pharetra facilisis, volutpat in, imperdiet sit amet, sem. Aliquam nec erat at purus cursus interdum. Vestibulum ligula augue, bibendum accumsan, vestibulum ut, commodo a, mi. Morbi ornare gravida elit. Integer congue, augue et malesuada iaculis, ipsum dui aliquet felis, at cursus magna nisl nec elit. Donec iaculis diam a nisi accumsan viverra. Duis sed tellus et tortor vestibulum gravida. Praesent elementum elit at tellus. Curabitur metus ipsum, luctus eu, malesuada ut, tincidunt sed, diam. Donec quis mi sed magna hendrerit accumsan. Suspendisse risus nibh, ultricies eu, volutpat non, condimentum hendrerit, augue. Etiam eleifend, metus vitae adipiscing semper, mauris ipsum iaculis elit, congue gravida elit mi egestas orci. Curabitur pede.

Maecenas aliquet velit vel turpis. Mauris neque metus, malesuada nec, ultricies sit amet, porttitor mattis, enim. In massa libero, interdum nec, interdum vel, blandit sed, nulla. In ullamcorper, eget tempor cursus, neque mi consectetuer mi, a ultricies massa est sed nisl. Class aptent taciti sociosqu ad litora torquent per conubia nostra, per inceptos hymenaeos. Proin nulla arcu, non-ummy luctus, dictum eget, fermentum et, lorem. Nunc porta convallis pede.

Capital-I shape
Read two or three lines at the top, look down the middle of the page, then read two or three lines at the bottom.

5 First and last

If you just read the first and last few lines on a page and omit the super-reading down the centre of the page, the pattern is called 'first and last'. In densely-written texts, you might also read the first and last lines of sections or even paragraphs.

If you find the text is written in such a way that key information is not contained in the beginnings and endings of sections or paragraphs, try reading just the **middles** (another pattern). When you apply the first and last pattern to a whole book, it is called **beginnings and endings** (#37).

First and last
Read just the beginning and ending lines on a page (or in paragraphs or sections).

Lorem ipsum dolor sit amet, consectetuer adipiscing elit. Nam cursus. Morbi ut mi. Nullam enim leo, egestas id, condimentum at, laoreet mattis, massa. Sed eleifend nonummy diam. Praesent mauris ante, elementum et, bibendum at, posuere sit amet, nibh. Duis tincidunt lectus quis dui viverra vestibulum. Suspendisse vulputate aliquam dui. Nulla elementum dui ut augue. Aliquam vehicula mi at mauris. Maecenas placerat, nisl at consequat rhoncus, sem nunc gravida justo, quis eleifend arcu velit quis lacus. Morbi magna magna, tincidunt a, mattis non, imperdiet vitae, tellus. Sed odio est, auctor ac, sollicitudin in, consequat vitae, orci. Fusce id felis. Vivamus sollicitudin metus eget eros.

Pellentesque habitant morbi tristique senectus et netus et malesuada fames ac turpis egestas. In posuere felis nec tortor. Pellentesque faucibus. Ut accumsan ultricies elit. Maecenas at justo id velit placerat molestie. Donec dictum lectus non odio. Cras a ante vitae enim iaculis aliquam. Mauris nunc quam, venenatis nec, euismod sit amet, egestas placerat, est. Pellentesque habitant morbi tristique senectus et netus et malesuada fames ac turpis egestas. Cras id elit. Integer quis urna. Ut ante enim, dapibus malesuada, fringilla eu, condimentum quis, tellus. Aenean porttitor eros vel dolor. Donec convallis pede venenatis nibh. Duis quam. Nam eget lacus. Aliquam erat volutpat. Quisque dignissim congue leo.

Mauris vel lacus vitae felis vestibulum volutpat. Etiam est nunc, venenatis in, tristique eu, imperdiet ac, nisl. Cum sociis natoque penatibus et magnis dis parturient montes, nascetur ridiculus mus. In iaculis facilisis massa. Etiam eu urna. Sed porta. Suspendisse quam leo, molestie sed, luctus quis, feugiat in, pede. Fusce tellus. Sed metus augue, convallis et, vehicula ut, pulvinar eu, ante. Integer orci tellus, tristique vitae, consequat nec, porta vel, lectus. Nulla sit amet diam. Duis non nunc. Nulla rhoncus dictum metus. Curabitur tristique mi condimentum orci. Phasellus pellentesque aliquam enim. Proin dui lectus, cursus eu, mattis laoreet, viverra sit amet, quam. Curabitur vel dolor ultrices ipsum dictum tristique. Praesent vitae lacus. Ut velit enim, vestibulum non, fermentum nec, hendrerit quis, leo. Pellentesque rutrum malesuada neque.

Nunc tempus felis vitae urna. Vivamus porttitor, neque at volutpat rutrum, purus nisi eleifend libero, a tempus libero lectus feugiat felis. Morbi diam mauris, viverra in, gravida eu, mattis in, ante. Morbi eget arcu. Morbi porta, libero id ullamcorper nonummy, nibh ligula pulvinar metus, eget consectetuer augue nisi quis lacus. Ut ac mi quis lacus mollis aliquam. Curabitur iaculis tempus eros. Curabitur vel mi sit amet magna malesuada ultrices. Ut nisi erat, fermentum vel, congue id, euismod in, elit. Fusce ultricies, orci ac feugiat suscipit, leo massa sodales velit, et scelerisque mi tortor at ipsum. Proin orci odio, commodo ac, gravida non, tristique vel, tellus. Pellentesque nibh libero, ultricies eu, sagittis non, mollis sed, justo. Praesent metus ipsum, pulvinar pulvinar, porta id, fringilla at, est.

Phasellus felis dolor, scelerisque a, tempus eget, lobortis id, libero. Donec scelerisque leo ac risus. Praesent sit amet est. In dictum, dolor eu dictum porttitor, enim felis viverra mi, eget luctus massa purus quis odio. Etiam nulla massa, pharetra facilisis, volutpat in, imperdiet sit amet, sem. Aliquam nec erat at purus cursus interdum. Vestibulum ligula augue, bibendum accumsan, vestibulum ut, commodo a, mi. Morbi ornare gravida elit. Integer congue, augue et malesuada iaculis, ipsum dui aliquet felis, at cursus magna nisl nec elit. Donec iaculis diam a nisi accumsan viverra. Duis sed tellus et tortor vestibulum gravida. Praesent elementum elit at tellus. Curabitur metus ipsum, luctus eu, malesuada ut, tincidunt sed, diam. Donec quis mi sed magna hendrerit accumsan. Suspendisse risus nibh, ultricies eu, volutpat non, condimentum hendrerit, augue. Etiam eleifend, metus vitae adipiscing semper, mauris ipsum iaculis elit, congue gravida elit mi egestas orci. Curabitur pede.

Maecenas aliquet velit vel turpis. Mauris neque metus, malesuada nec, ultricies sit amet, porttitor mattis, enim. In massa libero, interdum vel, interdum vel, blandit sed, nulla. In ullamcorper, est eget tempor cursus, neque mi consectetuer mi, a ultricies massa est sed nisl. Class aptent taciti sociosqu ad litora torquent per conubia nostra, per inceptos hymenaeos. Proin nulla arcu, nonummy luctus, dictum eget, fermentum et, lorem. Nunc porta convallis pede.

Very often you'll find that it's enough to do just 'firsts' – the first couple of lines on each page, or of each paragraph – and omit the 'last'. Try reading a whole book by reading only the first three lines on each page.

Lorem ipsum dolor sit amet, consectetuer adipiscing elit. Nam cursus. Morbi ut mi. Nullam enim leo, egestas id, condimentum at, laoreet mattis, massa. Sed eleifend nonummy diam. Praesent mauris ante, elementum et, bibendum at, posuere sit amet, nibh. Duis tincidunt lectus quis dui viverra vestibulum. Suspendisse vulputate aliquam dui. Nulla elementum dui ut augue. Aliquam vehicula mi at mauris. Maecenas placerat, nisl at consequat rhoncus, sem nunc gravida justo, quis eleifend arcu velit quis lacus. Morbi magna magna, tincidunt a, mattis non, imperdiet vitae, tellus. Sed odio est, auctor ac, sollicitudin in, consequat vitae, orci. Fusce id felis. Vivamus sollicitudin metus eget eros.

Pellentesque habitant morbi tristique senectus et netus et malesuada fames ac turpis egestas. In posuere felis nec tortor. Pellentesque faucibus. Ut accumsan ultricies elit. Maecenas at justo id velit placerat molestie. Donec dictum lectus non odio. Cras a ante vitae enim iaculis aliquam. Mauris nunc quam, venenatis nec, euismod sit amet, egestas placerat, est. Pellentesque habitant morbi tristique senectus et netus et malesuada fames ac turpis egestas. Cras id elit. Integer quis urna. Ut ante enim, dapibus malesuada, fringilla eu, condimentum quis, tellus. Aenean porttitor eros vel dolor. Donec convallis pede venenatis nibh. Duis quam. Nam eget lacus. Aliquam erat volutpat. Quisque dignissim congue leo.

Mauris vel lacus vitae felis vestibulum volutpat. Etiam est nunc, venenatis in, tristique eu, imperdiet ac, nisl. Cum sociis natoque penatibus et magnis dis parturient montes, nascetur ridiculus mus. In iaculis facilisis massa. Etiam eu urna. Sed porta. Suspendisse quam leo, molestie sed, luctus quis, feugiat in, pede. Fusce tellus. Sed metus augue, convallis et, vehicula ut, pulvinar eu, ante. Integer orci tellus, tristique vitae, consequat nec, porta vel, lectus. Nulla sit amet diam. Duis non nunc. Nulla rhoncus dictum metus. Curabitur tristique mi condimentum orci. Phasellus pellentesque aliquam enim. Proin dui lectus, cursus eu, mattis laoreet, viverra sit amet, quam. Curabitur vel dolor ultrices ipsum dictum tristique. Praesent vitae lacus. Ut velit enim, vestibulum non, fermentum nec, hendrerit quis, leo. Pellentesque rutrum malesuada neque.

Nunc tempus felis vitae urna. Vivamus porttitor, neque at volutpat rutrum, purus nisl eleifend libero, a tempus libero lectus feugiat felis. Morbi diam mauris, viverra in, gravida eu, mattis in, ante. Morbi eget arcu. Morbi porta, libero id ullamcorper nonummy, nibh ligula pulvinar metus, eget consectetuer augue nisi quis lacus. Ut ac mi quis lacus mollis aliquam. Curabitur iaculis tempus eros. Curabitur vel mi sit amet magna malesuada ultrices. Ut nisi erat, fermentum vel, congue id, euismod in, elit. Fusce ultricies, orci ac feugiat suscipit, leo massa sodales velit, et scelerisque mi tortor at ipsum. Proin orci odio, commodo ac, gravida non, tristique vel, tellus. Pellentesque nibh libero, ultricies eu, sagittis non, mollis sed, justo. Praesent metus ipsum, pulvinar pulvinar, porta id, fringilla at, est.

Phasellus felis dolor, scelerisque a, tempus eget, lobortis id, libero. Donec scelerisque leo ac risus. Praesent sit amet est. In dictum, dolor eu dictum porttitor, enim felis viverra mi, eget luctus massa purus quis odio. Etiam nulla massa, pharetra facilisis, volutpat in, imperdiet sit amet, sem. Aliquam nec erat at purus cursus interdum. Vestibulum ligula augue, bibendum accumsan, vestibulum ut, commodo a, mi. Morbi ornare gravida elit. Integer congue, augue et malesuada iaculis, ipsum dui aliquet felis, at cursus magna nisl nec elit. Donec iaculis diam a nisi accumsan viverra. Duis sed tellus et tortor vestibulum gravida. Praesent elementum elit at tellus. Curabitur metus ipsum, luctus eu, malesuada ut, tincidunt sed, diam. Donec quis mi sed magna hendrerit accumsan. Suspendisse risus nibh, ultricies eu, volutpat non, condimentum hendrerit, augue. Etiam eleifend, metus vitae adipiscing semper, mauris ipsum iaculis elit, congue gravida elit mi egestas orci. Curabitur pede.

Maecenas aliquet velit vel turpis. Mauris neque metus, malesuada nec, ultricies sit amet, porttitor mattis, enim. In massa libero, interdum nec, interdum vel, blandit sed, nulla. In ullamcorper, est eget tempor cursus, neque mi consectetuer mi, a ultricies massa est sed nisl. Class aptent taciti sociosqu ad litora torquent per conubia nostra, per inceptos hymenaeos. Proin nulla arcu, nonummy luctus, dictum eget, fermentum et, lorem. Nunc porta convallis pede.

Firts
It's often enough just to look at the first few lines of each paragraph (or even just of each page or section).

Which speed-reading pattern do I choose?

Sometimes the pattern you choose depends on personal preference – so try them all. Sometimes it depends on how the text is written – you start with one pattern to find out how the author presents information, and then you use the pattern which best suits the writing style.

It also doesn't really matter which pattern you choose and it's perfectly OK to move from one to another or to create a new one. Most experienced spd rdrs would be hard put to say which pattern they use – it might be any, all, or none of the above, depending on circumstances. The important thing is to look lightly over the text to find key information. This might mean reading the first and last chapter a bit more slowly, so you get a good idea of what the book's about, and then working out which pattern is going to suit you best.

You'll also notice that many of the patterns are just variations on one another. 'Zigzag' is a looser form of 'underlining backwards and forwards'. The 'capital-I shape' is a combination of 'first and

EXPERT TIP

Turn pages more quickly by getting ready in advance.

EXPERT TIP

Remember that you already use some version of speed-reading patterns when you look through a newspaper. It's just a case of transferring an existing skill to other forms of reading.

last' and 'super-reading'. As your confidence grows, you can move from the underlining pattern to super-reading over the course of a few pages (or a few days) simply by relying more and more on your peripheral vision and cutting off more words at the beginning and end of each line.

Remember, though, that you may only be using the patterns on specific pages which you have identified by using the contents list, chapter or section headings or the index. And remember too that you are using a skill you already possess – which you use every time you pick up a newspaper!

F-pattern / Online F-pattern

Eye-tracking devices have established that when people look at websites online they initially tend to look around the page randomly before settling down to read the first few lines of text. They then typically look down the left-hand side of the text, read a bit further into a few lines and continue down the left-hand side – roughly making the shape of the letter F. You might like to try this pattern, as one of the skittering techniques, but the research also serves to illustrate that people find it perfectly normal to let their eyes travel over the text to pick up information without feeling the need to read every word.

Online F-pattern
Online, people tend to look at text following the shape of the letter F.

Lorem ipsum dolor sit amet, consectetuer adipiscing elit. Nam cursus. Morbi ut mi. Nullam enim leo, egestas id, condimentum at, laoreet mattis, massa. Sed eleifend nonummy diam. Praesent mauris ante, elementum et, bibendum at, posuere sit amet, nibh. Duis tincidunt lectus quis dui viverra vestibulum. Suspendisse vulputate aliquam dui. Nulla elementum dui ut augue. Aliquam vehicula mi at mauris. Maecenas placerat, nisl at consequat rhoncus, sem nunc gravida justo, quis eleifend arcu velit quis lacus. Morbi magna magna, tincidunt a, mattis non, imperdiet vitae, tellus. Sed odio est, auctor ac, sollicitudin in, consequat vitae, orci. Fusce id felis. Vivamus sollicitudin metus eget eros.

Pellentesque habitant morbi tristique senectus et netus et malesuada fames ac turpis egestas. In posuere felis nec tortor. Pellentesque faucibus. Ut accumsan ultricies elit. Maecenas at justo id velit placerat molestie. Donec dictum lectus non odio. Cras a ante vitae enim iaculis aliquam. Mauris nunc quam, venenatis nec, euismod sit amet, egestas placerat, est. Pellentesque habitant morbi tristique senectus et netus et malesuada fames ac turpis egestas. Cras id elit. Integer quis urna. Ut ante enim, dapibus malesuada, fringilla eu, condimentum quis, tellus. Aenean porttitor eros vel dolor. Donec convallis pede venenatis nibh. Duis quam. Nam eget lacus. Aliquam erat volutpat. Quisque dignissim congue leo.

Mauris vel lacus vitae felis vestibulum volutpat. Etiam est nunc, venenatis in, tristique eu, imperdiet ac, nisl. Cum sociis natoque penatibus et magnis dis parturient montes, nascetur ridiculus mus. In iaculis facilisis massa. Etiam eu urna. Sed porta. Suspendisse quam leo, molestie sed, luctus quis, feugiat in, pede. Fusce tellus. Sed metus augue, convallis et, vehicula ut, pulvinar eu, ante. Integer orci tellus, tristique vitae, consequat nec, porta vel, lectus. Nulla sit amet diam. Duis non nunc. Nulla rhoncus dictum metus. Curabitur tristique mi condimentum orci. Phasellus pellentesque aliquam enim. Proin dui lectus, cursus eu, mattis laoreet, viverra sit amet, quam. Curabitur vel dolor ultrices ipsum dictum tristique. Praesent vitae lacus. Ut velit enim, vestibulum non, fermentum nec, hendrerit quis, leo. Pellentesque rutrum malesuada neque.

Nunc tempus felis vitae urna. Vivamus porttitor, neque at volutpat rutrum, purus nisi eleifend libero, a tempus libero lectus feugiat felis. Morbi diam mauris, viverra in, gravida eu, mattis in, ante. Morbi eget arcu. Morbi porta, libero id ullamcorper nonummy, nibh ligula pulvinar metus, eget consectetuer augue nisl quis lacus. Ut ac mi quis lacus mollis aliquam. Curabitur iaculis tempus eros. Curabitur vel mi sit amet magna malesuada ultrices. Ut nisi erat, fermentum vel, congue id, euismod in, elit. Fusce ultricies, orci ac feugiat suscipit, leo massa sodales velit, et scelerisque mi tortor at ipsum. Proin orci odio, commodo ac, gravida non, tristique vel, tellus. Pellentesque nibh libero, ultricies eu, sagittis non, mollis sed, justo. Praesent metus ipsum, pulvinar pulvinar, porta id, fringilla at, est.

Phasellus felis dolor, scelerisque a, tempus eget, lobortis id, libero. Donec scelerisque leo ac risus. Praesent sit amet est. In dictum, dolor eu dictum porttitor, enim felis viverra mi, eget luctus massa purus quis odio. Etiam nulla massa, pharetra facilisis, volutpat in, imperdiet sit amet, sem. Aliquam nec erat at purus cursus interdum. Vestibulum ligula augue, bibendum accumsan, vestibulum ut, commodo a, mi. Morbi ornare gravida elit. Integer congue, augue et malesuada iaculis, ipsum dui aliquet felis, at cursus magna nisl nec elit. Donec iaculis diam a nisl accumsan viverra. Duis sed tellus et tortor vestibulum gravida. Praesent elementum elit at tellus. Curabitur metus ipsum, luctus eu, malesuada ut, tincidunt sed, diam. Donec quis mi sed magna hendrerit accumsan. Suspendisse risus nibh, ultricies eu, volutpat non, condimentum hendrerit, augue. Etiam eleifend, metus vitae adipiscing semper, mauris ipsum iaculis elit, congue gravida elit mi egestas orci. Curabitur pede.

Maecenas aliquet velit vel turpis. Mauris neque metus, malesuada nec, ultricies sit amet, porttitor mattis, enim. In massa libero, interdum nec, interdum vel, blandit sed, nulla. In ullamcorper, est eget tempor cursus, neque mi consectetuer mi, a ultricies massa est sed nisl. Class aptent taciti sociosqu ad litora torquent per conubia nostra, per inceptos hymenaeos. Proin nulla arcu, nonummy luctus, dictum eget, fermentum et, lorem. Nunc porta convallis pede.

YES BUT ...

I've tried the patterns and I understand absolutely NOTHING of what I've read.

This is normal. People rarely 'get it' first time. When you first try out these techniques, part of your brain is focusing on the new technique rather than the information on the page. And it's something different and therefore strange.

Try out all the patterns at least twice over several pages – interspersed with super-duper-reading (#13) to speed up your brain. And once you get started, you'll find that you get more information by reading faster. When in doubt, speed up!

However, don't get bogged down in techniques. Your purpose is to find information as quickly as you can, so move on to other techniques, such as 20-minute work sessions (#18) and rapid reading (#24) to experience how they work in practice. Most people say that the patterns start to make more sense when they have a real purpose and they're looking for information they genuinely need.

Confidence builders

• Looking quickly through text to find information is a skill you already have – you do it every time you read a newspaper or look for a word you've found in the index. So why not build your confidence by doing just that – look up words you find in the index and experiment with the different patterns as you look for the words on the relevant page.

• Using your newspaper skills to find the message, use titles, headings and subtitles to guess in advance what the text will be about, and then use the patterns to look for information you expect to find. If it's not there, having a clear expectation also makes it easier to see what is there instead.

• See how quickly you can find these words in the article 'The History of Spd Rdng' on page 135 – one word per column (in order).
19th century • mathematics • White House • Norman Dixon • incubation • rhizome • mechanical exercises • visual language • successes

EXPERT TIP

When in doubt speed up, read faster.

To DO

Remember by doing something

SUMMARY *If you want to recall information you have read, take steps to fix it in your memory (read actively, take notes, talk about it) and then review it.*

It is not enough to take in information more quickly. You also need to remember it and be able to recall it when it is needed.

There are certain things you remember effortlessly: things which affect your survival (eg burns), things which had a big emotional impact on you (the birth of a child, someone's death, etc), things you do regularly (you don't have to 'remember' how to turn on the bathroom tap), and things you are really interested in (eg to do with yourself, your family, your hobby).

If you are an expert in a subject, you will also probably remember easily new information you read which is related to your subject. Because you already know a lot about the subject, your brain has a lot of 'hooks' to attach the new information to.

If you are a beginner in a subject, or if you are studying something which you do not find intrinsically fascinating, you will have to make more effort to remember new information.

Remembering is part of the learning process, so don't just think 'reading', think 'learning'. Many of the spd rdng techniques help you remember what you read, but there are some additional things you can do to help you retain information.

There's no such thing as a poor memory. There are just trained memories and untrained memories."

HOW TO remember what you read

- Make sure you're in a good **state** (#14). Stress is the biggest block to learning and remembering.
- Have a **purpose** (#4). Knowing why you're reading helps you identify important information, which is the first step to remembering it – your brain has something to hang on to.
- Only remember what you need to remember. ('Need' can be helpful to memory.) Decide which information is worth remembering before you start using memory techniques. Trying to remember 'everything' is a recipe for failure.
- Look for **difference** (#12). You learn more when things are new and different from what you already know.
- Read with an **active, questioning mind**. Think, summarise and articulate key messages to yourself, classify ideas in order of importance. Ask, 'What is new?' 'Do I agree?' 'What's missing?' You remember more when your brain is actively engaged.
- **Repeat** what you want to remember – preferably by doing

one of the other techniques here. Repetition builds memory.
- **Take notes** (#17) in your own words preferably as a mindmap or rhizomap. The action of taking notes helps you remember. Add **colour** and **pictures**.
- **Talk** to someone about what you've read (#19). Articulating your notes helps fix them in your mind. Blog or twitter.
- Take regular **breaks** (#27). You remember best things you read first and things you read last. Have more beginnings and endings. Feel energised.
- **Make links and associations** (mental and written) between new ideas and what you already know; link things to each other – the more links the better.
- Make up **stories** to connect facts; **visualise** them, use **colour, images, exaggeration** (make BIG pictures), something **funny**, strong **emotions** (surprise, horror, ecstasy, excitement, fear, joy), **sex** (people remember sex or lavatory humour), and **difference** ('different' things stand out in your memory).
- **Sleep, take naps** – sleep helps consolidate memories.
- **Review** your notes regularly (#20) – after 1 day, 1 week and 1 month.

Photographic memory – or not
There is a misconception that the ideal is to have a photographic memory – you just take one look at a page and it is imprinted on your mind. It doesn't happen quite like that – and are you sure that's what you want?

If you imagine having a library of books in your head, when you want the information, you will still need to look it up and read the relevant pages in your mind in order to access that information. It is much easier to remember information which is meaningful, so **process/distil the information before you make the effort to remember it.**

Recognition and recall
There is a difference between recognition and recall. It is much easier to recognise something (passively) you have read before than it is to recall it (actively). Think about it. How much of what you read do you normally remember 48 hours later? Anything more than 10% is well above average! It is probable, though, that you would recognise much of it if you saw it again. If you want recall, you need to follow the suggestions in this section.

Forgetting
Forgetting is healthy and natural. People with 'super memories' who cannot forget have to learn forgetting strategies – otherwise they are unable to function. Your memory can be compared to an in-tray – the important stuff, recent stuff, and stuff you use all the time stays at the top and is easy to find. The other stuff sinks down the pile and is less easy to access.

Use it or lose it – if you aren't actively using information, you will gradually forget it. If you don't want to forget, you need consciously to follow the suggestions in this section.

Have a good metaphor for your memory
It doesn't matter how many good techniques you use, if you have an overriding belief that you've got a bad memory, you're going to find it much harder to remember things.

What's your memory like? Think about it now. Ask yourself the question: 'What's my memory like?' Give an immediate answer: *My memory is like ....*

If your immediate response is something like 'I've got a memory like a sieve', it's no wonder that you tend to forget things. Change your metaphor to something positive, eg a **'powerful memory bank'**, or a **'memory like an elephant'**, or **'like a sponge'**. Write your positive metaphor on a piece of paper, illustrate it, put it up somewhere you'll see it frequently. Repeat the phrase to yourself every time you see it.

As you implement the ideas in this section, visualise yourself building powerful links in your brain to store the memories so that you can retrieve them easily. If you store facts well, you retrieve them more easily: **memory is reconstruction**, so the key to remembering is good **construction**.

It makes sense
Which of these could you remember most easily?

splzxxx fghyyooo drgh pqmai

heart leaf taste summary do top

A man slipped on a banana skin.

Before you make any effort to remember information, make sure it is meaningful and makes sense to you.

Take notes with mindmaps and rhizomaps

17

SUMMARY *Taking notes is the first step to fixing information in your memory. Mindmaps and rhizomaps are more memorable and lead to greater creativity than linear notes. If you're away from your desk, then write notes (on post-its) in your book.*

A tried and tested way of helping you remember what you read is to take notes. It engages your mind which makes it easier to take in information – you have to think critically to decide which notes to write. Noting which ideas are important to you helps fix them in your brain – and therefore helps you remember them. Also the physical act of writing itself helps form memories, since it brings into play additional parts of the brain and helps embody the information.

We suggest two ways of taking or making notes which improve on traditional linear note-taking:

- **mindmapping** (developed by Tony Buzan)
- **rhizomapping** (developed by Jan Cisek and Susan Norman based on philosopher Giles Deleuze's work on rhizomatic thinking)

There is a difference between **note-making** – generating ideas yourself – and **note-taking** – taking ideas from other sources such as books or lectures. You can use both mindmaps and rhizomaps for either.

MINDMAPPING

A mindmap (see example next page) starts with a picture or key word in the centre to represent the topic. Main 'branches' radiate out from the key word. On each branch is written a word or short phrase which encapsulates a key idea relating to the topic. Secondary ideas and examples are summarised on smaller branches and 'twigs' radiating out from the branches. Ideally use colour and pictures to make your mindmap more memorable.

The key to a good mindmap is to formulate your ideas clearly in the minimum number of words and use the branches and twigs to show relationships between ideas.

When to use mindmapping Mindmapping is very good for showing the connections between ideas. Produce a mindmap
- to set up a structure as a starting point for a 20-minute work

EXPERT TIP

The key to good note-taking is to choose carefully the key words which embody the ideas. Get out of the habit of writing long sentences in your notes – it avoids the thinking process which helps fix the ideas in your memory, and the longer your notes, the more you have to reread when you look at them again.

session (#18) or syntopic processing (#22)
- to clarify what you already know about a subject (and to identify possible gaps in your knowledge) before you start reading – as you read you add to the mindmap
- any time you are taking notes when you already know the structure of the subject and how things (do, or are likely to) fit together
- for sequential, step-by-step notes
- to organise the ideas from random notes (or from a rhizomap) so you can present them to someone else (eg to give a presentation or write an essay or a report)

For more information on mindmapping, google 'mindmapping', or 'Tony Buzan'. Buzan gives additional rules, such as only writing one word on each line, colour coding each branch, etc. We have found that the technique is effective even without following these secondary rules and may even be better when you make the technique your own.

This is a mindmap about mindmapping.

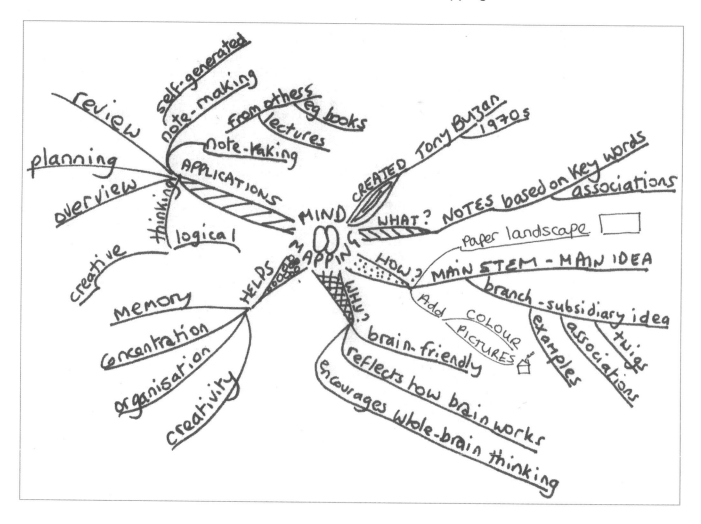

RHIZOMAPPING

With a rhizomap, you initially jot down ideas randomly on the page, and as you see additional ideas (or quotations, or examples) which seem to link with something you have already written, you write them nearby. If appropriate, you can reorganise the ideas afterwards by highlighting key ideas, or linking ideas using numbering, colour coding, stars, arrows, underlining, etc.

When to use rhizomapping Use rhizomapping when you do not know the structure of the subject before you start, eg when you are getting to grips with an overview (#25) of a completely new subject, or when you are not sure what useful information you will get from a book.

A rhizomap can also be a good way of presenting information, for example, this rhizomap presents key ideas on memory:

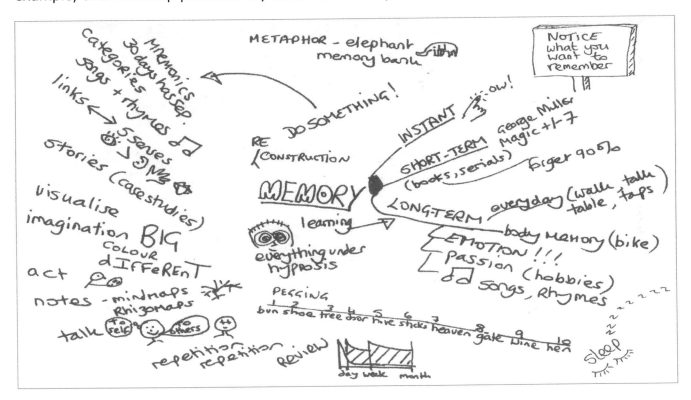

Tips

For both rhizomaps and mindmaps:

- Choose your key words carefully. Make sure they summarise the ideas succinctly in a way which will remain meaningful to you when you look back later.
- Use colours, quick pictures and symbols to make your notes more memorable.
- Research with children has shown that mindmaps are significantly more effective and memorable if the author of the mindmap explains the information in them to someone else as soon as possible after finishing it (see talking #19).

- By all means jot down page numbers so you can easily refer back to books, but make sure you link the page number to a key word or idea so you know what it refers to. A list of unconnected page numbers is of very little use.

Differences between mindmaps and rhizomaps

Mindmaps	Rhizomaps
arboric – like a tree; branches radiate from a central trunk, and subdivide into smaller branches	rhizomatic – like the complex root system of grasses
clear connections between ideas	everything potentially connected to everything else
start and finish points (usually start at '1 o'clock')	start and finish anywhere
need to know basic structure in advance	structure evolves
more sequential	open and organic
organised like a computer	same organisation as the human brain

EXPERT TIP

When you already know the structure of the information, use a mindmap. When you don't, use a rhizomap.

Write in your books

When you are away from your desk, eg reading on a train (we call it 'train reading'), and can't draw a rhizomap or mindmap, keep engaged in the reading process by highlighting or underlining key ideas, or making notes in the book. If the book isn't yours, if it is particularly precious, or if you just can't bear to write in books, then jot down your ideas on post-it notes and stick them in the book – which has the advantage that you can also find the relevant pages again more easily. You can make the notes more permanent by transferring them later to a mindmap or rhizomap – and the process of transferring the notes to a different format will help you remember better. Ebooks allow you to highlight text, make notes, add bookmarks, and search the content. You can also see what other people have underlined – so you can take advantage of 'crowd wisdom' by looking at popular highlights.

Have 20-minute work sessions

SUMMARY *Have work sessions of 20 minutes with one book and one clear purpose. If you feel you still need more from a book, don't go back to it until you've had a break.*

Limit the time you work with one book to 20 minutes. 'Working' with a book is when you 'put it all together' – when you combine all the spd rdng techniques suggested so far and actually sit down and read to get the information you need.

HOW TO do it

Before you start

- **Preview** the book (#2) to make sure it contains information you need.
- Decide on your **purpose** for reading the book (#4) – to look for specific information or to get a good idea of its message.
- Make sure you have **everything you need** to hand – paper, pens, your book. Sit comfortably at a table, in good light (#33).

The session

- Make sure you are in a **good state** for reading (#14) and that you have a relaxed, alert, questioning mind. You might also speed up your eyes and brain with super-duper-reading (#13).
- Set your **timer** (#23) for 20 minutes and keep it in view.
- Look through the book to **find the information to fulfil your purpose**. This might involve using the contents page and index, and using speed-reading patterns (#15) to look for hot spots of information (#11).
- **Take notes** (#17) of relevant information using a mindmap or rhizomap as you go along.
- Keep an eye on the time and make sure your purpose is clear in your mind – don't be seduced into slowing down and reading for leisure, keep looking only for the information to fulfil your purpose.
- When the 20 minutes is up, **stop**.

Afterwards

- **Evaluate** how much of your purpose you have achieved. Whatever you've got, you've got. (If you are a novice spd rdr, encourage yourself by asking yourself how long it would have taken you using your traditional reading methods to reach this level of understanding.)
- Ideally take three or four minutes to **talk** (#19) to someone else about the information you have gleaned.
- Re-evaluate how much of your purpose you have achieved

EXPERT TIP

Keep to time limits. Sticking to time saves you time!

> *Nothing is so fatiguing as the eternal hanging on of an uncompleted task."*
> *William James*

(talking can often increase your perception of what you have achieved). If you have achieved 80% or more of your purpose, accept that you have fully succeeded (80/20 rule #5); if less, decide how much longer you will need to complete your task.

- Learn from the experience and grow your reflective intelligence by thinking what you might do better or differently next time.
- Take a break of at least 5-10 minutes.
- After your break decide whether you need:
a) just a couple of minutes to complete your purpose (in which case, sit down and finish)
b) to plan another work session
c) to rapid read from cover to cover (#24) to get any further points – or
d) to do nothing because you have got enough information, in which case, celebrate your success (#35).

Although the 20-minute 'rule' is actually a guideline, we strongly recommend that in the early days you stick to it (#23). You will very quickly discover how much you get done in 20 minutes – which will also help you become better and better at clarifying your purpose.

Parkinson's Law

Parkinson's Law states that 'work expands to fill the time available'. So you won't necessarily do more even if you give yourself more time.

YES BUT ...

What happens if I don't fully achieve my purpose?

Our brains are designed to notice failure more than success, so novice spd rdrs frequently feel that they haven't achieved all or enough of their purpose. That is why it is a good idea to evaluate what you have got and ask yourself how long it would have taken you using traditional methods to reach this level of achievement. Many people find it would have taken up to 10 times longer.

Although with many books 20 minutes is easily long enough to extract and retain their message, there are obviously other books which need to be approached differently (#32). And in any case you still have the options of (a) working with the book for two or three more minutes, (b) rapid reading (#24) to pick up remaining bits of information, or (c) planning another 20-minute work session with a more realistic purpose.

There are also some books which contain a great deal of information which you are going to want to consult many times.

It can also be useful to think of such books as books of reference. Working with a book several times in 20-minute sessions is still usually much more efficient and effective than reading it through in the traditional way.

DO IT NOW

Put everything you have learnt so far into practice by working with one book for 20 minutes. Follow the sequence in 'how to do it' in this section.

Talk about what you read

SUMMARY *Talking about what you read helps crystallise your understandings in your mind – which is the first step to remembering. Do it twice:*

1) as you read, summarise the information to yourself – it keeps you actively engaged.

2) after reading, tell someone what you've read – it helps you understand and remember it better.

Although reading is traditionally viewed as a passive activity, it is important to engage with the material if you want to learn and remember things from it. Verbalising is an important part of clarifying, consolidating and retaining information you read.

Talk to yourself as you read

We're assuming that you're marking the book as you go along and/or taking notes (#17) – both techniques which help you engage with the material, help you crystallise ideas in your mind and therefore help you fix them in your memory. Another way to read actively and critically is to comment (internally or aloud) on what you're reading as you go along, eg *"OK, so the words are saying … but the underlying meaning is … and the author is clearly on the side of ….".* Alternatively you can ask questions about what you're reading:

* Is this important to me and my purpose? (if not, move on)
* Do I already know this? (if so, move on)
* Is there anything else which is not here? (in which case, where can I find it?)

Questions can also help clarify or amend your **purpose** (#4) – which in some cases you will do as you go along.

Subvocalising / vocalising

Talking to yourself as you read has the added benefit of stopping you from subvocalising. Mentally saying or mouthing the words to yourself as you read can slow you down to the speed of speaking (average 70-240 wpm) when you're reading for information. Subvocalising (or even vocalising, saying the words out loud) is a throw-back to when we first learnt to read. Many books on speed reading make a big deal about subvocalising, but it isn't a bad thing in itself – most of us do it some of the time. Sometimes you need to say the words aloud to check the pronunciation, or to make sense of something complicated. But subvocalising limits you to reading word by word, when you should be reading chunks of text at one time in order to speed up (see Read the message

#6 and Take fewer stops #8). As a first step, practise just saying the key words to yourself rather than the whole sentence (so for this last sentence you might say: 'first – say key words not whole sentence'). You might also use this habit productively by saying more important words and phrases more loudly. Then try speaking *about* what you're reading (making mental notes such as 'this bit's just another example' or 'this isn't important' or 'key words not whole sentence') which means that you can't read the words aloud to yourself and therefore it allows you to speed up. As you speed up, you'll find it easy to get out of the habit of saying the words to yourself as you read because you won't have time. It's the opposite of a vicious circle – a virtuous spiral.

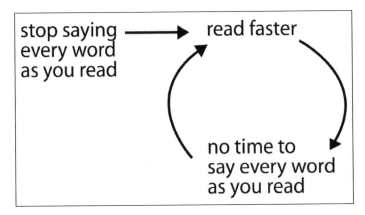

Talk to someone else
As well as talking to yourself while you read, talk to someone else after you've been reading. When you have finished a book and taken out the information you need, talking about what you have read will help you 'fix' the ideas in your mind so that you remember them.

If possible, share what you've read with an interested friend – preferably by telling them, although emailing, blogging and twittering also work (and provide you with a written copy you can refer to later). If you're short of (interested) friends then say the words out loud to yourself.

After talking about what they've read, many people find that they have achieved much more of their purpose than they initially thought when they first stopped reading.

EXPERT TIP

Talking about and sharing information helps you learn it.

Review information regularly

SUMMARY *Typically people forget 90% of what they read within 48 hours of finishing a book. But just by spending a few minutes reviewing your notes after 1 day, 1 week and 1 month, you can instead remember 80-90%.*

Since repetition is a key to remembering, in order to retain information you have studied, you need to revisit it regularly. Otherwise it is natural and healthy for your brain to forget. Each review need only take a few minutes, and the optimum times for reviewing notes are after:

- **1 day**
- **1 week**
- **1 month**

When you review material, we suggest that you start with a blank sheet of paper and jot down in note form what you can remember – and then compare it with what you wrote down before, sometimes going back to the original material to check any details you are not sure of. Testing your memory in this way makes it stronger (helps you recall information) than if you just look at your notes (recognition). Research shows that the only way to build recall is to practise recall.

By the way ...

We are assuming that you accepted 80% of your purpose in the first instance.

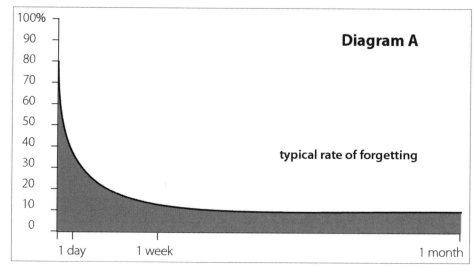

Diagram A shows the typical rate of forgetting new material which is only encountered once. As you see, after a very short time about 90% is forgotten.

Reviewing the material brings memory back up to near 100%, of what you remembered originally, and after a period of time it becomes easier and easier to recall it. The shaded area on Diagram B shows how much more you can expect to remember if you review material regularly – information which is available for your memory to 'hook into' as you learn other information on the subject.

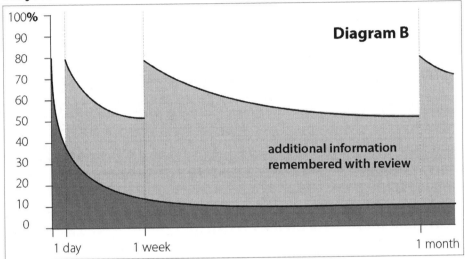

Remember
Once the information is 'yours', you no longer have to make any effort to remember it. You no longer have to remember basic things you learnt in primary school. So, as you learn more about a subject, things you initially had to make an effort to remember become 'second nature' to you – and you can focus on remembering new information.

Occasionally it might also be necessary to review after one year, for example in a modular course where you do nothing with the information for several months but then need it again for an exam later on.

EXPERT TIP

Put that small extra bit of effort into reviewing new information – otherwise you could be wasting all the early time savings.

Read different texts at different speeds

SUMMARY *People tend to read everything in the same (slow) way – which is like driving a car only in first gear. It is OK to read slowly if you are proof-reading for correctness, if you are savouring the sounds of the words, or if you are simply enjoying it. However, if you need information, then use other spd rdng techniques to get it as quickly as possible.*

As well as helping you read more quickly, spd rdng techniques also give you choices about how you read different materials differently.

Slow reading has its place

Spd rdng techniques are designed to help you acquire and retain the information you need from factual texts as quickly as possible – as well as actually reading more quickly. However, there are times when you will read more slowly. For example:

- When you first look at a new book or a new subject, you might initially read more slowly while you 'get your brain into gear'. But remember to speed up as soon as possible – don't get trapped into 'slow reading' – so that you quickly acquire enough information for your brain to make sense of.
- When ideas are complex, or expressed in unfamiliar jargon, you might need to read slowly – possibly even subvocalising or vocalising (saying the words to yourself, silently or aloud) in order for your brain to take in the meaning; this might also be the case if the writing style is cumbersome or ambiguous.
- Proof-reading, where you need to check all aspects of spelling, punctuation, grammar and sense as you read, needs to be done more slowly than information gathering.
- If you want to savour the sounds of words (eg in poetry) or focus on the pronunciation of words, you will read more slowly.
- If you want to enlarge your vocabulary, you will need to read slowly enough to notice the meanings of individual words.
- And of course, if you want to get engrossed in a story, there's nothing like curling up with a good book while you read sequentially at whatever speed gives you pleasure.

Reading more quickly

If you want to read in the traditional way, sequentially but more quickly, you can

- make sure you're in an optimal **state** (#14) to read with an alert, questioning mind
- **open your peripheral vision** (#9) and/or take your awareness

to your **concentration point** (#10)
- **speed up your brain** with **super-duper-reading** (#13)
- take **fewer 'stops'** per line with your eyes (#8)
- focus on **hot spots** of key information (#11)
- use **speed-reading patterns**: underlining, super-reading, skittering and capital-I shape (#15)
- concentrate on **reading the message**, rather than the words (#6)

Remember, if you read more quickly, you will understand more easily (your brain has more information to make sense of), you are less likely to subvocalise, and you are less likely to get bored – so your mind won't wander and you're more likely to persevere with books.

Beware!
You might find yourself reading slowly because you're tired or bored – or you might be tired or bored because you're reading slowly! Your state (#14) – having an alert, questioning mind – is crucial if you want to take in information quickly and easily. Take a break (#27), rest your eyes, breathe some fresh air, get some exercise – and come back to your reading refreshed and alert.

Deirdre's BIGGEST learning

"That I can enjoy reading different things in different ways."
I used to think that there was only one way of reading – in my case, slowly. But I loved reading and I suspect that I didn't want to learn any version of speed reading because I'd lose the pleasure of curling up with a good book. Now I use more useful techniques for getting the factual information quickly – and I have more time for pleasure reading.

Use 'syntopic processing' to work with several books

SUMMARY *Have a 75-minute work session with four books rather than one. Spend approximately 15 minutes per book to gather and compare information to fulfil one purpose, with a few spare minutes to take a break mid-way and evaluate at the end. Record information on a mindmap or rhizomap.*

Syntopic stands for 'synthesis of topic' and syntopic processing means working with at least two (ideally four) books at the same time on the same subject with the same purpose. You approach each book in the same way as when you work with one book for 20 minutes (#18) – but with the same purpose each time. When Mortimer Adler (author of 'How to Read a Book') developed 'syntopical reading', his purpose was to read two or more books in order to compare and contrast them. Spd rdng incorporates more techniques than he was aware of in the 1940s.

Sample purposes for syntopic processing (11 points each)
- information to answer one essay question
- information to write an article / report
- information for a presentation / talk
- overview of a new subject
- overview of all factors to consider before making a decision
- to get 11 specific techniques I can use at work to achieve a particular outcome (eg save time at work, negotiate with clients, ask for a rise)

By the way ...

While it is reasonable to set your purpose to look for 6 key ideas in a 20-minute session with one book, a good number for syntopic processing is 11 key ideas, giving you time to go into greater depth for each idea.

HOW TO do syntopic processing
Preparation
1 State your **purpose** (#4) – make sure it is clear, specific and contexualised.
2 Collect relevant books and preview them (#2) in 2-3 minutes per book. Choose the four best suited for your purpose.
3 Prepare the structure of your mindmap or rhizomap (#17) by thinking what questions you want to answer and how to display your notes.
4 Set a time frame for the task – a suggested time frame being 75 minutes for four books (15 minutes per book, plus 15 minutes). Set your timer for the first 15 minute session.

The work session
5 Get into a good state (#14).
6 Work with the books to find key information which fulfils your

purpose (#4) and write it on your mindmap or rhizomap. Move on to a new book every 15 minutes.

7 Take a short stretch-break half way through and get back into state.

8 Use the few minutes at the end of the session to evaluate your work – and possibly to look back at the book/s which gave you most for extra information.

Afterwards

9 When you finish, evaluate how much of your purpose you have achieved. Compare how much longer it would have taken using traditional reading and then celebrate your success (#35).

10 Tell/share with someone (#19) what you have learned.

Tips
- Use a timer to keep track of the time.
- If you find that a book contains very little relevant information, then move on early.
- Always move on to the next book at the appropriate time. Don't be tempted to go back to an earlier book, or stay longer than the 15 minutes with a book. You have time at the end to go back if necessary.

Organising your notes Whether you note down key information in a mindmap or a rhizomap (#17), decide before you start whether to divide the material:
- according to what is in each book, ie each 'branch' of your mindmap or section of your rhizomap will represent the information from one book
- according to key ideas in the subject matter – each section relating to a different topic. In this case, if it's relevant, you might like to use the initials of the title of each book to show where the information comes from. If you jot down page numbers (eg so you can go back to extract longer quotes direct to the computer later), note what the page number refers to.

Add a 'joker' to sharpen your focus
In addition to your four books, add a 'joker', a (short) book chosen at random not directly relevant to the subject to help you think more actively and creatively about your subject. Spend 5 minutes on your joker after your first book. Look through it and consider 'how it might make you think differently about your purpose and subject'. It might give you some actual **content** (as the other books do), it might give you **insights about the bigger picture**, it might help you **do the task differently**, or it might help you **present** the information more imaginatively.

The **purpose** of the joker is to connect you to **other areas** of expertise you might not have considered, to enhance your **creativity**, to help keep your **mind open**, to help you **think**

differently about the **process** or the **product**, and/or to **amuse** you and enhance your **positive state** for learning.

You can take a joker at random from your shelves, but we keep a collection which includes: a recipe book for children, simplified/ funny/ shortened books on various subjects, collections of quotations, essays, jokes or sayings, mini-dictionaries or phrase books, and small directories of wild flowers, birds, etc.

You can take ideas from the joker's
- **subject matter**, eg jokes might make you think 'I should approach this more lightly', 'The best state for learning is to enjoy myself'; recipes might suggest 'My work could be a collection of 'recipes', or 'I could give people recipes for how to complete tasks'.
- **layout and design** – you might get ideas such as: pictures might be helpful; 'I could think more clearly if each new idea was on a new page'; 'the joker's short and clear – am I being too verbose?'; 'how about lists or bullet points?'

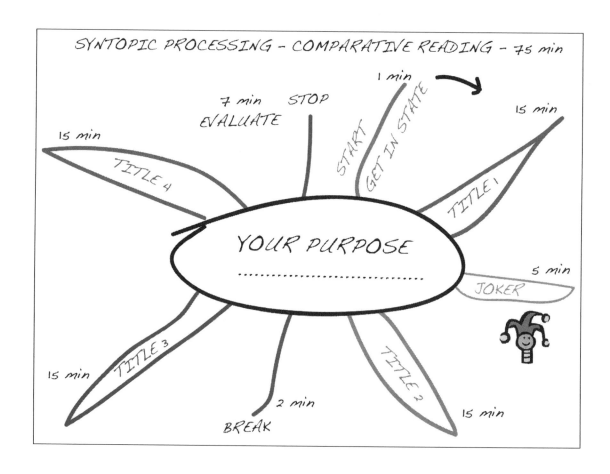

Your timing for syntopic processing will look like this:

- Choose your **purpose**
- Find and **preview** books
- Gather everything you need

09.59	Get into a good **state** (1 min)
10.00	Start. Work with **1st book**, take notes as you go (15 mins)
10.15	Look at **joker** to get a different view (5 mins)
10.20	Work with **2nd book** (15 mins)
10.35	Take a 2-minute stretch **break**
10.37	Work with **3rd book** (15 mins)
10.52	Work with **4th book** (15 mins)
11.07	**Review** – spend a final 7 mins to consult books again, or organise notes
11.14	STOP

- **Evaluate** how much you have achieved.
- **Learn** from experience. Build your reflective intelligence by asking yourself what you will do differently next time.
- **Tell** someone what you have learnt.
- **Celebrate** your success.

DO IT SOON

Set aside 75 minutes to reap the benefits of syntopic processing as soon as you can. If you haven't got a project to work on, choose to get an overview of a completely new subject you've always wanted to know something about. It's exhilarating to get so much information in such a short space of time.

EXPERT TIP

When comparing books, look for patterns. Ask yourself, 'What's repeated, what's missing, what changes, what's exaggerated the most?'

Set time frames and stick to them

SUMMARY *Time frames encourage you to work more quickly and focus on your purpose. Sticking to time encourages you to keep going with future work sessions.*

When you have internalised enough of the new techniques and approaches to reading, you will find that you begin to judge intuitively how long it will take you with any given material to get the information you need. However, when you are starting out and combating old habits and old ways of thinking, it is very useful to set yourself time frames, and a simple timer can be a very good investment.

EXPERT TIP

Invest in a timer – or use the timer on your smart phone.

Basic time recommendations are:
- 5 minutes maximum for previewing (#2)
- 20 minutes for a work session with one book (#18)
- 75 minutes for syntopic processing (#22) with four books (and a joker)

Initially people tend to find that they haven't managed to 'finish' in the time allowed. But this is often just a feeling based on old habits. When you look at how much you've done (rather than focusing on what you feel you've missed), you're likely to realise that you've actually achieved at least 80% of your purpose – and according to the 80/20 rule (#5), this is enough for most purposes. (If it's not, then it might be that you need to redefine your purpose #4.) You might also like to compare how much you would have achieved using your old system – and realise just how much time you've saved using these new techniques.

When you work to a deadline (such as that imposed by the timer), you'll find that you work faster and faster as the time goes by and you realise how little time you have left. After doing this a few times, most people are able to work at this 'faster' pace from the beginning of the work period, and therefore get much more done in the time. But it is the experience of working within time limits that gets you to this point. (Remember Parkinson's Law.)

> **Warning**
> Don't be tempted to extend the time to 'just finish this bit'. 'This bit' gets longer and longer and in no time you find you're back to your old habits. And worse – the next time you think about reading a book, you remember that it didn't really only take 20 minutes, it took much longer. The result is that you don't start.

The other benefit of working within time limits and realising how much you can get done within a relatively short space of time is that you start the task in the first place. Most people could get a lot of information out of a book if they just spent 10 minutes looking at it (eg while waiting for a bus or a dentist appointment) – but because they feel they 'can't read it properly', they don't even start.

Susan's experience

Susan was at a seminar where they were going to discuss a book everyone was supposed to have read – and she hadn't read it. However, after working with it in the 20-minute coffee break, she was able to make more pertinent comments than anyone else. Why? Everyone who'd taken several hours to read the book over a number of days had not given themselves a clear purpose to begin with and had forgotten a lot of the information. And the other person who hadn't read it didn't realise that it was possible to get so much information in 20 minutes so didn't try.

'Rapid read' from cover to cover

SUMMARY *Look quickly (2-10 seconds per page) at every page, searching for 'hot spots' of key information. Do this after a work session to collect any final bits of information.*

Reading from cover to cover means going quickly through the book sequentially looking at every page for key information. This is what most people think speed reading is (whereas it is just as valid to go backwards and forwards through the book or only go to specific sections to look for relevant information.)

HOW TO rapid read

Look quickly through the book, looking consciously at every page (2-10 seconds per page). Use the speed-reading patterns (#15) to look for hot spots (#11) of key information. Any time you find key information you can slow down and read around it (dip) until you have grasped the point, and then resume rapid reading.

By the way

Rapid reading is the technique of choice for text with a continuous story line, eg novels, biographies and historical account.

Why read from cover to cover?
- Less experienced spd rdrs will typically rapid read after they've worked with a book for 20 minutes, checking for information they may have missed. Because you are already familiar with the book from previewing it and having a work session, it is relatively easy to spot new information. Rapid reading can be helpful in the early days for getting over the **feeling of having missed something** if you don't read from cover to cover. As you grow to trust (#31) your ability to gather the information you need and accept the 80/20 rule (#5), you are likely to use rapid reading less for this purpose and use your time for moving on to new books.
- Experienced spd rdrs often rapid read a book instead of doing a work session when their purpose is to **understand its message** or **to get an overview** of the information it contains.

However, both experienced and inexperienced spd rdrs need to do something with the information (take notes #17, talk about the information #19) if they want to be sure of remembering it (#16).

When you have understood the downloading process (#28), you can be confident that as you consciously take in information using rapid reading, you will also be taking all the information into your non-conscious mind. This is why experienced spd rdrs sometimes use rapid reading in place of downloading since it is more satisfying to the conscious mind.

If you still feel you're missing something

You're not alone. It is very common in the early days to feel that we have to read word for word to get all the information. This often stems from the way we were taught to read as children. And at times you may experience irritation, disappointment or tension – which seems to be an inevitable part of a successful learning experience. Avoid getting cross or criticizing yourself. Instead …

- Trust the 80/20 rule. You probably don't need everything in the book, and even if you did, you wouldn't need it all in one go, and reading sequentially is not the best way to get it.
- Do not judge the process by your first experiences. New skills may take a bit of time to become second nature. Keep going.
- Switch on your inner smile and relax. The more you practise getting into a good state, the easier it gets and the more often you feel good 'for no obvious reason'.
- Notice what is already working. Focus on what you have achieved and build on that.
- Check what you think you've missed. Once you've used the spd rdng to work with a book, read it sequentially to see what you've missed. It's likely that you will have gleaned at least 80% of the information you need (not the same as all the information it contains), but what you might have 'missed' is the feeling of reading conventionally. Feel free to read conventionally for pleasure, alongside using spd rdng techniques for information.
- Go on to read all those other books you haven't even started yet.

Reading in a new way

Cross your arms. Now cross them the other way (with the 'wrong' arm on top). Most people find this uncomfortable. (Some can't do it at all.)

We get used to doing something (eg reading) in one way and when we first try a new way, it feels wrong. Or we feel we haven't got enough – there may be something else in the book that we've missed. Or we feel guilty because we're not doing it the way we were taught. But it's just a feeling.

In school, the teaching of reading stops once you can decipher letters and words. Thereafter you're on your own. Some people develop their own reading strategies, but most of us don't. Most of us learn them later in life. You're learning them now. You can always go back to reading in the old way if you want to (in first gear) – or you can choose to use spd rdng techniques to read quickly and easily for the rest of your life. Once they become second nature, they're just as comfortable as (and much more effective than) your old conventional reading.

Adams's BIGGEST learning

"that I could read 30 books a week."
I went into my first seminar on my masters degree course having done a syntopic processing session with five books on the subject. None of the other students had read more than half a book and they knew almost nothing about the subject. I already knew at least 80% of what the tutor told us, which meant I was able to take part in a meaningful discussion. In lectures, I'm able to listen critically and just take occasional notes, while everyone else is frantically writing down everything. They don't know which bits are important. I do.
Now I'm regularly working with up to 30 books a week – including 'extra' books, which means I can challenge some of the tutors!
And I still have a bit of time for leisure reading just for fun.

YES BUT ...

All this isn't proper reading!!!!!

You're absolutely right, if by 'proper reading' you mean conventional reading.

With conventional reading, you take three or more days to read a book.

With spd rdng you can usually get the important information from a book in less than half an hour.

With conventional reading, you usually forget 90% of what you read within 48 hours.

With spd rdng you can retain as much information as you need for as long as you need it.

With conventional reading, you read everything in the same way.

With spd rdng you have a variety of techniques and strategies which you can adapt for different types of reading materials.

With conventional reading it is easy for your attention to wander.

With spd rdng it is easy to stay focused.

With conventional reading, the author determines how you get the information – whether you need it or not.

With spd rdng you are in control of how and when you get the information – and you only spend time on information which is relevant.

Conventional reading implies that reading something is enough to make you an expert.

Spd rdng gives you the techniques to genuinely build your expertise quickly and easily.

Get the overview before the details

25

SUMMARY *When learning a new subject, make sure you understand the overview, the big picture, before you look at the details. Since most books are written sequentially (ie detail following detail), this usually means starting by previewing and looking at chapter and section headings and first and last chapters for a general understanding. Syntopic processing is excellent for getting an overview of a new subject.*

Although this is not strictly speaking about reading, this technique is the key to getting a good purpose (#4) and can make the difference between success and failure when putting other techniques into practice.

When you are learning something new, the brain learns most easily if it starts by getting an overall picture of what the subject is about before you go into detail. Unfortunately, information is more usually presented bit by bit, supposedly 'to make it easier'. But this is like doing a jigsaw by taking individual pieces out of the box and trying to put them together. It's much easier if you start by looking at the picture on the box to see what you're aiming at, and then work on 'obvious' areas (eg the red dress, the blue umbrella, all the faces). If a particular piece is difficult, you compare it with the picture again. Then you notice how different sections fit together, and finally you fill in the larger expanses of sky and grass (the difficult bits or final details).

Most people read word by word as if they were looking at a building like this: "brick, brick, brick, brick, window, brick, brick, door – oh yes, it's a building." This is a very inefficient way for our brains to process information. Start by noticing the main features of the building, before going into as much detail as you need to later.

HOW TO get an overview
Assuming that you know (almost) nothing about the subject, there are various ways to get an initial overview:
- google the subject online and read introductory articles or definitions
- ask for guidance from an expert or a mentor
- read simplified (children's) books and/or summaries
- get hold of a college course first-year booklist for your subject and preview (#2) all the books on the list
- go to a library or bookshop and preview introductory books on

Ania's success story

Ania was doing a one-year course in nutrition to complement her work as an osteopath. For whatever reason, she failed to do any work at all until just before the exam. At that point, she sat down with all the relevant books and worked for three days to produce mindmap after mindmap which she pinned up round the walls. She started with the general overview, then got an overview of each key area of the subject, and finally got into more and more detail. She was the only person on the course who got more than 90%.

your subject (3-5 minutes each) and choose the one/s you think will be most useful
- if you have several books on the subject, do syntopic processing (#22), drawing a mindmap/rhizomap (#17) of the subject overview.

Your purpose (#4) is to write down all the key areas of your subject (the ones an author might make the chapter headings in a book) and know in general what each area refers to (much of your time may be spent just making sure you understand the contents list). Once you have this big picture, you can then get an overall idea of what each 'chapter' is about. After which you can go into as much detail as you like in any of the areas, confident that you know how they relate to other areas of the subject.

Sometimes the details are not important, in which case, the big picture is enough. But even if you need all the details, it is easier to fit them into a pattern than to get them separately and sequentially.

YES BUT ...
I need all the details.
1   Even if this is true, you can't get them all at once and it is much harder to learn them sequentially. Start with the big picture – and then go into as much detail as you like.
2   Remember that reading is only part of the process of building up expertise. You need to intersperse your reading with putting the information into practice in some practical way.

Rd smrys

SUMMARY *Reading summaries is the quickest way of getting the book's message.*

Research shows that people remember more (and for longer) after reading a summary than they do after reading the whole book. When you are previewing a book, always check whether it contains chapter summaries which quickly give you an overview of what the book is about.

As you read, look out for phrases which indicate that the author is giving a summary, eg **'to sum up'**, **'in summary'**, **'in short'**, **'in a nutshell'** , **'in conclusion'.**

Even better, find a summary of the complete book – there are lots of compilations of summaries published as books or online. Often a good review will give you a summary of the book's key message. (See 'Resources' at the end of this book)

Take notes from the summaries on a mindmap or rhizomap (#17) as you would from the whole book.

By the way ...
You will usually read a summary more slowly than you would read a 'normal' book because the information is so dense. But if you think of reading as 'information gained in relation to time spent' rather than 'how fast am I reading?' (#3), summaries are an excellent investment of time.

Take frequent breaks

SUMMARY *You remember more from the beginnings and ends of work sessions (the primacy and recency effects). By taking more breaks you have more beginnings and ends – and you refresh your eyes, body and mind to improve your state.*

Did you know ...

- ... most people cannot listen or read and take in new information for more than 8-20 minutes at a time? (The actual time depends on their age and physical/emotional/mental state, their schema or current knowledge of the subject, and the difficulty or interest of the subject matter.)
- ... according to research by Zeigarnek, you tend to remember more from the beginning and end of a learning session than from the middle? These are known as the 'primacy and recency effects'. (However, beware the 'suffix effect' – if you start doing things other than your work at the end of your session, this is what you will remember, rather than the subject matter. Effectively, therefore, you remember most from the beginnings of sessions.)

It therefore makes sense to read for concentrated periods of up to 20 minutes and then take a break (for a minimum of five to ten minutes) before resuming your reading/study – you wake up your brain, and you have more beginnings and endings to help your memory.

During your breaks, do some eye exercises, and wake up your brain by taking deep breaths of fresh air, sipping water, and doing physical exercises. When you start work again, remember to get into the best state (#14) for taking in information – take a deep breath in, focus on your concentration point (#10) and feel your peripheral vision opening up, pause and plan what you are going to do, take a deep breath, and smile.

Meenal's BIGGEST learning

"**to work in 20-minute chunks.**" Now I live my life by this principle (20 minutes is definitely enough for housework!) and I get so much done.

Exercises for eyes

It's harder to read when your eyes are tired. Keep your eyes in an optimal state for reading by doing eye exercises from time to time:

• Change focus
Look up from what you're reading and alternate a few times between focusing on something in the distance and on something up close.

• Palm your eyes
Briskly rub the palms of your hands together to warm them slightly. Place the palms over your closed eyes and with the outsides of your palms gently massage the bony areas around the eyes (not directly onto the eyeballs) for about 30 seconds. Open your eyes under your hands, and create a seal with your palms so that you're looking at complete darkness for a moment or two.

• Clock gazing
Sit comfortably with an erect spine and both feet on the floor. Imagine a huge clock face about 30 cms away directly in front of you. Without moving your head, look up to 12 o'clock – then down to 6 o'clock.
Up to 1, down to 7
Up to 2, down to 8
Right to 3, left to 9
Down to 4, up to 10
Down to 5, up to 11.
Close your eyes and rest (or palm them) for 30 seconds.

• Lazy eights
Make a fist with your thumb sticking up. Hold it out at arm's length in front of you. Draw a figure 8 on its side – start in the middle, move up to the right, round, down the outside, up towards the middle again and then round over the top on the left, down the outside, up into the middle again. Keep going. Make sure you're going up in the middle and down round the outsides. Keep your head still and follow your thumb with your eyes

Fizzical challenges

During breaks, challenge yourself by trying (and perfecting) one or more of the following:

• **Feet/thumbs crossover**   Stand with your feet pointing inwards (like a letter A) and your hands at your sides, thumbs pointing out. Jump and change over, ie feet pointing out (like a letter V) and thumbs pointing in. Keep jumping and changing over.
Hint The brain doesn't like opposites. Mentally link your thumbs to your heels – so they both go the same way. Don't jump initially. Swivel your heels, keeping your weight on your toes.

• **Ear and nose**   Clap your hands on your knees. Bring one hand up to your nose and the other hand up to the opposite ear. Clap hands on knees, then bring the opposite hands to your nose and other ear. Continue.
Hint Forget about the knee clap initially. Place one hand on your nose and the other on the opposite ear. Slowly bring your ear hand to just in front of your nose. Take your nose hand around the other hand to the opposite ear. Repeat this process several times till it feels natural. Then add in the knee clap between each change.

• **Circling toe**   Cross your legs, left over right. Circle your left big toe in a clockwise direction. Keep that going as you draw a figure 6 in the air with your left hand.

• **2/3 time**   Put your right hand straight up in the air, then bring it down to your side. Keep going in a regular one-two rhythm. Stop.
Keep your right hand still. Put your left hand straight up in the air, then straight out to the side horizontally, then down to your side. Keep going in a regular one-two-three rhythm.
Put the two actions together, arms moving at the same time: R/L up, R down – L out, R up – L down, R down – L up, R up – L out, R/L down ... and keep going.

• **Moving alphabet**   Read the alphabet aloud as written on the chart. As you do so, raise your Right hand if the letter below is R, raise your Left hand if the letter below is L, and raise both hands Together if the letter below is T.
It's harder than it looks, but if you can do it easily, then read the alphabet backwards – or read up and down the columns – or additionally lift your opposite knee (ie R = raise your right hand and left knee, L = raise your left hand and right knee, T = raise both hands and both legs/jump).

A	B	C	D	E	F	G	H	I
R	R	L	R	T	R	L	L	T

J	K	L	M	N	O	P	Q	R
R	L	R	L	T	R	L	R	L

S	T	U	V	W	X	Y	Z
T	R	L	R	T	L	R	L

Brain Gym

Any physical challenges similar to those above (rubbing your tummy while patting your head, etc) help wake you up by stimulating both hemispheres of the brain, but certain exercises, known as Brain Gym, have additional positive effects (by working on the body's energy system). Try the following:

• **Brain buttons**   Find these acupuncture kidney points on either side of your breast bone just below the ends of your collar bones. They're easier to find if you hunch your shoulders forwards. Place one hand over your tummy button and the thumb and middle finger of the other hand on your two brain buttons. Sit or stand straight and gently massage your brain buttons for about 30 seconds.

• **Cross crawl**   Lift your left leg and touch your left knee with your right hand (arm crosses the body). Then lift your right leg and touch your right knee with your left hand. Keep going, touching alternate knees – as slowly as possible. (A more energetic variation is to touch elbows to the opposite knee.)

• **Gorilla thumps**   Take a deep breath in. Pound the centre of your chest with loose fists as you breathe out making a loud 'aaaaaaargh' sound.

• **Cook's hook ups**   Put both hands out in front of you, backs of your hands together, thumbs facing down. Place one hand over the other so palms are facing, then interlace your fingers. Swivel your interlocked hands together towards you, and bring them up under your chin. Cross one leg over the other. Relax shoulders, tummy and face. Put the tip of your tongue on the roof of your mouth and take several deep breaths. This is a particularly calming and focusing exercise to end with before going back to work.

Download the book into your non-conscious mind

SUMMARY *Download the book into your non-conscious mind by looking quickly at each double page without making any conscious effort to see or understand the text. Trust that the information has gone into your non-conscious mind. Use the other conscious spd rdng techniques as before and gradually notice how much more information you know as the downloaded knowledge comes to conscious awareness.*

This is the easiest technique in the book to do – and possibly the hardest to understand. It is different from all the other techniques and strategies in that you rely on your **non-conscious mind**. You do not consciously have to 'read' anything. The purpose of downloading is to expose your non-conscious mind to all the information in the book so that it can go directly into your long-term memory. It 'primes' your brain with the information in the text.

HOW TO download
- Hold your book in such a way that, when it is open, you can easily see all four corners of the book.
- Focus on your concentration point, smile and relax. (The more you enjoy it, the better.)
- Turn over the pages one at time from cover to cover at the rate of about one per second (ie quickly – the faster the better) making sure that the four corners of the book remain within your peripheral vision. Don't try to 'read' – just make sure the words pass in front of your eyes quickly.
- If you get tired before you finish the book, you can turn it upside down and continue to the end using the other hand (your brain can interpret the words whichever way up they are).
- When you get to the end of the book, flick through it backwards and forward a few times as you look at it.
- Do something else for at least 20 minutes (ideally you will sleep before doing any further work). It's important to give the brain time to sort out the information you have downloaded.

That's all there is to it. You'll almost certainly feel as if you haven't understood a word. That's the usual response. And consciously you haven't 'read' the book. But your non-conscious mind has taken the information directly into long-term memory.

The words can be clear or blurred   It doesn't matter whether you see the words clearly or not – the technique still works, even if the words are slightly blurred. This is because the brain can make sense of information even if it's not complete (#6). It is perfectly OK, too, if you see words consciously – but don't be tempted to slow down to start 'reading'.

You don't have to concentrate   It doesn't matter whether or not you concentrate on the material – you are going too quickly to consciously understand everything (or anything) anyway. So it's quite possible to concentrate on something else (eg having a conversation or listening to the radio – Jan likes to watch TV over the top of the book) as long as you hold the book so that you can still see all four corners in your peripheral vision.

Make sure that what you download has meaning to you.
If you don't understand what you are downloading, your mind has nothing to 'hold on to'. It will still work – eventually – but it will take much longer for the brain to make sense of the information.

If you are downloading a new and complex subject with **specialised vocabulary**, then as well as downloading an explanatory textbook, you might also download a glossary of terms. Downloading descriptive texts and glossaries or (specialist) dictionaries will also help you build your vocabulary – which will make reading easier.

If you are **learning a new language**, then initially download story books with pictures, phrase books with translations, dictionaries with definitions in your mother tongue, and articles or stories where the translation appears alongside (as in airline magazines). This is particularly important when the new language is in an unfamiliar script. Once you understand the script and some of the basics of the language, then you can download extended texts. (**By the way ...** As well as downloading, make sure you also listen to native speakers in real situations, eg films, or listen to children's stories while following the text – otherwise you will tend to make up your own pronunciation which you will then have to unlearn.)

Rapid reading for downloading
Rather than downloading per se, we (Jan and Susan) frequently rapid read a book (#24), ie consciously look at every page – knowing that the whole book is going into our non-conscious mind. It takes very little extra time, and it feels satisfying because it gives conscious as well as non-conscious input.

When to download
You can download books (or other materials) at any time. However, here are some of our recommendations.

By the way ...

Downloading and direct learning (#29) are the only non-conscious techniques in the book. Do everything else with conscious awareness.

Susan's experience

Susan was planning to attend a beginner's Spanish course through suggestopedia. Before the course she downloaded lots of Spanish dictionaries, children's books, phrase books, bilingual articles, etc. On the course she made such good progress that another participant left, saying that she wasn't getting it. Susan tried to reassure her by explaining about all the preparation she'd done, to which the angry response was: 'You cheated!' The difference was that the woman was there to test the system, while Susan was there to learn Spanish.

- **Download when you have determined your purpose for reading**   Download after you've previewed the book (#2) and decided on your purpose (#4). Having a purpose gives the mind something to latch on to.
- **Download after working with a book**   After you have worked with a book with a specific purpose for 20 minutes (#18), you will have a clear idea of what the book contains and how it can be useful to you, and you will have created many more 'hooks' in your brain for new information.
- **Download in advance of needing the information**   Your brain needs 'down time' in order to process the information you download. The ideal is to 'sleep on it' – but if you can't sleep between downloading and wanting to use the information, then take a break of at least 20 minutes, doing something unconnected with the information.
- **Download just before you go to sleep**   Sleep is when your brain does its best processing.
- **Download only when you need the information**   We suggest that you download material that you will need to use within the next week or so. If you leave it too long between downloading and using new information, it can be harder for the brain to retrieve it.

How downloaded information comes to conscious awareness

Downloaded material goes straight into your long-term memory, bypassing conscious awareness. However, you don't consciously know what you know – and you can't guarantee **when** the information will come to conscious awareness. But the information can come into conscious awareness in the same way as any other information stored in your long-term memory, through:

- **association** – something else reminds you of the information
- **need** – when you have a genuine need for the information (eg while writing an essay or giving a presentation), you might suddenly find that you know something you didn't know you knew
- **recognition** – you suddenly recognise something you didn't know you'd encountered before

All of these things prod the non-conscious mind into releasing the information. Other 'prods' are:

- **passion** – you're really interested in something
- **repetition** – you keep working consciously with the information

Assuming that you're not truly interested in this information (which is why you're working at it), then the best way to bring downloaded information to conscious awareness is to continue doing all the other (conscious) spd rdng techniques. The repetition gives the non-conscious mind the message that you are interested and stimulates it to bring information to your conscious attention.

Although it is possible (and we know of cases) for people to do nothing other than download information from books before successfully passing exams or job interviews, we strongly recommend that you use downloading as one of the steps of the learning process. Once you have practised the technique for a while and understood how the information comes to conscious awareness, you will know the extent to which you can rely on it working for you when you need it.

The more you use it, the better it works. The more relaxed you are about retrieving the information, the more likely you are to remember it. The more you trust the process, the more likely it is that the information will be available to you when you need it. Stress accounts for 80% of learning difficulties and is also the biggest factor in stopping downloaded information from coming to conscious awareness. Since exams and jobs interviews can be very stressful, it's better not to rely only on downloaded information in these situations. Do other preparation too.

Remember that it is the **information** which comes back when you need it, not the book. So even though you might become aware of individual bits of information, you may not know where it came from originally, and you probably still won't feel as if you know what's in the book.

Downloading can also be used for **direct learning**, or learning without learning (#29).

HOW TO guarantee that you WON'T remember downloaded information

It takes most people some time to realise for themselves how the non-conscious mind works and therefore what you can expect from downloading. However, there are certain things NOT to do if you want to give the process a chance:

- Don't respond to challenges from friends to show off how much you remember. (You're almost bound to fail.)
- Don't rely on information coming to mind when you are under stress, eg in an examination. (Stress is the biggest cause of difficulties with learning and memory.)
- Don't give up after one try. (You need to give everything new a fair chance – and the less you know about something, the more you need to practise.)
- Don't focus on testing the technique rather than using it. (The non-conscious mind responds to real need, not to manufactured tests.)
- Don't try it only with information you don't need to use. (Information tends to come back when you really need it.)

By the way ...

Downloading is known as 'mental photography' or 'subliminal photography' in the system originally developed by Dr Richard Welch (www. subdyn.com). Paul Scheele called it the 'photoreading' step in the PhotoReading Whole Mind System where you are told to consciously defocus your eyes as you do it – mainly to break the habit of 'reading' slowly, and because the non-conscious mind responds well to 'weak' signals. We (Jan and Susan) don't defocus because it takes a moment or two to refocus when we want to read consciously again and we (along with others) find defocusing uncomfortable or tiring.

Q&A

What's the most number of books I can download?
Physically the only limit is time. We often download 5-10 books at a time when we're working on a new subject. It is perfectly feasible, for example, to preview (#2) and download all the books on a study course booklist in about a week to give you a head start on your course.

How many times should I download a book?
Once – on the basis that it has gone into your long-term memory. But if you are coming back to a book after a long break, you might profitably download it again, or if you are working on a complex subject which is new to you, then you might download it two or three times over a period of weeks to give your brain more 'hooks' to help you understand it. In between each download, though, do other work (eg consciously use other spd rdng techniques) on the subject.

Do I have to use the other conscious spd rdng techniques or will I eventually be able to rely on the downloading technique?
The more you use the downloading technique together with the other conscious spd rdng techniques, the more you will come to understand how it works and the more you will be able to rely on it. Initially it works best if you rely on all the conscious techniques and do downloading as a 'bonus'.

You could also rapid read from cover to cover (#24) after you've worked with a book, confident that while you consciously look for hot spots (#11) of information, your non-conscious mind is taking in everything else.

Can I download from the computer screen/mobile device?
Yes. Downloading digital texts is easy. Make sure you can see the four corners of the page/s, and set your computer or reading device to scroll the text in front of your eyes at a rate of approximately one second per page to begin with. As your experience and confidence grow, you can go faster.

DO IT NOW

Download this Spd Rdng book now or shortly before you go to bed tonight. If you're doing it properly it won't take you more than three or four minutes.

SUMMARY OF TERMS

Aaargh! I'm getting lost in all these different terms. What's the difference between super-reading and rapid reading, for example?
Firstly, don't worry about the terms. Focus on getting the information you need from your reading material. If you're doing that quickly and easily, then do more of whatever is going right. If you'd like more help, then focus on putting different techniques into practice rather than worrying about what they're called. But if you'd like a quick reminder about the differences, then …

Speed reading is an approach to reading and includes anything which helps you read faster.

Super-reading is a speed-reading pattern when you look down the middle of a page to find hot spots of information.

Super-duper-reading is similar to super-reading in that you look down the middle of the page, but you do it faster than you can consciously take in the information and your purpose is to speed up your brain. After about 10 pages, you slow down slightly and start looking for information, possibly using a speed reading pattern such as super-reading, skittering, etc.

Skimming (newspaper technique) means looking quickly through a text using a variety of spd rdng techniques with the intention of getting an understanding of what an unfamiliar text is about.

Scanning (dictionary technique) is similar to skimming, except you are looking for specific information which you hope or believe is in the text. (The difference between skimming and scanning is purpose.)

Downloading (or **photoreading**) means turning the pages as quickly as possible while making sure that you can see all four corners of the book. You are not consciously reading, just looking at both pages at once, confident that the information is going directly to your non-conscious mind.

Rapid reading is when you look quickly at every single page from cover to cover – usually after you've had a purpose-driven 20-minute work session – with the aim of consciously noticing any additional information you might have missed. (Experienced spd rdrs might rapid read a whole book at the rate of 4-10 seconds per page to get its message or notice things they don't already know about a subject – confident that while they look consciously for information, everything is simultaneously going into their non-conscious downloading.)

Spd Rdng is the name of the comprehensive and flexible approach to reading developed by Susan Norman and Jan Cisek which brings all these different techniques and strategies together to allow you to get the information you need from whatever you read.

Download books for 'direct learning'

SUMMARY *Download several books containing strategies for a physical skill you wish to acquire (eg improve golf swing) or information for a specific purpose (eg quiz night). Continue with your normal activities (playing golf, taking part in the quiz) and notice improvements.*

Direct learning means downloading (#28) books to gain specific skills or results without doing anything to bring the information to conscious awareness. It relies on the power of the non-conscious mind to recognise and implement the information or skill you need without the intervention of the conscious mind.

HOW TO do it

- Identify the skill you want to improve. Set that as your purpose (#4), eg "To have a strong tennis backhand." "To make better decisions at work."
- Close your eyes and visualise yourself with the desired outcome (this helps clarify your purpose – and means you'll know when you've achieved it).
- Preview (#2) several books and find the two or three that are most likely to teach you the skill – make sure they give practical instructions and not just theoretical information.
- Download (#28) all the books. (The immediate feeling is that you don't consciously know anything from the books.)
- Put the skill into practice without thinking about it, ie carry on with your normal activities involving the skill (play tennis, keep making decisions).
- Over time notice improvements

The usual stages of learning

Normally, we approach the learning of a new skill as a conscious process which goes through the stages of:

1. **Unconscious incompetence** You don't know what it is you don't know. (You have no idea how to drive a car.)
2. **Conscious incompetence** You learn what it is you don't know, but you can't actually do it yet. (You start taking driving lessons and you become aware of what is involved.)
3. **Conscious competence** Practice, practice and more practice! (You can drive, but you're not confident and still need to concentrate.)
4. **Unconscious competence** You are proficient and able to use the new skill without thinking about it.

The usual learning sequence

Usually when you learn something new in a sport, things get worse before they get better, because you are consciously trying to remember and put into practice things you have learnt. But when a tennis ball is coming towards you, there isn't time consciously to decide what stroke to play, move your body into the correct place, take your arm back and swing the racquet forwards at the exact fraction of a second required to hit it back. As you practise more, the movements get into 'body memory' and you do them 'automatically' – this is known as 'unconscious competence'.

Direct learning bypasses the conscious mind and goes directly to unconscious competence – you can do it, but you don't know how. You still need to use the skill and you probably won't become an expert overnight. Malcolm Gladwell quotes in his book 'Outliers' that it takes 10,000 hours of practice (about 10 years) to become an outstanding world-class expert. With direct learning and speed-reading techniques you can achieve a normal level of expertise much more quickly – as long as you keep applying your chosen skill.

How direct learning worked for some people

Poor circulation   Ania was doing an exercise to see how much information she could glean just from downloading a book – the cover, contents and title pages had been removed. When she'd finished downloading, she thought she was getting a cold because she was feeling very hot – and she did indeed look flushed. After lunch when she picked up the book again, she immediately got the sensation of heat. When she checked, she discovered that the book was 'Beyond the relaxation response' by Herbert Benson. In it he describes a practice called 'fierce woman' in which Tibetan monks strip and sit out in the Himalayas in sub-zero temperatures and cover themselves with wet sheets. They dry the sheets by generating heat, starting in their abdomen. (The winner is the one who dries the most sheets – what those monks will do for fun!) The point of the story, though, is that Ania had always had poor circulation, and suffered from cold hands and feet. Her non-conscious mind had picked up on this technique as a useful one for improving her circulation – which it did. And the effect lasted.

Bad back   Ania's second experience was when she had a bad back. She didn't have time to go to an osteopath, so she downloaded a book on osteopathy – during the course of which something 'clicked' in her spine and she was fine. It was possibly helpful that she was herself an experienced osteopath, so she was simply reminding her body, via her non-conscious mind, that it knew what to do to be well. But nonetheless, there was no way that she could have consciously manipulated her own spine in order to achieve the desired result.

By the way ...

If you have been putting into practice the spd rdng skills in the book so far, you are almost certainly at the conscious competence stage. With a bit more practice, you'll be spd rdng.

95

Fixing the computer *Jan transferred all his data to a new computer – which promptly stopped working. He spent a couple of hours on the phone with expert technicians, who eventually advised him that the computer must be broken. Jan really needed the computer to work so he downloaded the manual. Then he had a cup of coffee (to relax), played a game on his mobile phone (to remind himself that he could work things out), then sat down and started playing with the computer. Within 10 minutes it was working again – but he doesn't know what he did to fix it.*

Job interview *Howard wanted a job doing video editing – which he knew very little about although he was an enthusiastic amateur. He did our Spd Rdng course at the weekend, downloaded appropriate books on the Monday morning, went for the interview in the afternoon – and got the job.*

Golfing *A group of golfers who came on the course specifically to learn the direct learning technique all downloaded a range of golfing books. Over the course of the next few weeks, many of them said that their golf had improved significantly.*

Exams *One man who'd done very little work at university downloaded all his coursework in the final week before the exam and passed. (We don't recommend this!)*

Language learning *Jan was planning to attend a seminar on hypnosis in Spain and decided that three months would be enough time to learn enough Spanish to attend the course. Things didn't work out that way and he'd done nothing about learning Spanish, so on the three-hour flight he downloaded a lot of books, worked through an article in the bilingual in-flight magazine, and listened to a Michel Thomas language-learning tape. Jan understood about 80% of the seminar. He didn't get the jokes, but he understood the seminar enough to get the information he'd gone for.*

Pub quiz *In 2008, there was a TV showing of a Derren Brown programme in which Derren Brown taught a man his version of the downloading technique. The man downloaded numerous books of information he thought might be appropriate for a pub quiz. He entered the quiz. He was alone, even though the quiz was for teams, and he came second.*

DO IT NOW

Whether or not you did it at the end of the previous section, download this Spd Rdng book (again) with the intention of letting go of your attachment to traditional reading habits and becoming an efficient and effective spd rdr.

By the way

People frequently ask how to use spd rdng with mathematical formulae. While it can be effective to download mathematical books which explain the formulae in context, it is also necessary to work with a formula in order to understand it fully. Certain memory techniques might also be useful in the early days.

Read a book three or more times

SUMMARY *Working with a book several times, using different spd rdng techniques, will give you a much greater knowledge of its contents than if you read it only once. It should also be much quicker than reading it once in the traditional way.*

Many people read factual books as if they're novels – slowly and sequentially. But this is the least effective way of getting the information you need and it's not helping you remember it.

Just by using the spd rdng techniques already described in this book, you will be working through a book several times:
- Previewing (#2) gives you an overview.
- One 20-minute session (#18) with a clear purpose (#4) will give you much more usable information than you would normally get from one traditional reading – and you can do more than one 20-minute session if the material warrants it.
- You also have the option of rapid reading from cover to cover (#24) or downloading (#28) the book, either of which will enable your non-conscious mind to take in further details.

Even doing all three processes should be quicker than reading in the traditional way – and since repetition is one of the keys to remembering, you will certainly retain much more of the information than from traditional reading, particularly if you review it after 1 day, 1 week and 1 month (#20).

Notice how much better you know a film if you watch it a second time, or a book if you read it through again. On the first read/ viewing, you are trying to make sense of the message or the story. On the second read/viewing you know the story and you are better able to focus on what is important or how the story/information is presented. The first time, all the information was of equal value. By the third time, you really know it! With spd rdng you reach that level of understanding much more quickly.

31 Trust the process

SUMMARY *Trust that the more you use the spd rdng techniques, the more effective your skills will become, and the more you will be able to trust the process – and your intuition – in relation to books and reading.*

Richard's BIGGEST learning

"That I can trust myself (and the process) to get the information I need."
In the early days I wasn't sure I could trust my intuition. So I checked. I went through books thoroughly to see what I'd missed – and time and again I found that I'd got everything I needed from my work sessions. Now I no longer have to read every word in a book in case I've missed something. I can usually get the message of a book within 20 minutes or so – and it's much more efficient than my old system of reading over three or four days. I used to forget the beginning before I'd got to the end. And I find that since I started downloading those huge computer manuals, I seem to have become much more intuitive about what to do to fix problems.

As you use the spd rdng techniques regularly, you will notice that it becomes easier and easier to find the information you want. As you start to trust the process, you will lose the fear of 'having missed something'. You may even find that you 'just happen' to open the book at the page you need. Or you quickly get a feeling about whether a book contains the information you need. This is your non-conscious mind at work.

As you work with books, you will notice information more quickly, be confident that you have understood enough to put the book down without 'finishing' it, and trust that the information you need will come to you when you need it. As you use the techniques, your trust will grow as you see results, and as your trust grows, you will get better results.

Use different techniques with different materials

32

SUMMARY *Because you read different materials with different purposes, experiment with using the spd rdng techniques in different combinations.*

Books are different and you will need to use different techniques with different books and according to your different purposes – which is why spd rdng doesn't offer a 'one-size-fits-all' approach.

Putting it all together
Books with a good index, informative titles and subheads, chapter summaries, etc, are easy to exploit using any of the techniques in this book. Others can be less easy. With all of the following practical suggestions we recommend that you get into a good state (#14) before reading – and in addition you can download (#28) any of the books into your non-conscious mind – or rapid read from cover to cover (#24), knowing that the information will go into your non-conscious mind.

- **When a book is written descriptively** with lots of stories and examples, you can use any of the techniques – especially previewing (#2), purpose (#4), 20-minute work session (#18) and note-taking (#17) – with the aim of cutting through the details to get the key ideas down in note form. Read one or two (but not all) examples to bring the information to life and make it more memorable.

- **When a book has a continuous story line** (eg novels, biographies, most historical material) you probably need to read sequentially. The techniques you need are super-duper-reading (#13) to speed up your brain, rapid reading (#24) – looking quickly at every page while using patterns (#15) such as super-reading and/or skittering (eg zigzag) to look for hot spots (#11) of key information. You may also (or instead) find it useful to use beginnings and endings (#37). You can also profitably preview (#2) and download (#28) these books. We call these books 'train reading' – they are ideal for reading on public transport. Highlight or make notes in the book as you go along – or write on post-it notes. Transfer your notes to a mindmap or directly to your computer (article, reports, essay, etc) later.

- **When books are very dense and information heavy** (eg textbooks and manuals which give lots of facts and summaries), the key is to add your own examples to make the information more meaningful and memorable. To do this, you need to:
1) get an overview (#25) of the subject, first by previewing (#2) and then having a 20-minute work session (#18) with the specific purpose (#4) of getting a subject overview

Jeannie's experience

Jeannie was starting to work with a book on feng shui (the Chinese art of placement). She opened it at random, and in the middle of the page she read 'There's nothing here'. Since she was already quite adept at feng shui, she felt that this meant there was nothing in the book relevant to her, but decided to check it out anyway. Sure enough, when she read through the whole book, her initial impression was confirmed – she already knew everything in the book. Thereafter she was much more confident about trusting her intuition.

EXPERT TIP

Use reading as just one step in a process where you build up expertise in a subject.

2) work with the book in several 20-minute sessions, each with a purpose related to a specific real example.

After working with one focus, do the same with another and then another, and you will see that information from one area overlaps with information from another, so you are gaining greater and greater knowledge. The key in each case is to think of one specific context in which you apply the information. When you have a clear context in mind, it is easy to evaluate whether the information is going to work or be appropriate.

This approach works with any subject, eg:

• **Medicine**   Focus on a specific disease and collect the information which would enable you to identify this disease in, for example, a middle-aged female, or a child – and identify which other diseases or factors might cause you initially to make a wrong diagnosis. If you are studying a particular area of the body, gather the information you would need to explain to a novice how it works and what can go wrong with it.

• **IT**   Have you noticed how much quicker it is to learn on the job? Use that experience to work on a practical specific example of something you are likely to do in real life when, for example, programming or checking for faults. Guess or look up in the manual the sequence of commands you need to carry out the task. Intersperse working practically at the computer and using your 20-minute session (#18) (which may be less than 20 minutes) to check and correct your thinking.

EXPERT TIP

Focus on getting information you can use – and then put it into practice.

• **Personal development**   Focus in each 20-minute session (#18) on gathering a specific number of techniques or strategies (eg 6 or 7) in relation to a specific aspect of your life (eg time management at work, decluttering at home, giving up smoking, etc) that you can immediately put into action. Then do them! Move quickly past problems you don't have, situations which don't apply to you and 'solutions' you know already or that you won't actually use. Only write down the ones you can put into practice.

• **Coaching**   In an area you know little about, follow the instructions above for personal development and work initially on solutions for yourself (you know yourself best and this approach will help you understand the topic's relevance to real life). If you don't have the particular challenges you're reading about, or if you already know the subject, then use each 20-minute session to look for several possible solutions for a different particular client each time. Relating information to a specific person – rather than thinking about it in the abstract, allows you to bring the information to life, which makes it both more memorable and more immediately practical. The information you glean in relation to one person is bound to be useful to others too. As you have different work sessions relating to different individuals, your experience grows and you are more and more likely to understand other people as they present their problems. If you're very experienced or you don't know anyone with the specific problems you want to read about, then imagine how those problems would manifest in someone's life. Make them real.

• **Acting** Get an overview (#25) of all the factors you need to consider when looking at a part in a new script – or all the different things to include when portraying a character. Then work on one individual character at a time as you prepare to play them – use your 20-minute session (#18) to get all the information you need to help you portray this one character. Take a similar approach with each character you are asked to play. Notice how quickly your repertoire builds.

• **Finance / investment** Make sure you have an overview (#25) of all the factors involved in your topic – probably by doing syntopic processing (#22) with several books. Then use your 20-minute session (#18) to look for specific factors relating to a specific type of investment that you are interested in. The result you want is to be able to use this information when you next buy or sell shares or property. If you're advising or investing on behalf of clients, focus on the needs of one client at a time – the needs of an individual investor are very different from those of a big corporation, for example. (Please note that no-one can as yet accurately foresee the future, so knowing the strategies recommended in books is no guarantee that you will make a fortune from your investments!)

In all the above examples notice how focusing on one real person or situation in context allows you quickly and easily to evaluate whether strategies or techniques will really work in practice. Once you've gained strategies in relation to one situation, you often find that you don't actually need to read more. A small amount of thinking will allow you to adapt what you've learnt to different situations.

By the way ...

Almost all reading techniques are effective when used appropriately. What is not effective or efficient is to use the same technique (eg slow reading) all the time.

Study skills

Since so many people need reading for study purposes at different times through their lives, it's worth thinking about how to apply the spd rdng techniques. Jan had the opportunity to see how well the advice we'd been giving to students actually worked in practice while he was preparing for his MSc in Environmental Psychology. It worked well. This is what he did.

- For each of his subject areas he spent about a day in the library previewing all the books on his reading list and making brief notes next to each. While other students were daunted by the thought of 'reading' 70 books, after one day Jan knew which ones contained what sort of information, which ones were worth buying, where to find relevant information, and in addition he'd got a really good overview of the subject.

- Before each lecture or seminar, he would either rapid read or have a 20-minute session on one (introductory) book on the subject. During the lecture he was then free to listen, evaluate, and add to his mindmap things he'd missed or misunderstood from his initial read. Other students were frantically writing down everything, since they were in no position to judge which bits were important.

- He did syntopic processing with four books (plus joker) to gather information for each essay he had to write (the title of the essay was his purpose).

- He used the search facility online to find the relevant websites and to identify and download papers containing relevant information to his dissertation.

Unfortunately, we don't know of too many spd wrtng techniques – once the information had been gathered and organized in mindmaps, writing the dissertation had to be done one letter, one word, one sentence at a time.

The statistics experience At his initial interview, Jan had 'exaggerated' how much he knew about statistics (in reality nothing), so the first (compulsory) statistics exam (for which there was no teaching) promised to be something of challenge. Since he knew absolutely nothing, it took him four false starts with books purporting to be for beginners before he found the one it was possible to get the information from easily. (The worst book was one which kept adding in jokey comments about the author's life – they looked more interesting, but actually proved to be very distracting and unhelpful.)

First he downloaded all the books.

Then, using the one comprehensive book, he started by making an overview mindmap of the key aspects of the subject and stuck it in the middle of an empty wall. (The purpose was 'to make an overview of the six main aspects of statistics' – the number was dictated by the number of chapters in the book, each of which focused on a particular area.) This process actually took 27 minutes rather than 20, because although each branch of the mindmap was pretty much the title of a chapter, he spent enough time on each chapter to understand approximately what the chapter was about and to add a few ideas to each branch. (The six were: variables and research design; SPSS; descriptive statistics; probability, sampling and distributions; hypothesis testing and statistical significance. This was not a complete overview of the subject, but he was only aiming at getting enough information to pass the exam.)

He then spent six 20-minute sessions getting a more in-depth overview of each of the key areas on the initial mindmap – and added each to the wall display in its relevant position.

Next he started at the end of each chapter and worked through the 'study questions'. Each question was the 'purpose' for a 20-minute session (ie to get 6 key ideas to answer the question "[title of question]"). The first question in each section he found hard, but since subsequent questions began to include information he'd found for an earlier question, they got easier and/or took less time to answer.

On the evening before the exam he downloaded all the books again and then went to bed early and got a good night's sleep. In the morning he ate a healthy and substantial breakfast. In the exam room, he got into a good state (smile, breathe, open peripheral vision, pause and plan) before he turned over the paper – and sipped water throughout the exam. With the multiple-choice answers, if he wasn't sure he guessed. (Many of his guesses proved to be right – possibly due to having downloaded the information?)

He passed the exam with 70%, while some people who had previously studied statistics for three years failed. And his whole study process, once he'd found the right book, took a day and a half. He started at lunchtime on the Saturday, worked in 20-minute chunks through the rest of the weekend (with breaks of 5 to 15 minutes between sessions) and sat the exam on Monday morning. He would scarcely have been able to read once through the book in that time if he'd been using traditional reading techniques.

Revise using past exam questions
When preparing for exams, get past papers for your subject. Write the first question as your purpose, spend five minutes jotting down anything you already know on a mindmap, then have a 20-minute session with your books to collect six additional points you would

EXPERT TIP

Always remember why you are reading. Keep your purpose at the forefront of your mind.

include in your answer. Then do the same with the next question, and the next, etc.

You will find that almost everything for the first question will be new information. The second question will possibly overlap slightly with the first, the third with both the previous two, and by about question five or six it will just be a case of rearranging material you already know.

Collaborative learning

We recommend that you teach these spd rdng techniques to a friend (or two). As well as helping you consolidate your new skills, it will also allow you to study collaboratively, which will bring immense benefits. Try syntopic processing (#22) using different books, or the same books in a different order – particularly for subject overviews, or on revision exam questions. You can take notes on different aspects of a subject and share your results or prepare questions on different texts for one another. You can collaborate face to face or online.

DO IT NOW My Own Unique Spd Rdng System
Before you look at the mindmap of the Spd Rdng System on the next page, spend five minutes flicking through this book and jotting down all the techniques that you will be combining when you work with your own material. You can present your ideas as a sequential list, a mindmap or rhizomap. In effect, you are putting the techniques together to form your own Spd Rdng System.

The Spd Rdng System

This computer-generated infographic shows how the individual spd rdng techniques can be combined to provide a coherent system.

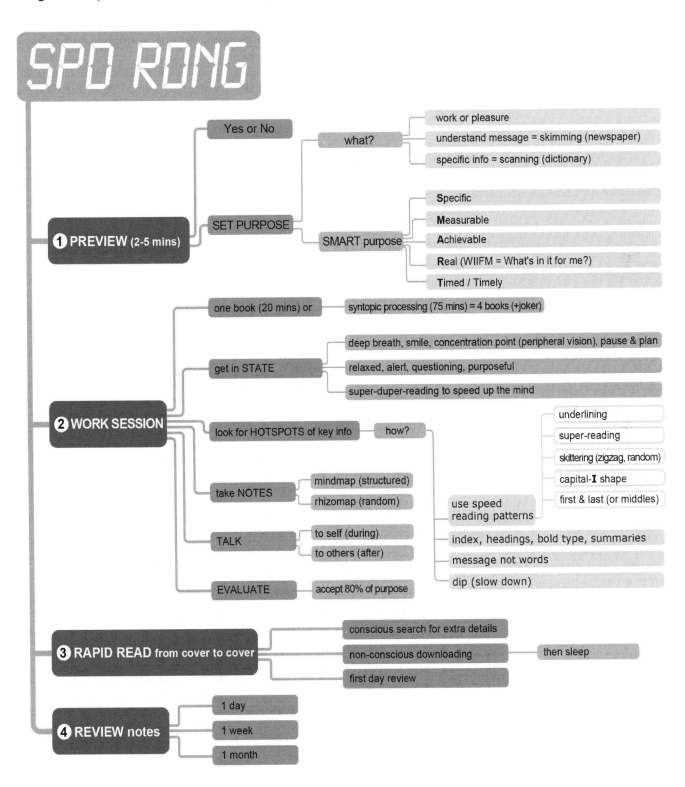

SPD RDNG

1 PREVIEW (2-5 mins)
- Yes or No
- SET PURPOSE
  - what?
    - work or pleasure
    - understand message = skimming (newspaper)
    - specific info = scanning (dictionary)
  - SMART purpose
    - **S**pecific
    - **M**easurable
    - **A**chievable
    - **R**eal (WIIFM = What's in it for me?)
    - **T**imed / Timely

2 WORK SESSION
- one book (20 mins) or → syntopic processing (75 mins) = 4 books (+joker)
- get in STATE
  - deep breath, smile, concentration point (peripheral vision), pause & plan
  - relaxed, alert, questioning, purposeful
  - super-duper-reading to speed up the mind
- look for HOTSPOTS of key info → how?
  - use speed reading patterns
    - underlining
    - super-reading
    - skittering (zigzag, random)
    - capital-**I** shape
    - first & last (or middles)
  - index, headings, bold type, summaries
  - message not words
  - dip (slow down)
- take NOTES
  - mindmap (structured)
  - rhizomap (random)
- TALK
  - to self (during)
  - to others (after)
- EVALUATE → accept 80% of purpose

3 RAPID READ from cover to cover
- conscious search for extra details
- non-conscious downloading → then sleep
- first day review

4 REVIEW notes
- 1 day
- 1 week
- 1 month

Ensure that physical factors are in your favour

SUMMARY *When you're working with a book, sit comfortably at a table with pen and paper for taking notes, in good lighting. Hold your book at a 45 degree angle towards you (rather than flat on the table). Make sure you're in a good state.*

Although it is quite possible to read at almost any time under almost any circumstances, there are several physical factors which can make quite a difference to your ability to read quickly and efficiently.

If you are reading for pleasure, then choose your physical circumstances to suit yourself. However, if you are reading for work or study purposes, then sit upright at a table or desk in what you consider to be pleasant surroundings with everything you need to hand – pencil, post-it notes, spectacles and whatever else (water, fruit, etc).

Also consider the following:
- Good **lighting** can make a significant difference to reading ability. Make sure you have a reasonable level of ambient lighting as well as direct/task light on your book. Natural light is preferable. Fluorescent light is least preferable.
- Whether or not you play **music** is entirely a matter of personal choice – people are different. However there are some recommendations:
  - choose music without words – words are more likely to distract you
  - Baroque music and Mozart have been particularly recommended to enhance concentration and learning
  - there is also some evidence to suggest that heavy metal (or any overloud discordant music) can damage living organisms (including you) and is therefore not helpful for learning
- Take frequent breaks (#27), **drink water**, and **rest/exercise your eyes** from time to time.
- Experiment with the **position in which you hold the book** to see whether it makes a difference to your fluency or ease of understanding. Holding it at a 45% angle to the table rather than flat gives the eyes and brain less work. Also try holding it to your right (test by reading a few sentences aloud) – and then to the left (again read a few sentences aloud). Most people notice some difference, although it is not the same for everyone. If you're not sure, read aloud to

EXPERT TIP

Be in the habit of getting into a good state (#14) before you start reading – every time, until it becomes second nature. Open your peripheral vision by focusing on your concentration point (#10), pause and plan, take a deep breath, smile.

someone else in the different positions – often there is one position where they will notice that you read more fluently and with more warmth in your voice. That's the position where you will also take in new information more easily.

- Some people find that viewing a page through a **coloured filter** can have a significant effect on their reading. Experiment by placing different coloured sheets of acetate (or coloured see-through plastic folders from any stationer) over the page. If one makes a significant difference, find out more by googling 'coloured overlays'.
- **Crossing your legs or ankles** while reading can help comprehension. (Many people find that they do this naturally.)
- **Sleep –** ideally for 7-8 hours per night. Sleep is particularly important when you are taking in a lot of new information. It is the time when your brain makes sense of your learning and consolidates memories.

By the way

We have noticed that people who initially have problems in applying some of the spd rdng techniques often sit very close to the text. This tends to slow down their reading because they are more likely to focus on details and read word by word.

The remedy is to **sit back** and hold the book a bit further away so you can see all four corners of the page as you read. Make this part of your habit of getting into a good state (#14) before you start reading.

Harry's BIGGEST learning

"That I can read much better just by holding the book to my left." I learnt lots of useful techniques on the spd rdng course, but I was amazed to discover just how big an improvement there was when I held my book on the left rather than straight in front of me. I've always found it difficult to read aloud, which makes it difficult to give prepared speeches, but somehow I could just see the words much more clearly when they were on my left.

Set high expectations

SUMMARY *Expectations (what you want) usually exceed your actual results – which tends to lead people to reduce their expectations. But then results go down again – until you're back to old, slow traditional reading habits. Increase your expectations, set tighter time limits, strive for more, read faster and see your results improve.*

As you put the techniques in this book into practice, make sure you raise your expectations about what you can achieve in a limited amount of time. If you have already experienced how much you can achieve in a 20-minute session (#18) working with a book or in a 75-minute syntopic processing session (#22) working with several books, you will also have noticed how much more you achieve in the last third of the time compared to the first two-thirds.

Although you are always likely to be a bit slower when you first start a work session (while your brain speeds up), with practice you will realise that:

- the way to get more information is to speed up and look at more pages
- the way to get your brain working more quickly is to speed up (#13)
- if you're not fully understanding, it is better to go forwards and look at more pages (so you have more information for clarification) rather than looking back at what you have already read.

The more pages you look at and the quicker you read, the quicker your brain will begin to make sense of the material.

Did you know ...
... that simply believing that you can improve can lead to improvement? Research (reported in Carol Dweck's book *'Mindset: The New Psychology of Success'*) has shown that there are two types of people – those who think that intelligence is fixed (**fixed mindset** – you are either smart, or good at things, or you're not) or people who understand that intelligence changes as you learn new things (**growth mindset**). One result is that people who think that their intelligence is fixed tend to try something once and then give up if they don't succeed immediately. People who know that they can improve if they keep practising, do just that – keep practising, and getting better.

> **"** *A woman went up to Gary Player, the golfer, after he'd just played a particularly difficult shot very successfully. 'You were lucky there,' she said. Gary Player looked at her thoughtfully and replied, 'You know, it's a funny thing. I find that the more I practise, the luckier I get.'*

Raise your expectations

Actual performance almost always falls short of expectation. You rarely do quite as well as you think you're going to. Initially, while you are gaining expertise and experience, this is not so obvious because you can see growth. However, as you gain in expertise, there usually comes a point when you 'plateau' – you don't feel you've learnt everything there is to learn, but you don't seem to be making progress (see graphs).

A common response at this 'crisis point' is to feel a sense of failure and to lower expectations.

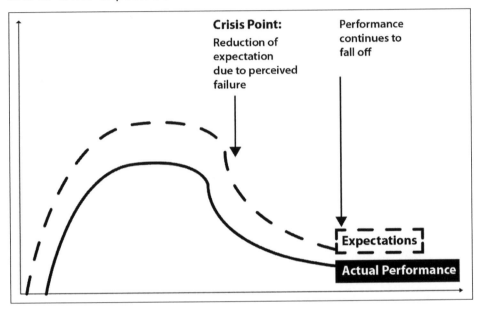

Crisis Point:
Reduction of expectation due to perceived failure

Performance continues to fall off

Expectations

Actual Performance

Unfortunately, if you lower your expectations, then your actual performance is likely once again to fall short of the revised lower expectation, leading to fewer and fewer positive results.

The way to break out of this vicious circle is to raise your expectations (see diagram on the next page). Even if your performance doesn't match your expectation, you will still be improving.

By the way, if you combine raising your expectations with being satisfied when you achieve 80% of your purpose (see 80/20 rule #5), you will continue both to improve your actual success rate, as well as feeling good about your progress – turning a vicious circle into a virtuous spiral.

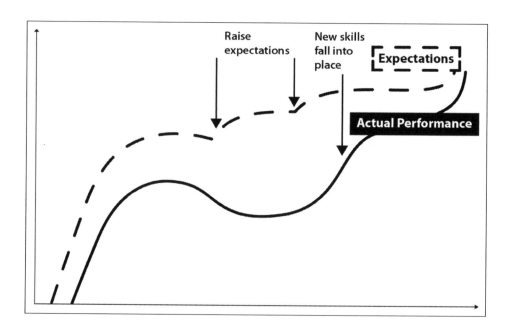

EXPERT TIP

In order to understand, go quicker, not slower; read more, not less.

Develop good habits
Initially, when you learn any new skill, it usually takes quite a lot of effort (see diagram below). After that you don't need to put in more effort, but you do need to sustain the effort for a while. Then gradually you need to make less and less effort as your new skill becomes a habit.

99 *We are what we repeatedly do. Excellence, then, is not an act, but a habit."*
Aristotle

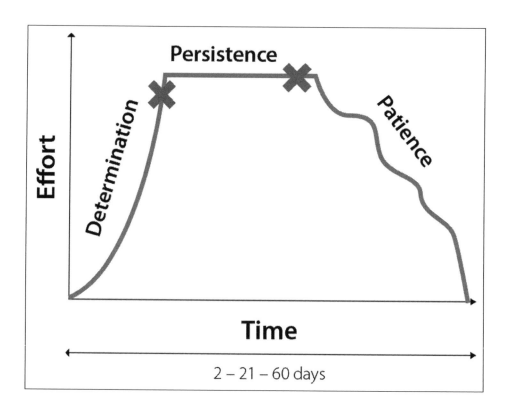

Ironically, people tend to give up just before things start getting easier (see crosses in diagram) – especially if they haven't seen this diagram. They think that if they have to keep putting in effort, then it isn't worth carrying on. Whereas all you need to do is keep putting the new skill into practice and maintain some initial **determination**, followed by **persistence** and **patience**, and at some point you will notice that this is something you can do effortlessly.

Celebrate success

SUMMARY *Your brain is programmed to notice when you fail or make mistakes – but if you train yourself to notice when you succeed, you encourage further success.*

The natural tendency of human beings is to notice when they fail or when things don't go as well as they'd hoped. This is good for our evolution, since it teaches us what to avoid in the future. It is always a good idea to ask yourself 'what could I do better next time?' However, it can be a limitation in learning terms if it discourages us, so it is equally, if not more, important to notice successes. Noticing even small improvements can encourage you to improve even more.

After every work session, make it a habit to **pause and evaluate** how much have you achieved. As well as noting things you can do better next time, make sure you also celebrate any successes.

Reflective intelligence

David Perkins of Harvard University says that 'reflective intelligence' (RI) is key to learning. RI means being aware of your habitual ways of thinking and learning so that you can improve them as well as doing more of what's working. So start noticing when you have learnt something new. After each reading experience, ask yourself what you will do better or differently next time. Notice too each time you succeed at something. Ask yourself what you're doing well. Realise how much more quickly you are gathering information using these new techniques compared to your old traditional reading. The more you do it, the more it becomes second nature – and the insights you gain give you strategies you can apply in future learning situations.

Good or new

If noticing success is not a natural state for you, take a couple of minutes each day to feel good about 'anything good and/or new' that has happened in the previous 24 hours. This is more effective if you write them down or tell someone else. The things you notice don't have to be huge things – a pretty colour, an evocative smell, or a delicious meal can all bring pleasure. Nor do they have to be connected with reading – but make a point of noticing improvements in your reading too.

Reward yourself

If you are sticking to time (#23) and reading with a purpose (#4) while in a good state (#14), then celebrate all the successes you have by giving yourself small rewards – a walk, a game, a chat, whatever works for you. With time, however, you'll find that the greatest reward is being in control of your reading and knowing that you can get the information you need in the time available.

DO IT NOW Just to get you started ...
... jot down anything you have already learnt from spd rdng which is saving you reading time.

....

....

....

....

Also jot down the ways in which you can reward yourself – and the rewards you are noticing from putting the techniques into practice.

....

....

....

....

Read more

SUMMARY *Simply reading more of anything – particularly if you use spd rdng techniques – will make you a better reader. The more you read, the more words you will learn – the more words you know, the easier it is to read.*

Did you know ...
- the biggest indicator of how successful people will be in later life is the amount they read for pleasure when they are younger? (You can read anything - as long as you enjoy it.)
- that the biggest influence on a child's reading ability in later life is how much they were read to when very young? (That's how much you read to them and with them, not how much they themselves read.)
- that, on average, good readers make more money?

Good readers read a lot The brain gets good at what it's used to, so reading gets easier the more you do it.

Build your vocabulary Reading is one of the best ways of building your vocabulary – keep a dictionary to hand for words you can't guess from the context, or use the ebook online dictionary.

Make it easy on yourself You'll find it easier to read things that you read regularly – 'your' newspaper is easier than one you don't read so regularly. And you'll do more if it's easy and pleasurable.

Background reading
This book is primarily about building up good spd-rdng habits so that you get the information you need in the time you have available. But there's a lot to be said for 'unfocused' reading too. By this we mean leisure reading, reading for pleasure, or just reading to see what's going on in the world (newspapers, magazines) or in your field (journals).

It's like the difference between men and women shopping. Men typically go with a list, go directly to the items on the list and buy them. Women may make a list, but they still walk round the shelves and notice what else is on offer so they have items ready in advance or ideas about what get do next time. Reading 'extra stuff' builds up extra levels of knowledge which may come in handy. Your default purpose (#4) for background reading will be 'to find six interesting facts in this article/book'.

EXPERT TIP

Read as much as you can of anything you like – the only criterion is that you enjoy it.

Read beginnings and endings

37

SUMMARY *Very often key information can be found at the beginnings and endings of books or chapters. So look there first.*

Check out the first chapter
There are two kinds of first chapter (or introduction). One is very helpful. It grabs your attention. It lays out what the book is about and where it's going – effectively giving you an overview (#25) of the subject. If it's this kind of first chapter, it can pay dividends to read it first.

However, as you read the first chapter, you may find it's one of the other kind, which gets bogged down in too much tedious detail. (It is this kind of first chapter which stops many people from ever getting past the first chapter of a book!) As an expert reader, feel free to skip it – and try out the second approach to beginnings (or move on to the final chapter – see below).

The second approach to beginnings
Read enough of the first paragraph of each chapter to get an overview (#25) of what the book is about. Then look at the top couple of lines on each page. This may be enough to give you an understanding of the book's message, or you might use it as a way of finding hot spots (#11) of information – which might lead you to look further down the page for more details. If you need to go into greater detail on a page (or in an article or report), then look at the beginning of each section or paragraph (see patterns #15).

Read the end first
Many people naturally flick to the end of a book before they start reading 'properly' – but not so many realise what an effective technique this can be.

Try reading the last chapter of a book first. It often summarises the main point the author wishes to make – so then you only need to look back through the book for the explanation of things you don't understand. Make sure you look for summaries at the end of other chapters too.

It's like reading the end of a thriller to find out whodunnit. If you then read the book sequentially, you are reading in a different way – not to be surprised by the ending, but to see how clever the author has been in giving subtle clues and in setting up red herrings. As you read you know what's important and what's not. If you read sequentially without knowing the ending, then

EXPERT TIP

Read summaries. Research shows that readers remember more from summaries than from reading the book.

everything seems to be of equal importance – you have to work a lot harder to make sense of it.

Similarly, with many subject textbooks it can be very helpful to read the last unit first and then work backwards. Although the information may initially seem hard to understand, you are starting with the big picture, the overview (#25), and as you work backwards filling in details, the information is getting easier and easier to understand. Think how much more motivating that is!

THE END of the techniques

Actually it's just the beginning of your new approach to reading.

But ... if you find a better way, use it ... and let us know!

Excellent readers are constantly looking for ways to read and implement these techniques more effectively. We are always on the lookout for ways to improve our reading, the techniques, and the book. Please let us know if you have any suggestions – or if you would like to share successes.

Contact us via our website – and check for updated information too: **www.spdrdng.com**

PRACTICE TEXTS

The texts on the following pages are for practising your spd rdng techniques.

The texts are:
- *The Extended Mind – The Sense of Being Stared At*
- *The Wise Teacher and the Jar*
- *A History of Speed Reading*

You can also use your spd rdng techniques to read the whole section 'More About Reading'. (p 141) All the texts have word counts at the ends of sections in case you want to use them to check your reading speed.

1 **Expectation** Before you start work on any of the texts, look at the title and ask yourself what you expect it to be about. Jot down a few words, phrases or sentences about what you expect to read. (Whether you're right or not this activity will prime your brain to be more receptive to the information you do read.)

2 **Previewing** We recommend that you start by previewing (#2) each text, spending not more than 3 minutes, just to give you an idea of what it is about and to set your purpose.

3 **Hot spots** Use the first page of 'The Extended Mind' article to determine what a hot spot is. Read it as slowly or as quickly as you like for this task, as you ask yourself:
- What is the key information on this page?
- Which actual words give you that information? (How often are they repeated?)
- What are all the other words (the cool spots?) doing? Which words is it safe to overlook when you're reading quickly?

Compare your answers with ours at the end of the article. (p 129)

4 **Speed-reading patterns** Use other pages to practise the different speed-reading patterns (#15). Your purpose is simply to find out what the article is about.
- Start by getting into a good state (#14). (Don't do super-duper-reading at this stage.)
- First do super-reading (use a pacer to guide your eyes down the middle of the page). Use the first page which you've already read to get you into the technique, and continue for two or three more pages at the rate of 15 seconds per column. Use a timer. After about 7 seconds you should be halfway down the column. Don't worry about it too much. Just see what you notice.
- Now speed up your brain by super-duper-reading (#13) through the whole article at the rate of 4 seconds per column. Then repeat the super-reading of the first three pages at 15 seconds

per column and notice how much more time you seem to have. The aim of this activity is not for you to think that you've cracked it (we've only met a couple of people who've managed to get the information first time at this rate), but for you to believe that it might be possible: that there are people who can read at this rate (and faster), and that with a bit of practice you're going to be one of them.

- Now try out the other patterns, still at the rate of 15 seconds per column, going over the last page you went through with the previous pattern and then continuing for two or three more pages.

Remember to look at headings no matter which pattern you are using:

- zigzag
- capital-I shape
- underlining (leaving off the beginning and end of lines)
- make up your own pattern and try that

Just practising the patterns is a good way of learning them, but they really only to start working well once you are reading with a genuine need for the information. Remember too that this is something you already do naturally when you're reading a newspaper. So …

- Try looking through the texts as if you are reading a newspaper – just to get an idea of what they're about. Slow down when you find information which really interests you (dip) and speed up again once you've got that piece of information.

Very often we are just using the patterns (or some variation of our own) to look for specific information we think is there, so try looking for the answers to the following questions in 'The Extended Mind'. (There are other questions and suggested purposes at the beginning of each text.) The questions are effectively your purpose for reading.

QUESTIONS on 'The Extended Mind'
Use speed-reading patterns to look for the answers to the following questions on 'The Extended Mind'. (p 121) The questions are in the order the information appears in the text.

Finding the answers to the questions is your purpose for reading. Ignore any information which does not answer these questions.

Get into a good state before you start. Set your timer for 20 minutes. Read through all the questions before you start reading the article. Jot down the answers in note form as you find them. Stop as soon as you have the answers to all the questions. Compare your answers with ours at the end of the article.

1 Does Sheldrake think the mind is contained within the brain or that it extends beyond it?

2 What is the 'hard problem'?

3 Whose theory is it that vision is a two-way process: Sheldrake's or conventional scientists?

4 What percentage of people say they've had the experience of knowing that they're being stared at (even before they look)?

5 Name three professions that Sheldrake interviewed about the phenomenon of being stared at.

6 How many people have taken part in the experiment in the NEMO centre in Amsterdam?

7 How long ago did eyes evolve?

6 How many of the veterinary clinics in North London regularly had problems with people missing appointments for their cats?

9 At what moment does the evidence show that dogs first start waiting for their owners to come home?

10 What's the name of Aimee Morgana's parrot?

11 What does Sheldrake say is the problem with most of the para-psychological research?

12 Give one example of the sorts of people who are likely to have the strongest telepathic links.

13 What's the success rate of the telephone experiment (guessing in advance which of four people is calling)?

14 What are morphic fields?

15 What does Sheldrake call the ability of morphic fields to evolve and communicate?

16 Why might it be easier to do the Times crossword puzzle later in the week?

17 What did Sheldrake's son do to give himself a chance of getting better grades in his exams?

18 What is/are the main point/s of this article? What does Sheldrake want us to believe that's different from the conventional scientific view?

The Extended Mind – The Sense of Being Stared At
Rupert Sheldrake

True story? Tall Story?

What is the true nature of our minds? Which of the following do you think is the tall story? Which one do you think is true?

Are our minds confined within our heads? Are all our thoughts, feelings and sensations located inside our brain tissue? Does this sound like the tall story? Or do our minds extend beyond the confines of our heads? Our thoughts, feelings and sensations are rooted within the brain but can extend far beyond them. Is this perhaps the tall story?

Some of my colleagues in the scientific world would have no doubt that the second is the tall story, and strenuously promote the idea that all the thought products of our brains remain within the brain.

I, on the other hand, am definitely rooting for the second idea, that our minds extend beyond our heads. But you will have to make your own decision. *(164 words)*

Fields of influence

In this article, I am suggesting that the mind is much more extensive than the brain and that our minds stretch out beyond our brains through what I term 'morphic fields'.

This is not a new concept to us. Everyone now is familiar with mobile phones. We all accept that in order to work they must involve some kind of energy field which extends far beyond the electronic circuits and plastic casing you hold in your hand. We're all used to the idea of invisible fields of influence which stretch beyond their source.

We accept that a magnet contains within it a magnetic field, and that this field stretches beyond the magnet itself to exert its pull on other objects. There's nothing unscientific about magnetism. Similarly the earth's gravitational field stretches out far beyond the surface of the earth – it's what keeps the moon in orbit around it. Gravity is invisible, it moves through empty space and yet it's real.

Sir Karl Popper, science philosopher, acknowledged that matter is no longer the fundamental explanatory principle in science. Matter is explained in terms of energy found within fields. So fields and energy are the most fundamental explanatory principles in modern science.

Similarly, then, I am suggesting that our minds are systems of fields that stretch far beyond our brains. They are rooted in our brains but they are not confined to the inside of our heads. This is no more a dualistic theory, in the traditional sense of dualism, than mobile phones, magnetism or gravitational fields. It is a scientific view of the mind, even though it goes way beyond the current scientific model.

So I'm going to discuss the 'extended mind' and some of the evidence that supports this view.

Perhaps one of the easiest ways of seeing how this different view of things might work is by considering vision. Not visionary experience, just ordinary vision – how you look with your eyes at whatever is in front of you.
(332 words; total 496)

How we see

Now the conventional theory of vision (which corresponds with the view that the mind is confined to the brain) is that light is reflected from whatever you are looking at and enters your eyes. Inverted images form on your retinas, changes happen in the cone cells, and electrical impulses travel up the optic nerve and stimulate electrical and chemical activity in the various visual regions of the brain.

All this has been studied in great detail and it's all very good – as far as it goes. The trouble is that that's as far as it does go. Seeing something involves more than just electrical and chemical changes in the brain. There is also a conscious experience. And science has almost nothing to tell us about conscious experiences.

It's only in the last 15 or 20 years that scientific research has focused on consciousness and even now most people still think that consciousness is nothing but a by-product of chemical and electrical activity in the brain. It doesn't actually do anything. So that's the first mystery, what people call the 'hard problem', the fact that there's consciousness at all. Science can't explain it. If your brain is like a computer, then how come you are conscious when your computer isn't?

The second mystery is that all this change is supposedly happening inside your head and yet I imagine that you are experiencing what you are looking at where it actually is, out in front of you, rather than inside your head.

The theory I'm putting forward is so simple that it's quite hard to understand. I'm proposing that your image of what you are looking at is out there in front of you. It's in your mind, constructed by your mind, but it's not inside your brain. *(299 words; total 794)*

Vision: a two-way process

I suggest that vision is a two-way process. Light comes in, changes happen in the brain, and the images are projected out to where they seem to be – which corresponds exactly with our experience because we experience the images outside ourselves.

But that's not the official scientific view. The official scientific view is that everything you can see is actually inside your head. There's a kind of virtual reality display going on inside your brain. You're having an experience inside your head and falsely imagining that it's out there. So when you look at the sky, that's an image inside your head too. So in some way your phenomenal skull must be beyond the sky.

That's the official view and that's what's taught in practically every university in the world.

So what do you think? Which of these two views is the tall story?

My theory that vision involves a two-way process is not an original one. It was put forward by Plato, believed by most of the ancient Greeks and taught in medieval universities. It's what traditional people all over the world believe. It's taught by Hindu and Buddhist sages. And it's what European children under the age of about ten believe – until they are taught the 'correct' view. It's what most of us have believed at some point in our lives, because it's this kind of view that has been incorporated into the 'scientific' world view as an unspoken assumption, but on very slender evidence.

I'm not discussing philosophy here, but science. If we have a theory, can we test it? And the way we might test it is to see whether by looking at something we can affect it. If my image of anything in the world is projected to where that thing is, then by looking at it, in a sense my mind touches it. So is it possible for me to affect something by looking at it?

At first it seems improbable, but think about it from your own experience. If you look at somebody from behind and they don't know you're there, can they tell when you're looking at them? You can look at them through a window so they can't see you, hear you or smell you. You can look through lace curtains so there's no chance of them knowing you're there. Can they detect when they are being looked at? Can you?

Well, the answer is that many people can. Surveys show that more than 90% of people have had the experience of being looked at from behind; you turn round and someone is staring at you. Most people have had the other side of the experience too; staring at someone from behind and seeing them turn round. *(460 words; total 1255)*

The 'scientific' view

So what does science have to tell us about the sense of being stared at? The answer is, until recently, almost nothing.

There's been an almost complete taboo on this subject, even among parapsychologists. Until recently, there has been virtually no research on the subject; the number of published papers over the 100 years from 1890 to 1990 is four. There's been very little investigation because it fits so badly with the standard paradigm, the model of reality that it's all happening inside the brain. It ought not to happen. So although everybody knows it does happen, as a phenomenon it's been completely filtered out of science, psychology and the academic world. It's a very good example of how a paradigm can limit your thinking so you don't even consider something – you know it happens, but you don't think about it. It doesn't fit on the intellectual map so it's just dismissed. Or you turn around all the time anyway, and you only remember it when somebody's staring at you, so it's not really a phenomenon, it's just a coincidence, and it's very easy to dismiss it.

All educated people have been educated to dismiss these kinds of things, not to take them seriously. In fact that's almost how being educated is defined in our culture – as rejecting these kinds of things that unsophisticated people take for granted. But children are very familiar with the phenomenon, not because they have been told about it – they just notice it. *(251 words; total 1506)*

The sense of being stared at

To find out if it really happens, I've applied several lines of research. One is to talk to people who know a lot about watching other people. I've interviewed private detectives, surveillance officers and security personnel, including the drug squad at Heathrow Airport in London, and others who are paid to watch other people as a job. They are in no doubt about the reality of this. On the first day of a training course to be a private detective, you'd need to learn a few skills, and one of them is that if you're following someone, if you're trailing them, you don't stare at their back. Because if you do they are likely to turn round, catch your eye and your cover is blown. Of course you have to look at them a little bit, otherwise you'd lose them, but you look at them as little as possible. In the SAS, when you're being trained to creep up behind people to stab them in the back, you're taught not to stare at their back before stabbing them, because they are likely to turn around and shoot you first! These things are well known by people to whom it matters, even though they are denied within the scientific world.

But in science we need more than what's called 'anecdotal experience'. Anecdotal experience is simply experience. Science is meant to be based on experience, but for some reason anecdotes tend to be dismissed. Incidentally, the Greek root of the word anecdote, which is 'anekdotos', means 'not published'. An anecdote is an unpublished story. Medicine is based on anecdotes, but when they are published, they are promoted to the rank of 'case histories'. *(287 words; total 1793)*

The staring experiment

However in science it's important to be able to test things experimentally. On this I agree with my colleagues in science: you need controlled experiments and proper statistics. And you can test it very simply. I've developed an extremely simple experiment, so simple a child can do it – in fact, thousands of children have already done it. This research has mainly taken place in primary schools, where there are willing subjects, and children turn out to be more sensitive than adults. It has also been done in laboratories with adults.

The experiment works like this:
• You need two pieces of apparatus – a blindfold (I use airline blindfolds, or eye masks) and a mechanical stimulus, a click or a beep. I use mechanical clickers that give a standard click.
• You work in pairs, and one person, who is the subject, wears the blindfold, the other person sits behind them, and in a random series of trials they either stare at the back of the

person's neck or look away and think of something else. So you're sitting there with the blindfold on, you hear a click which signals the beginning of the trial and you have to guess if you're being stared at.

So you're right or you're wrong. By pure chance you'd be right 50% of the time on average. These experiments show a small but highly significant effect; on average when people are being stared at they are right about 60% of the time, and this result is quite consistent over tens of thousands of trials. This becomes massively significant statistically. And this of course is only an average, because we take all-comers for this test, and some people are much more sensitive than others and score much higher.

This experiment has now been replicated in many schools; more than 19,000 people have taken part in the NEMO Centre in Amsterdam. You can also do the experiment online, it's on my website: www.sheldrake.org.

If you're a school teacher and want to do it for your class, it's really fun; you can do it in a single period. People swap places after 20 trials. It only takes about 10 minutes or less to do 20 trials and so the children can swap places and experience doing it both as a 'looker' and a 'guesser'. You can find all the details on my website, where you can download the pre-randomised instruction sheet. And if you do decide to do it, please let me know what you find, because I compile all these results. It's a simple experiment with dozens of independent replications, and the evidence seems very strong that this really happens. The sense of being stared at seems to be for real, just as most people assumed.
(462 words; total 2255)

CCTV – do you know they're watching?

It turns out that it also works, rather surprisingly, through closed circuit television. First of all, in the real world there are now millions of CCTV cameras. Britain has the highest number per capita of any country in the world. We're all being watched – in hotels, in airports, in the street, in shopping centres, by hidden security personnel. In my experience since I've been to interview some of them in their security booths, mostly they are not watching us very hard; I usually find them drinking tea and reading the newspaper. But nevertheless there are all these banks of screens and they can watch you. Some security guards have noticed that if they stare at somebody intently enough, that person often gets quite shifty and starts looking around to see where the hidden cameras are. Shoplifters and people who are security conscious are apparently particularly sensitive.

Experiments have also been done in several universities using closed circuit television. In those experiments, a person is either looked at or not looked at on a TV screen in another room, or even in another building. The question is – can you tell when someone is looking at your image on a TV screen? In these tests, which are quite

sophisticated, people don't even have to guess. Their skin resistance is monitored using electrodes – an electro-dermal response, like in a lie detector – and people's skin resistance changes significantly when someone looks at their image in another room. They are not conscious of it, but their body, their physiology is picking this up. These things are primarily bodily, physiological, emotional responses.

In my own experiments people have to guess. They have to turn it into consciousness, which is the hard bit, because the mind gets in the way. It's more sophisticated to measure people just physiologically; it's also more complicated. I prefer the guessing method. It's simple. It's cheap – in fact it's free – and anyone can do it. But this more sophisticated test shows that it really works through CCTV as well. *(343 words; total 2597)*

Staring at animals

It also works with animals. Many people have found that animals can tell when they are being stared at. A lot of pet owners have found that they can waken their sleeping dogs or cats by staring at them. Some people have found that their dogs or cats can waken them by staring at them. In the wild it's well known to hunters and to wildlife photographers that although you are concealed when you look at an animal, even through a telescope or a telescopic lens, the animals can often pick up when they are being looked at, even if they can't see the person looking at them.

So this seems to be very widespread in the animal kingdom, and I think that it is a basic physiological thing, which has primarily evolved in connection with predator-prey relations. A prey that can tell when a predator is looking at it, and get out of the way, would obviously survive better than one that couldn't. So there are probably very strong natural selection reasons for the development of this sensitivity.

I think that it is not just human vision that works on the projection of images into the world outside them. It is something we share with all animals. I think it is the way eyes work.

Eyes first evolved about 530 million years ago in the Cambrian period and probably this ability evolved soon after, so it's very ancient, very widespread, and it is part of our biological nature. It's present in modern people, even though it is never mentioned in the educational system. Every effort is made in our culture to discourage people from taking it seriously, and yet almost everybody has it. It's very deep, and it comes into its own when people are in threatening situations, when it becomes very useful.

There is fear about the baleful effects of envious or angry gazes; traditions about the 'evil eye' are predominant in many parts of the world including Southern Europe, the Arab world and India. The belief is that the power of the gaze can have a harmful effect. I consider that this folklore and these beliefs are related to a background in predator/prey relations. People usually find stares threatening in some way, and often they are.

I think we are dealing here with a very basic biological ability that's to do with the two-way nature of vision in people and in animals involving extended fields of perception which stretch out far beyond the brain.
(420 words; total 3018)

Telepathy

Similarly I think that our minds and especially our emotions stretch out beyond our brains and our bodies too, and this is what we call 'telepathy'. I think telepathy, like the sense of being stared at, is grounded in biology. It is an evolutionary feature that we share with many species of animals. It's not paranormal, beyond the normal, it is normal. It's not supernatural, beyond the natural, it is natural. It's part of our biological nature.

Because I think it is part of animal nature, I have initially investigated it mainly in animals, and I started my investigations on animal telepathy with the animals we know best, namely pets. I did this in several ways, firstly by looking at the natural history of telepathy, and to do that I appealed for information: I asked people to tell me their experiences that suggested their pets might be telepathic. I had appeals throughout the media, and I have thousands of these stories. When you hear one story you can say it's just an anecdote. But the plural of anecdotes is 'data' – and if you have hundreds of similar stories where people all over the world are telling you the same kind of thing about their dogs or cats, this seems to be a repeatable phenomenon.

I found there were certain repeatable categories of behaviour that suggest that pets are picking up people's intentions or emotions, not necessarily telepathically, but suggesting that it might be so. For example, many cat owners told me that their animals seem to know when they are planning to take the cat to the vet. The cat disappears. And after it has happened a number of times, people try not to give the cat any clues. They don't let it see the carrying basket, they don't talk about the vet, some of them even desperately try not to think about the vet – and the cat still seems to know. Some people even go so far as to ring up the vet from work to make the appointment, so that the cat can't overhear them! Then they swing by home on the way back from work to pick it up – but it's not there.

To find out if this really was as common as it seemed to be, we did a survey of all the veterinary clinics listed in the North London Yellow Pages: 64 out of 65 said they had a regular problem with people missing their appointments with their cats – they would ring up to say they couldn't come because they couldn't find the cat. The one exception said it happened so often they had given up appointments for cats completely! *(446 words; total 3464)*

Do pets know when you're coming home?

The principal phenomenon I've concentrated on in the animal world is the ability of many animals to know when their owners are coming home. Many cat and dog owners have found that their animal will go and wait at a door or a window when the person they are attached to is on the way home. No one thinks this odd if it happens only a minute or two before, because they could just be hearing footsteps on the street or the crunch of car wheels on the gravel, or if it always happens at a routine time, because it could be a biological clock. No one thinks it's odd if the person at home says, 'So and so's coming home' and the animal gets excited, because it could be picking it up from them.

In many households, though, when people return at non-routine times, it's the animal that knows first, and the people at home know when the person is coming back from the animal's behaviour. I have over 800 stories of this kind concerning dogs, and more than 500 about cats. The stories have a lot in common, in many cases it happens ten minutes or more in advance, and if people have been on holiday for weeks, sometimes the animals are responding hours before they come home.

So what's going on? When I first got interested in this, I discussed it with a sceptical friend of mine in Cambridge, Nicholas Humphrey. To my surprise, he didn't deny the phenomenon. He said, 'Oh, my dog used to do that. It knew when I was coming home half an hour in advance. My mother could always tell.' So I asked him how it could have done that. It couldn't possibly have been hearing his car on the other side of Cambridge 20 miles way across all the traffic and motorways and things, and he said, 'On the contrary. It just shows what sharp hearing they've got.'

And that's what led to the idea of the experiment. I said, 'OK, Nick. What would happen if you came home on the train, borrowed a bicycle and cycled from the station, so there were no familiar car sounds. If your mother didn't know when you were coming, would the dog still respond in advance?' He said, 'Of course not.' I said, 'Well, perhaps it would.' And that's the key experiment.

We've done hundreds of experiments. We videotape the place the dog waits when the person is out. The person goes at least five miles away and they come home at randomly chosen times. We page them on a pager so it's not a routine time. No-one at home knows when they are coming. Sometimes there is no-one at home. In the most rigorous experiments, to avoid familiar car sounds, they come home in taxis, in a different taxi every time.

We've found repeatedly, hundreds of times, these dogs start waiting when the person decides to come home, before they have even got into the taxi. It's the intention that seems to be involved in this, from miles away. We have it all on film, and we've also published papers in scientific journals.

In experiments on telepathy with human beings, the scores often fall off after a while because people get bored with doing repetitive tests. Luckily, dogs never get bored with their owners coming home, so you can do this experiment over and over again. We were challenged by sceptics who thought there were various flaws in the method, so I invited one of Britain's leading sceptics, Richard Wiseman, to do experiments with one of these dogs himself, and he got exactly the same results as we did. These results are described in my book, *'Dogs That Know When Their Owners Are Coming Home'*.

There seems to be good evidence for telepathy in pets. There are many ways in which pets pick up people's thoughts, intentions and emotions. That is because they form bonds with us as if we are part of their group. This is not because they are pets, since animals do this with each other in the wild. There is evidence from the natural history of wolf behaviour that they communicate telepathically over great distances, and they are the ancestors of dogs. These things are very widespread. *(725 words; total 4189)*

A psychic parrot

One of the most impressive examples that came to my attention concerned a parrot. Parrots, especially African greys, are often exceptionally telepathic with their owners. With dogs and cats people often say, 'If only they could speak.' Well, a lot of parrots actually can. The most remarkable parrot I know of is one called N'kisi who lives in New York with his owner Aimee Morgana. Aimee got in touch with me five years ago and told me that her parrot had a phenomenal vocabulary and she was training it mainly to see how far she could go with language use. This parrot speaks in grammatically correct sentences, it speaks meaningfully in relation to what is going on, and it even has conversations with her and comments on what is happening. This in itself is astonishing enough.

Aimee's primary aim was to study language in the parrot, inspired by an American researcher called Irene Pepperberg who has already demonstrated that African greys can use language meaningfully. Aimee had shown this with her parrot, but what she noticed was that it actually seemed to pick up what she was thinking. She kept a log book which now has hundreds of entries. For example, she'd be thinking of ringing a friend called Bob, and she'd go to look up his number, and the parrot would say, 'Ring Bob now.' And she hadn't said anything about Bob, and she hadn't rung him for weeks, months. But most remarkable of all is that the parrot sleeps in her bedroom and it often interrupts her dreams by commenting on them loudly and waking her up!

All this was off the scale of anything I'd heard of before, so at the first possible opportunity I went to visit her in Manhattan, and to my amazement it was all true. The parrot was talking, it was speaking grammatically, it was responding to what was going on.

We set up an immediate telepathic test, where I had Aimee go into another room, and look at a picture selected at random. It was a picture of a girl. While she was holding it and looking at it, from the next room the parrot said, 'That's a girl.' I was astonished, so we set up a formal set of controlled experiments to test this parrot for telepathy. You can find details of this extraordinarily successful experiment at my website (www.sheldrake.org). We had all the tapes transcribed independently and analysed by a Dutch professor of statistics in Amsterdam. The data is massively significant. It was published in a scientific journal and the results are summarised in my book, *'The Sense of Being Stared At'*.

N'kisi continues to learn and his vocabulary now in 2005 is over 1000 words, which is the highest ever recorded for a language-using parrot, and he was only seven years old. Parrots live to an average of about 75, so we may hear a lot more about N'kisi. *(494 words; total 4683)*

Testing telepathy

I've conducted extensive research on telepathy in animals, which I am convinced shows that this is a widespread ability among them. The key feature in animals is that it happens within social groups, and I think the same principles apply to people. In our society there is a taboo about telepathy among educated people, particularly among scientists. Although privately they may know it happens as they have experienced it, publicly they feel they have to deny it exists, or pretend it doesn't occur at all. So we have a taboo on the subject, but nevertheless, it's widespread in the modern world.

The same principles apply in the human world as in the animal world. Telepathy seems to occur primarily between people who are strongly bonded – mothers and children, lovers, husbands and wives, twins, and close friends. It also happens between therapists and their clients, if they have transference. You get strong emotional bonds in other situations too. It doesn't typically happen between complete strangers.

Unfortunately, much of the para-psychological research on telepathy has involved complete strangers guessing meaningless cards in separate rooms. You could hardly think of conditions less likely to reveal the existence of telepathy, and they usually give much weaker results than real life events seem to show.

Let me just give one example of a case that's been investigated in the literature which seems to be a really good piece of psychical research. This one is relevant to the larger question of learning, because I think telepathy can play an unsuspected part in the way we learn. There is a kind of resonant transmission involved in many forms of learning which I think is quasi-telepathic.

This case involves a child who was severely mentally challenged and almost blind. He had a very close bond with his mother, and he first came to the attention of a biochemist colleague of mine at Cambridge, Sir Rudolph Peters, and his colleagues. One of his colleagues who is an ophthalmologist tested this boy when he was about five, and this boy did far better in the eye tests than he knew was possible. He then sent the mother out of the room and the boy's ability collapsed. He just couldn't do it. When the mother was there, he could do it, when she wasn't there, he couldn't. They then did other tests, and asked him various simple questions and puzzles, and if the mother was with him he could answer them, if the mother wasn't there or if she didn't know the answer, he couldn't. So they came to the conclusion that this boy must be working telepathically through his mother. She loved him very dearly and spent hours a day with him and here was real biological need.

They set up an experiment between the Babraham Institute and Cambridge, five or six miles apart, in laboratories with telephones. The boy was in one laboratory, and the mother was five miles away. The mother was shown a series of cards with letters and numbers on them, and the boy had to guess what card the mother was looking at. His results were spectacular, billions to one against chance, unlike these card-guessing games with strangers in laboratories. These were spectacular results, because it is working with the grain of the phenomenon.

What this experiment shows is in the ordinary learning of ordinary parents and children that this kind of thing probably occurs. We take it for granted. We don't really think about it. And usually people say things like, 'Well, if there are visual clues, if there is body language, if there's a communication going on it can't be telepathy because these other things explain it. I don't think so. I think that telepathy is going on all the time in ordinary communication and we don't usually notice it because there are other channels as well. It's not as if when we can see somebody we don't listen, or when we can smell something we don't hear. The channels all work together and telepathy is part of it, and I think telepathy plays an unsuspected role in learning and in the transmission of information from parents to children, and from teachers to those they are teaching.
(706 words; total 5389)

Telepathic bonding

I've looked at telepathy in cases where there are strong social bonds, and one of the strongest and most biological bonds that exists is between nursing mothers and their babies. Many nursing mothers feel they have a telepathic link with their baby.

I did a survey and I found that many nursing mothers have had the following experience. Typically, they have been away from the baby, not at a usual feeding time, for example, shopping in a supermarket, and then they feel their milk let down. That's what happens when a baby needs

feeding. The breasts get ready to feed the baby by squeezing out the milk. It's mediated by the hormone oxytocin and normally triggered by the sound of the baby crying. It's a distinct physiological response: the milk let-down reflex. When women are away from their baby and for no reason feel their milk let down, most of them assume their baby needs them. Usually they are right, and this seems to be a very common experience, it is not just a matter of regular feeding times. To test this I recruited ten women in North London and we monitored them for two months – every time their milk let down it was recorded, and every time the baby cried it was recorded. We did a statistical analysis, and it showed that they weren't right every time, there were some false alarms, but far above the chance level the women's milk was letting down when the baby really did need them. The odds against chance were a billion to one. It was a highly significant effect.

Many mothers find they retain a telepathic link with their children as they grow older. For example many of them have had the experience of just feeling that something is wrong, so they phone home or go home and something has happened, the child has had an accident. It even happens with grown-up children.

Women are better at this than men. All the literature and all the surveys I've done reinforce the common everyday assumption that women are, on average, more intuitive than men. And so the best telepathic links often happen between mothers and daughters, and many mothers and daughters have the experience that the mother will know when the daughter is upset and distressed and ring up and ask what's wrong.

There are many examples of human telepathy, and I have studied and investigated various kinds. Telephone telepathy is the commonest kind of telepathy in the modern world. About 80% of people in random samples have had this experience that seems to be telepathic: you think of someone and then for no apparent reason they ring, or you just know who it is when the phone rings. Most people don't think this is odd. Of course it's not odd if you know someone is going to ring at a particular time, or if it is a habit, but when it is unexpected it is more impressive. *(497 words; total 5886)*

The telephone experiment

What does science have to tell us about this? The answer is that until recently, absolutely nothing, because it had been uninvestigated even by parapsychologists. The standard armchair argument that educated people have been trained in, this kind of armchair scepticism, just says well, of course, it's just a coincidence. You think about other people all the time, and sometimes someone rings and you think it is telepathy but you forget the millions of times you are wrong. They don't have any statistics about how many times you've been wrong, they just make it up, but it sounds scientific.

Does it really happen? Once again, the only way to find out for sure is to do controlled experiments. I've devised a very simple experimental test to see if people really can tell who is calling. Of course, like any experiment, it is artificial which probably reduces the intensity of the experience. But this is how it works.

If you were the subject, you would give me the names of four people you might be telepathic with and who you might know when they are calling. You sit at home, we videotape you to make sure you are not getting any other phone calls or email messages. The whole time in this research we have to deal with sceptics who are eager to point out possible flaws, and the one they are most keen on is that people simply cheat.

You're videotaped, you're sitting there, the phone is on the table. It is a landline, because mobile phones have caller ID displays, so it is a landline without a caller ID display. You know that you will be getting calls from these four people during this experimental session. For each test we pick the caller at random by the throw of a die, so you can't know in advance who is going to call.

We call them up and say please call your friend in about five minutes, the phone rings and before you pick it up you have to say which of the four people you think it is. You say, 'I think it's Mary', pick it up and say, 'Hello Mary.' You're right or you're wrong.

By chance, you'd be right one time in four, 25%. We've done more than a thousand of these tests and the average success rate is 42%, massively significant statistically, and it would probably be higher if we could think of a more natural way of doing this experiment. Some people do better than that, some do worse. Some people are at chance levels, but that's the average over many different subjects.

This work has been replicated independently at a University in Amsterdam and the University of Capetown. The experiment shows a robust, strong, telepathic effect. It is published in peer review journals; you can read all the statistics in my book and in the published papers which are on my website.

We've done similar experiments with email – the latest development of evolutionary telepathy. The success rate there, in more than 600 tests, is 45%; highly significant, slightly higher than the telephone telepathy tests. I now have a telepathic online experiment and this is where I'd like you to help me. You can log onto my website www.sheldrake.org to find out more and participate. *(553 words; total 6439)*

Morphic fields

So this new view, this view which differs from the traditional scientific view, is possible. It's even probable. The theories of two-way vision and telepathy certainly have some robust scientific evidence to back them up. They are normal. It is the so-far-unchallenged traditional view that is looking more like the tall story.

So now I would further like to suggest what might underlie these theories; what it is that makes these things possible. And my answer is 'morphic fields'.

What are morphic fields? They are part of a new field of study of nature. They manifest through things like telepathy and the sense of being stared at. They also underlie the development of organisms – they organize the growth of embryos and plants. They act like invisible fields or moulds within or around the organism which help it develop in the same way as others of its type or family. This work I describe in detail in my books *'The New Science of Life'*, and especially in *'The Presence of the Past'*, which is my main theoretical book.

Morphic fields work rather like quantum fields, by patterning otherwise indeterminate or probabilistic processes. They organise the activities of our brains, they underlie our learning, our instincts, and our behaviour. That is the hypothesis. One of the features of morphic fields is that they have a built-in memory, they evolve, and this process of evolution and communication I call 'morphic resonance', where similar things influence subsequent similar things across space and time. What this means is that each species has a collective memory. Each individual draws on the collective memory of its own species and in turn contributes to it. The instincts of spiders to spin webs are a type of collective habit that spiders have built up over many generations. The genes that organisms inherit enable them to tune in to the right fields, although not all this material is coded in the genes.

Your TV set has to have the right components in order to work. If you change or remove some of the condensers or transistors it won't work properly, showing that these components are important. But the pictures and the sounds that come out of the set are not generated from inside it, from the components, and similarly I don't think the forms of organisms or their instinctive behaviour are generated from inside the organism by the genes. What the genes do is code for proteins, or code for the control of protein synthesis, they don't contain forms, patterns, instructions. A lot of fantasy has been put into the genes; they are credited with the whole of heredity. They play an important part, but they are not all of it, any more than the components are all there is to your TV set. I think genes are grossly overrated. Similarly I think brains are grossly overrated, because there is more to the activity of the mind than is contained within the brain. The brain is the TV set. The mind is much more than that. *(508 words; total 6947)*

Learning through morphic fields

I think that through morphic fields and morphic resonance we humans have a kind of collective memory, and this collective memory can express itself in learning. So it means that if some people learn something, others should find that thing easier to learn. And to support this theory, there is already evidence (summarized in my books '*The Presence of the Past*' and '*The New Science of Life*') that rats trained to learn new tricks make it easier for other rats of the same breed all around the world to learn the same tricks more quickly.

Special tests for morphic resonance with humans have also shown that if some people learn something, others can do it quicker. One of these tests involved crossword puzzles. This came to my attention because several people wrote to me and told me they found the Times crossword easier to do if they left it until the next day. If my theory is correct, then the reason might be that thousands of people have already done it on the day it was published, so it's easier to do the next day. A student in Nottingham University did some actual tests with crossword puzzles. We had to get them before they were published in order to do the tests before and after, and the results suggest this effect really does happen.

One interesting area where research suggests the morphic resonance hypothesis really works is in IQ tests. When I first developed this theory, I was looking for standard tests that are done year after year. The prediction should be that people get better at doing them, because millions have already done them. I predicted IQ scores should rise. Of course, they are tabled by definition to an average of 100 every year, but the absolute scores should go up. However, I couldn't have access to the relevant data.

A few years later, a New Zealand psychologist called James Flynn discovered what is now called the Flynn Effect, which is that average IQ scores have been rising in all countries all over the world for the last 50 years, or in fact since IQ tests were introduced. This was a big puzzle for psychologists because there is no independent evidence that people are getting smarter. And they're not. They are not actually getting more intelligent, they are just getting better at doing IQ tests. I think the reason is that so many people have already done IQ tests, that they have created a strong IQ test morphic field. By morphic resonance, people are being helped in doing the tests by people who have done them before.

A new way of testing for morphic resonance was suggested by my 17-year-old son last year when, in the run up to exams, he and his friends were discussing how they could actually apply these ideas. They hit on what is actually a brilliant idea which provides a wonderful test for morphic resonance. He and his friends decided that in their physics and maths papers, they would answer questions 7 and 8, the last two questions, first, and then go back to the earlier ones. He said that in this way they would be about a quarter of an hour behind thousands of other people doing the exam and should get a boost from morphic resonance for the first six questions. 'And even if morphic resonance doesn't exist,' he

added pragmatically, 'we won't lose anything.' This is a wonderful idea, and one could actually test this nationally on a huge scale. If I were in charge of GCSE exams I'd make sure that some schools, although they'd still have the same questions, would get them in a different order.

Morphic resonance plays a major part in learning, and when we learn something there is a resonant transmission from the teacher and from all the people who have learned it before. That means that the most effective learning techniques based on this principle should be ones which facilitate this resonance. The least effective would be the ones which minimise it.

For example, if you want to learn French in the least effective way, you'd learn it in the way totally unlike French babies learn it. You'd sit down in front of a desk with a text book, you'd learn lists of words and irregular verbs, and grammar which ordinary French people never bother with – they just pick it up. You'd learn it the way it's actually taught in most British schools – very ineffectively. To do it effectively, you'd be exposed to people talking in meaningful situations, you'd hear the sounds, more like the language laboratory method or just being thrown in at the deep end in France. You'd learn it much more quickly because you would resonate with the people speaking it. I think when babies learn languages they pick it up largely by a resonance with those around them. It's not innate, genetically-programmed grammar as Chomsky suggested, but it is innate in the sense that it is inherited through a kind of resonance.

There are many aspects of the mind that we don't understand. There is a great deal that is not known, and this is the big new frontier within science. There is no reason that scientific methods shouldn't be extended to these areas, as I hope I've illustrated, and as some others are already doing. There is a huge amount we can learn about ourselves. It would help to break down the artificial gulf between our own experience and the official mechanistic view of us as mere machines, with minds that are nothing but the activities of our brains.

It will be an exciting healing process as we make these discoveries. I hope that some of you, by taking part in these experiments and by encouraging others to do so, will join in this process of discovery.

© 2005/2012 Rupert Sheldrake
(981 words; total 7928)

This article reproduces a talk given by Rupert Sheldrake at the Liverpool 2005 Conference of SEAL (Society for Effective Affective Learning). The talk was written up by Christine Miller and appeared over two issues of ReSource Magazine (July and September 2005).
Contact www.yourultimateresource.com
It is reproduced here with the permission of Rupert Sheldrake.
(53 words; total 7981)

Rupert Sheldrake is a biologist and author of more than 75 technical papers and several books, including 'The Presence of the Past', 'A New Science of Life', 'The Sense of Being Stared At, And Other Aspects of the Extended Mind', and 'The Science Delusion: Freeing the Spirit of Enquiry' (2012). His book 'Dogs That Know When Their Owners Are Coming Home, And Other Unexplained Powers of Animals' (1999) was selected as Book of The Year by the British Scientific and Medical Network. He studied natural sciences at Cambridge University and philosophy at Harvard, where he was a Frank Knox Fellow. He took a PhD in biochemistry at Cambridge and was a Fellow of Clare College, Cambridge, where he was Director of Studies in biochemistry and cell biology. As a Research Fellow of the Royal Society, he carried out research at Cambridge in developmental biology. He is currently a Fellow of the Institute of Noetic Sciences, in California, and lives in London. Contact: www.sheldrake.org

(167 words; total 8148)

Our ANSWER to 'What is a Hot Spot' – on the first page of 'The Extended Mind' article

The message of the first page is that Sheldrake proposes that:

• The activity of the mind extends beyond the physical brain (whereas conventional scientists believe that the activity of the mind is contained within the physical brain).
• This happens because of morphic fields.
• Fields and energy (not matter) are the most fundamental explanatory principles in modern science.
• The secondary idea (which is a sort of example) is that vision is a two-way process and not confined within the brain.
• Vision involves consciousness (science cannot explain consciousness)

The actual words (hot spots) that say this are highlighted in the copy on the next page.

Notice that the ideas are **repeated** several times (including in the title), and if you are reading with an open accepting mind until you understand the article, then you only need to read something once to understand it. You can then skim quickly past the repetitions.

The remaining words are **explanation** (how vision extends beyond the brain), **examples** of other fields we are familiar with (paragraphs about gravity, mobile phones, magnets), giving **credibility** (Karl Popper, your own experience), **grammatical words** to make the language flow (is, the, does, that, to, etc), and **literary devices** (Which is the tall story? The first/second mystery … etc) to make it more interesting to read.

How much you personally need to read will depend mostly on your existing knowledge and experience (and therefore to some extent on your age).

The Extended Mind – The Sense of Being Stared At
Rupert Sheldrake

True story? Tall Story?

What is the true nature of our minds? Which of the following do you think is the tall story? Which one do you think is true? Are our minds confined within our heads? Are all our thoughts, feelings and sensations located inside our brain tissue? Does this sound like the tall story? Or do our minds extend beyond the confines of our heads? Our thoughts, feelings and sensations are rooted within the brain but can extend far beyond them? Is this perhaps the tall story?

Some of my colleagues in the scientific world would have no doubt that the second is the tall story, and strenuously promote the idea that all the thought products of our brains remain within the brain.

I, on the other hand, am definitely rooting for the second idea, that our minds extend beyond our heads. But you will have to make your own decision. *(164 words)*

Fields of influence

In this article, I am suggesting that the mind is much more extensive than the brain and that our minds stretch out beyond our brains through what I term 'morphic fields'.

This is not a new concept to us. Everyone now is familiar with mobile phones. We all accept that in order to work they must involve some kind of energy field which extends far beyond the electronic circuits and plastic casing you hold in your hand. We're all used to the idea of invisible fields of influence which stretch beyond their source.

We accept that a magnet contains within it a magnetic field, and that this field stretches beyond the magnet itself to exert its pull on other objects. There's nothing unscientific about magnetism. Similarly the earth's gravitational field stretches out far beyond the surface of the earth – it's what keeps the moon in orbit around it. Gravity is invisible, it moves through empty space and yet it's real.

Sir Karl Popper, science philosopher, acknowledged that matter is no longer the fundamental explanatory principle in science. Matter is explained in terms of energy found within fields. So fields and energy are the most fundamental explanatory principles in modern science.

Similarly, then, I am suggesting that our minds are systems of fields that stretch far beyond our brains. They are rooted in our brains but they are not confined to the inside of our heads. This is no more a dualistic theory, in the traditional sense of dualism, than mobile phones, magnetism or gravitational fields. It is a scientific view of the mind, even though it goes way beyond the current scientific model.

So I'm going to discuss the 'extended mind' and some of the evidence that supports this view.

Perhaps one of the easiest ways of seeing how this different view of things might work is by considering vision. Not visionary experience, just ordinary vision – how you look with your eyes at whatever is in front of you. *(332 words; total 496)*

How we see

Now the conventional theory of vision (which corresponds with the view that the mind is confined to the brain) is that light is reflected from whatever you are looking at and enters your eyes. Inverted images form on your retinas, changes happen in the cone cells, and electrical impulses travel up the optic nerve and stimulate electrical and chemical activity in the various visual regions of the brain.

All this has been studied in great detail and it's all very good – as far as it goes. The trouble is that that's as far as it does go. Seeing something involves more than just electrical and chemical changes in the brain. There is also a conscious experience. And science has almost nothing to tell us about conscious experiences.

It's only in the last 15 or 20 years that scientific research has focused on consciousness and even now most people still think that consciousness is nothing but a by-product of chemical and electrical activity in the brain. It doesn't actually do anything. So that's the first mystery, what people call the 'hard problem', the fact that there's consciousness at all. Science can't explain it. If your brain is like a computer, then how come you are conscious when your computer isn't?

The second mystery is that all this change is supposedly happening inside your head and yet I imagine that you are experiencing what you are looking at where it actually is, out in front of you, rather than inside your head.

The theory I'm putting forward is so simple that it's quite hard to understand. I'm proposing that your image of what you are looking at is out there in front of you. It's in your mind, constructed by your mind, but it's not inside your brain. *(299 words; total 794)*

Vision: a two-way process

I suggest that vision is a two-way process. Light comes in, changes happen in the brain, and the images are projected out to where they seem to be – which corresponds exactly with our experience because we experience the images outside ourselves.

But that's not the official scientific view. The official scientific view is that everything you can see is actually inside your head. There's a kind of virtual reality display going on inside your brain. You're having an experience inside your head and falsely imagining that it's out there. So when you look at the sky, that's an image inside your head too. So in some way your phenomenal skull must be beyond the sky.

That's the official view and that's what's taught in practically every university in the world.

So what do you think? Which of these two views is the tall story?

My theory that vision involves a two-way process is not an original one. It was put forward by Plato, believed

Our ANSWERS to the QUESTIONS on 'The Extended Mind'
(p 119)
Please note that this is not an easy text to read, particularly if you
don't already know something about it, nor did all the questions
ask for easy answers. Also we have given very full answers (often
more than the questions asked for). So if you got the answers to
more than 10 of the questions in 20 minutes, and particularly if
you were able to give a reasonable summary of some of the main
points in Question 18, please count yourself successful!
1 Sheldrake thinks the mind extends beyond the brain.
2 The hard problem is to define 'consciousness'. Why does
   consciousness exist at all?
3 Sheldrake thinks vision is a two-way process. The conventional
   view is that vision is interpreted within the brain and everything
   we see is therefore contained in some way within the brain.
4 90%
5 Sheldrake interviewed private detectives, surveillance officers
   and security personnel, including the drug squad at Heathrow
   airport. It is not clear whether he also interviewed members of
   the SAS.
6 More than 19,000 people have taken part in the experiment in
   the NEMO centre in Amsterdam.
7 Eyes evolved about 530 million years ago in the Cambrian
   period.
8 All 65 of the veterinary clinics in North London regularly had
   problems with people missing appointments for their cats. (If
   you wrote 64 out of 65, count it as a right answer. The other
   one also had so much of a problem that it stopped
   appointments for cats altogether. But you got the important
   point which is that cats tend to know and run away when their
   owners are planning to take them to the vet.)
9 Evidence shows that, in many cases, dogs first start waiting at
   the moment when the owners make the decision to come home.
10 Aimee Morgana's parrot is called N'kisi.
11 The problem with most of the para-psychological research is
    that it involves complete strangers guessing meaningless
    cards – which are the conditions least likely to reveal
    the existence of telepathy.
12 The sorts of people who are likely to have the strongest
    telepathic links are nursing mothers with their babies,
    mothers with their children, particularly mothers and
    daughters because in general women are better at telepathy
    than men. (You only had to give one example.)
13 The avarage success rate of the telephone experiment is 42%
    (by chance you'd expect a 25% success rate).
14 (Morphic fields aren't easy to define – Sheldrake doesn't
    explain what they are, he compares them to other things and
    says how they might work.) Morphic fields are like quantum
    fields, they act like invisible fields around living organisms
    and contain a sort of memory or blueprint of the organism

which helps their growth and development to be like others of their kind. Morphic fields are what allow things like telepathy and the sense of being stared at to happen.

15 Sheldrake calls the ability of morphic fields to evolve and communicate 'morphic resonance'.

16 It might be easier to do the Times crossword puzzle later in the week because more people will have completed it and therefore the morphic resonance will be stronger.

17 Sheldrake's son did the last two questions first, then did the other questions in order starting at the first in the hope that the morphic field of right answers would be stronger with all the earlier questions because a lot of people would have done them.

18 The main point of this article is that Sheldrake says the activity of the mind extends beyond the actual brain and manifests in things like telepathy (conventional science says that all thinking processes happen within the brain and that telepathy doesn't exist). Sheldrake also says that when we see things, not all the activity stays within our brain (the conventional view), something also goes out from our eyes which can be detected by other living beings. He has conducted simple experiments to show that both of these things are true. The principle that makes both of these things possible, he calls 'morphic fields' and the ability of morphic fields to evolve and communicate he calls 'morphic resonance'.

QUESTIONS on The Wise Teacher and the Jar

Look for the answers to the following questions in The Wise Teacher and the Jar. (next page)
Finding the answers to the questions is your purpose for reading. Ignore any information which does not answer these questions. Get into a good state before you start. Set your timer for 8 minutes. Read through all the questions before you start reading the text. Jot down the answers in note form as you find them. Stop as soon as you have the answers to all the questions. Compare your answers with ours at the end of the text.

1 Jot down in order the things the teacher dropped into the jar.
2 What do you think is the main meaning or message of the story?
3 How many different meanings can you think of in the remaining time available?

Our suggested answers are on page 134.

The Wise Teacher and the Jar

There was once a very wise teacher, whose words of wisdom students would come from far and wide to hear. One day as usual, many students began to gather in the teaching room. They came in and sat down very quietly, looking to the front with keen anticipation, ready to hear what the teacher had to say.

Eventually the teacher came in and sat down in front of the students. The room was so quiet you could hear a pin drop. On one side of the teacher was a large glass jar. On the other side was a pile of dark grey rocks. Without saying a word, the teacher began to pick up the rocks one by one and place them very carefully in the glass jar. (Plonk. Plonk.) When all the rocks were in the jar, the teacher turned to the students and asked, 'Is the jar full?' 'Yes,' said the students. 'Yes, teacher, the jar is full.'

Without saying a word, the teacher began to drop small round pink pebbles carefully into the large glass jar so that they fell down between the rocks. (Clickety click. Clickety click.) When all the pebbles were in the jar, the teacher turned to the students and asked, 'Is the jar now full?' The students looked at one another and then some of them started nodding and saying, 'Yes. Yes, teacher, the jar is now full. Yes.'

Without saying a word, the teacher took some fine silver sand and let it trickle with a gentle sighing sound into the large glass jar (whoosh) where it settled around the pink pebbles and the dark grey rocks. When all the sand was in the jar, the teacher turned to the students and asked, 'Is the jar now full?'

The students were not so confident this time, but the sand had clearly filled all the space in the jar, so a few still nodded and said, 'Yes, teacher, the jar is now full. Now it's full.'

Without saying a word, the teacher took a jug of water and poured it carefully, without splashing a drop, into the large glass jar. (Gloog. Gloog.) When the water reached the brim, the teacher turned to the students and asked, 'Is the jar now full?' Most of the students were silent, but two or three ventured to answer, 'Yes, teacher, the jar is now full. Now it is.'

Without saying a word, the teacher took a handful of salt and sprinkled it slowly over the top of the water with a very quiet whishing sound. (Whish.) When all the salt had dissolved into the water, the teacher turned to the students and asked once more, 'Is the jar now full?' The students were totally silent. Eventually one brave student said, 'Yes, teacher. The jar is now full.' 'Yes,' said the teacher. "The jar is now full.'

The teacher then said, 'A story always has many meanings and you will each have understood many things from this demonstration. Discuss quietly amongst yourselves what meanings the story has for you. How many different messages can you find in it and take from it?'

The students looked at the wise teacher and at the beautiful glass jar filled with grey rocks, pink pebbles, silver sand, water and salt. Then they quietly discussed with one another the meanings the story had for them. After a few minutes the wise teacher raised one hand and the room fell silent. The teacher said, 'Remember that there is never just one interpretation of anything. You have all taken away many meanings and messages from the story, and each meaning is as important and as valid as any other.' And without saying another word, the teacher got up and left the room.

From *'In Your Hands, NLP for teaching and learning'* by Jane Revell & Susan Norman, Saffire Press 1997
(349 words; total 649)

Our ANSWERS to the QUESTIONS on The Wise Teacher and the Jar (p 132)

1 Rocks, pebbles, sand, water, salt
2 Possibly that you shouldn't accept the first right answer, or that the message anyone takes from the story is as valid as anyone else's. This story is often used in NLP courses and the usual message given is 'get the big rocks in first'.
   (NLP – Neuro-Linguistic Programming – started by looking at how to copy the strategies used by people who are very good at different things. It describes how the brain works and how different brains work differently, and suggests ways to think and behave in ways which are more beneficial to you. It is a good starting point for self-development.)
3 Possible meanings: the teacher (or the author) wanted students to look beyond the first (right) answer and think of other possibilities; the teacher didn't know the meaning of the story; the teacher was a sadist who wanted to make the students feel silly; people tend not to offer an opinion when they think they might be wrong; it is important to do things in the right order; it is important to do things carefully; the writer of the story wanted to teach students how to behave quietly and respectfully in class; the colour and sound of things (how we experience things sensually) is important; the teacher was so wise that the real meaning is impossible for us to understand; the teacher had an urgent appointment so didn't have time to stay and explain the real meaning of the story. Any other meanings you come up with are valid as long as they are supported by evidence from the story (otherwise they might be classified as 'creative thinking').

A History of Spd Rdng

Before you start reading the article on the next page think (predict) what sort of information you would expect to find in this article. Then spend two minutes previewing the article and setting your purpose.

After getting into a good state, set your timer for 20 minutes and jot down information from the article which fulfils your purpose. As you read notice in particular information you can ignore.

Sample purposes

Choose only one, or something better of your own.
1 Write a timeline of 6 key developments in spd rdng
2 Find 6 spd rdng techniques I will definitely use
3 Identify 6 spd rdng techniques and the names (and approximate dates) of the 6 different people who originally developed them

A History of Spd Rdng

Ever since people have been reading, many of them have been trying to read faster and more effectively. Oddly, though, apart from some early exploration by the US Air Force who held the first formal speed reading course at Syracuse University in 1925, there has been little or no support from educational establishments or governments. Even though you would think there were academic plaudits or increased educational attainments to be gained by the first organization or country to implement a reading programme which could take students beyond the basics, all advances seem to have been made by committed individuals who have remained outside the formal education system, and that is still the situation today.

Some of these individual innovations have become accepted within the field, but even within the 'field' (if it exists), many individuals remain unaware of the work and advances of others, so it's possible, probable even, that some 'discoveries' have been made by more than one person, some techniques have remained unique to their inventor, and some may have flourished briefly but then been lost. So what follows is a partial, incomplete summary of the ideas which we (Jan Cisek and Susan Norman) have built on, discovered or rediscovered for ourselves, and developed into the reading system we now call 'Spd Rdng'. This is also by way of an acknowledgement of our debt to those who have taught and inspired us. As Isaac Newton said, 'If I have seen further, it is only by standing on the shoulders of giants.' *(258 words)*

Earliest references to faster reading
The third quarter of the 19th century saw some of the earliest references to speed reading techniques. Around 1878, Emil Javel, a French ophthalmologist who is remembered for his work on correcting squints, did some experiments into how the eye is involved in reading. It was he who established that the eye does a series of 'jumps' (called 'saccades') along the line and pauses to take in information at each 'stop' ('fixation'). He also established that it was possible to take in information to either side of the fixation, ie that people could understand chunks of text, rather than reading every single word. Some six years later, articles began to appear in journals (including *'The Education Review'*) about enhanced reading skills acquired by reading groups of words without vocalising (saying the words to yourself as you read).

Things then go quiet for a while, until around 1921, John Anthony O'Brien wrote a book called *'Silent Reading: with special reference to methods for developing speed, a study in the psychology and pedagogy of reading'*, which

reiterated the point that it was possible to read groups of words without vocalising.

In the 1940s, experiments on 'rapid' reading were done at Harvard University using a tachistoscope. This device, first described by A W Volkman, a German physiologist in 1859, used to be used (before computers) for experiments which involved showing subjects visual stimuli for controlled durations. They have been used to encourage recognition speed (and could therefore be used to help people test or increase their reading speed) and also to show items for too short a period for them to register consciously (which might be useful for experiments on 'downloading', also known as 'photoreading'). *(287 words; total 545)*

Mortimer Adler
It is also worth noting that 1940 saw the publication of a book called *'How to Read a Book'* by American professor, philosopher, and educational theorist, Dr Mortimer J Adler. This was more about how books should be classified and how to read books in depth than it was about reading faster. However, in the revised 1966 edition, he refers to 'syntopical reading' (the basis of the comparative reading of several books with one purpose at one time, which we refer to as 'syntopic processing'), which he defines as 'reading in' the whole set of great books as contrasted with 'reading through' a single work.

The set of great books is those books from which Adler extracted the ideas on which western civilization is based. He indexed these ideas and called it the 'Syntopicon' – which he hoped readers would use to compare the thoughts of great thinkers of the previous 3000 years in a matter of moments. (If you're interested, Adler's 102 'great ideas' are: Angel, Animal, Aristocracy, Art, Astronomy, Beauty, Being, Cause, Chance, Change, Citizen, Constitution, Courage, Custom and Convention, Definition, Democracy, Desire, Dialectic, Duty, Education, Element, Emotion, Eternity, Evolution, Experience, Family, Fate, Form, God, Good and Evil, Government, Habit, Happiness, History, Honor, Hypothesis, Idea, Immortality, Induction, Infinity, Judgment, Justice, Knowledge, Labor, Language, Law, Liberty, Life and Death, Logic, Love, Man, Mathematics, Matter, Mechanics, Medicine, Memory and Imagination, Metaphysics, Mind, Monarchy, Nature, Necessity and Contingency, Oligarchy, One and Many, Opinion, Opposition, Philosophy, Physics, Pleasure and Pain, Poetry, Principle, Progress, Prophecy, Prudence, Punishment, Quality, Quantity, Reasoning, Relation, Religion, Revolution, Rhetoric, Same and Other, Science, Sense, Sign and Symbol, Sin, Slavery, Soul,

Space, State, Temperance, Theology, Time, Truth, Tyranny, Universal and Particular, Virtue and Vice, War and Peace, Wealth, Will, Wisdom, World.) The 72 authors from which he took these ideas are listed under 'Great Books of the Western World' (although for most of the authors he recommends more than one book, and for several – including Shakespeare, Hippocrates, Archimedes, Sophocles, and others – he recommends reading 'the complete works'), and these are supplemented by a further 153 listed under topic headings in the section 'Gateway to the Great Books'.

Adler was also a proponent of holistic reading or 'global to detail' reading (although he didn't use either of those terms). He wrote, 'To understand a book, you must approach it, first, as a whole, having a unity and a structure of part; and second, in terms of its elements, its units of language and thought.' And he encouraged keeping an open mind: 'Understanding an author must always precede criticizing or judging him.' *(432 words; total 977)*

Evelyn Wood names 'speed reading'

It wasn't until the 1950s that the phrase 'speed reading' was coined by Evelyn Nielsen Wood, who published her book, *'Reading Skills'*, in 1959. Originally a school teacher, she studied exceptional readers (including President John Kennedy) and discovered people who could read between 1500 and 6000 words per minute, often by reading down the page rather than from side to side (what we call super-reading), reading meaningful groups of words rather than individual words and avoiding rereading texts (regression). She also noticed that faster readers were also more efficient and effective.

Together with her husband, Evelyn Wood created a system which increased a reader's speed on average from a rate of 230-300 wpm (words per minute) by a factor of two to five times that, with increased retention. They named the system Evelyn Wood Speed Reading Dynamics and taught the programme throughout the USA. White House staff members took her course and her classes were taught on college campuses until the late 1990s. She is credited with introducing the use of a 'pacer' (a finger or capped pen which encourages the eye to move quickly down the text) and she discouraged subvocalisation. *(199 words; total 1178)*

Tony Buzan and mindmapping

Although *'Speed Reading'* by Tony Buzan was published in 1971, his greater contribution to the Spd Rdng system was the development of mindmapping as a way of taking non-linear notes which he writes about in numerous other books. However, in his speed reading book, his 'Mind Map Organic Study Technique' (MMOST) is made up of two sections: Preparation (setting a time for your study period, deciding on the amount of material to be covered, checking how much knowledge you already have, and setting down goals

in the form of questions) and Application (Survey, Preview, Inview and Review). Buzan gives some interesting insights into reading and some of the problems which hold back slow readers, but much of his book is given over to mechanical number-spotting exercises and textual comprehension tests. He recommends building vocabulary, and, to that end, lists the meanings of 80 prefixes and 51 suffixes.
(151 words; total 1327)

The non-conscious mind

The next giant leap in the history of spd rdng was the focus on the amazing abilities of the non-conscious mind. In 1966, Georgi Lozanov, a Bulgarian doctor, psychotherapist and educationist, founded his Suggestology Research Institute in Sofia. He developed a method of teaching which he called Suggestopedia (suggestion + pedagogy) in which learning became a pleasurable, natural experience which reflected the way children learn while drawing on the huge capacity of the non-conscious mind. When Lozanov's approach was taken up in the west, it was referred to as Accelerated – or Accelerative – Learning. Many of these ideas have been incorporated into the Spd Rdng approach with its emphasis of putting reading (the taking in and processing of ideas) into the wider context of learning (putting those ideas into practice).

Norman Dixon's book *'Preconscious processing'* was published in 1981. It details his work on the ability of the brain to take in information without conscious awareness and the effect that 'priming' can have on a person's behaviour without their knowledge. One of his conclusions, which is particularly relevant to the downloading (photoreading) technique where the 'reader' looks quickly (approximately one second per page) at every page of a book without consciously reading it is that 'Words ... do not have to be consciously perceived in order to be recognised'.

This conclusion had been previously recognised by Richard Welch, the self-styled 'father of mental photography' who went on from running Evelyn-Wood-type speed-reading courses to develop 'Subliminal Dynamics'. He made incredible claims for the system which involved eliminating subvocalisation completely – including a 16-year old dyslexic boy who could take in 606,000 wpm and then scoring 90% on a 100-question in-depth test. Welch said that it was not necessary to read and reread information until it 'sinks in'. 'Sinks in to where?' he asked. He said that participants on his courses were regularly taking in information at the rate of two seconds per page, or faster, sometimes holding the book upside down, since the subconscious mind knows no bounds. Although the 'readers' had no sensation of 'reading', the information found a direct path through the brain to the part of the subconscious which 'gets it'.

After attending a course with Richard Welch, Paul Scheele developed his own system which he called 'The

PhotoReading Whole Mind System', which again depended heavily on downloading, which he called the 'photoreading step', although in his system the information which had gone direct to the non-conscious mind then needed 'activating' in order for it to be useful. The five photoreading steps were: Prepare (set your purpose and get into a good state), Preview, Photoread (including going into photofocus), Postview (similar to preview), and Activate. The challenge for people learning this system was to understand the 'activation' process, which seemed to be of equal value to the other four steps, but which in reality can take more than twice as long as the other four steps put together. It starts with 'incubation' – which means waiting at least 20 minutes, and preferably overnight, for the non-conscious mind to process the information, after which readers work with the book using super-reading, making mindmaps and rapid reading. After doing this people typically expected to remember the book in the same way as they might do after traditional reading, whereas downloaded information tends to come back piecemeal as it is needed. Secondly, although in reality versions of many of the spd rdng techniques are mentioned in Scheele's PhotoReading book (published 1993), the system seems to imply that it should be applied rigidly to any and every book. Learners typically spend a disproportionate amount of time worrying about 'getting the system right' rather than focusing on getting the information they want from the text, and they worry about deviating from that system, even though one will clearly use a variety of different approaches depending on the type of material, the reader's existing knowledge, their purpose, the time available, etc. A one-size-fits-all system just doesn't.
(663 words; total 1990)

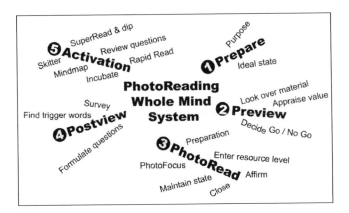

Additional contributions

Numerous other people need to be mentioned in this 'partial history'. John Duns Scotus was the 13th century monk who asked children to focus on the concentration point above and behind their head to help them read. This point was rediscovered by Ron Davis who taught it to people with dyslexia and helped them to read (his book *'The Gift of Dyslexia'* was published in 1997).

The 80/20 rule was posited by the management consultant Joseph M Juran (1904-2008), who named it 'the Pareto Principle' after the Italian economist Vilfredo Pareto (1848-1923). Then Dr Russell Stauffer's book *'Teaching Reading as a Thinking Process'*, in which he states that 4-11% of words in most books carry all the meaning, was published in 1969.

'Rhizome' and 'rhizomatic' are terms used by Gilles Deleuze and Félix Guattari to describe the philosophical concept they developed in their 'Capitalism and Schizophrenia' project (1972-1980). The botanical rhizome was used as an analogy for a non-hierarchical organizational structure which can be entered and exited at any point. Additionally all points within it have the potential to be connected. This is in contrast to the more common arboreal (tree-like) structure which implies hierarchy and binary (yes-no) choices. We (Jan Cisek and Susan Norman) used the concept to develop a freer note-taking alternative to mindmapping, for which the name 'rhizomapping' was suggested by Susan's husband, Hugh L'Estrange.

Norman and Cisek also added the idea of the 'joker' to syntopic processing (which was first posited by Adler – see above) which we came across in our work on accelerated learning and creative thinking. We also believe we are the first people to offer a range of strategies to control sub-vocalisation (most books just say 'stop doing it'!)

The 'fizzical' challenges and eye exercises were taken from Brain Gym (developed by Paul and Gail Dennison), Hatha Yoga and NLP (Neuro-Linguistic Programming).

Additionally, although we didn't take the idea of collaborative learning from Howard Stephen Berg, it is something he recommends to students in his Maximum Power Reading system – and it gives us the opportunity to mention the man who claims to be the fastest reader in the world. *(358 words; total 2348)*

Detractors

We are well aware that speed reading and photoreading are somewhat controversial and have their detractors. Despite excellent results and a proven track record, some people don't believe speed reading works, or don't believe it can work for them. Some fail to 'get it' (usually because of a rigid mindset, or because they have unrealistic expectations or won't try something more than once before giving up), or they fail to keep it up (usually because old habits feel more comfortable) and then blame whichever system they chose to learn. Claiming that something doesn't work is can be more comfortable than accepting that they haven't persevered with learning something new. But it's also true that some techniques work better for some people than others.

Some people just can't see the need – either because they have worked out a satisfactory system for themselves, or because they don't want to try it (in case they fail?), or can't spare the time.

We ourselves would like to add a warning about online and computer-driven exercises which claim to improve reading speeds. By definition, these tests are mechanical. The brain on the other hand thrives on meaning. Although it is possible to improve reading speeds by working at mechanical exercises, what you tend to get better at is doing mechanical exercises and that skill does not necessarily transfer to the task of deriving meaning from a text. This may also be the reason why some independently-run tests of speed reading do not produce exceptional results. It may not seem to work particularly well when people are given objective tests on information which has no intrinsic value to the reader. What the experimenters miss is that speed reading can work in practice. It works when people have a real need for the information they're looking for.
(301 words; total 2649)

Promoters

On every Spd Rdng course we run, you can be sure that at some point at least one person will say something like, 'How I wish I'd known this when I was younger,' usually followed by 'Why on earth isn't this a compulsory course in schools?' Occasionally there is some follow-up by an individual working within education who tries to run a Spd Rdng course, and yet not one of them has come to fruition. Even when courses are offered free to university students, the people whose lives could be transformed by using these techniques and strategies, there is never enough take up from the students to make it worthwhile. Perhaps it's badly presented. Or perhaps the students just see it as 'one more thing to do', without realizing that this one thing could save them hours and hours of time. So spd rdng still remains the private secret of those with the wisdom to know that, in a world where everything is changing at an ever-increasing rate and where almost no aspect of life can be taken for granted any more, those who will survive are the ones who are able to access, process and react to new information in the shortest possible time. *(206 words; total 2835)*

Spd Rdng

Jan Cisek was the first qualified PhotoReading instructor in the UK and he started teaching PhotoReading in 1999. Courses generally went quite well, but in 2004 he approached Susan Norman, an expert in accelerated learning, to see if they could be improved. Jan and Susan regularly ran courses together over the next five years, during which time we took note of all the difficulties different individuals had and devised new approaches to make it easier for people to learn the new skills. Within a year the course was significantly

different enough for us to rename it VIP (Visual Information Processing), since the biggest shift we ask people to make is to change their thinking from 'reading' to 'information processing'. As we started writing the course in book form, it evolved into the 37 separate techniques and we (at the suggestion of a friend, Holly Craigs) renamed the new system Spd Rdng.

Spd Rdng includes the best aspects of everything that has gone before, takes advantage of the latest research and insights into reading and learning, and is presented in a unique format which allows it to be applied to any reading material. One key difference with the Spd Rdng approach is that it is flexible. It allows for people to use different techniques with different material, people are free to combine the different techniques to produce their own system, and they are actively encouraged to find better ways to do things.

The first version of the book '*Spd Rdng - the Speed Reading Bible*' was published online in a Kindle edition in 2010 and has been selling well ever since. This revised edition of the book was published as a paperback book in 2012. Translations into eight languages are completed or in preparation. More are planned. *(298 words; total 3133)*

What's next?

We are aware that the world is changing in unpredictable ways at an ever-increasing rate. Spd Rdng is a flexible, dynamic approach to reading which takes account of the different ways in which the human brain works, while being ready to adapt to whatever changes occur in reading, learning, technology and human understanding in the coming years. We are particularly watching the development of visual language, the singularity and direct learning.

Robert E Horn's book '*Visual Language*' (published 1998) explains and shows how through infographics (information graphics) images and words can be combined to express ideas much more clearly and directly than either images or words can do alone. You can already see these ideas at work in certain TV commercials, and all the spd rdng techniques will work even more effectively if and when these ideas become more widely adopted. At the very least we are encouraged to see that more books are now being written and published with clearer navigation, descriptive titles, more subtitles, helpful glossaries, summaries, and more – all things to help the reader extract the message more easily.

Technology is also developing at an exponential rate, and it is possible that the 'technological singularity' (a greater-than-human superintelligence) will emerge in the foreseeable future. The term was popularized in science fiction by Vernor Vinge, who proposed that this superintelligence might come about through the development of artificial intelligence, human biological enhancement (genetic engineering?) or some kind of brain-computer interface. Read more in *'The Singularity is Near'* by Ray Kurzweil. But we can only imagine what that might mean for reading and learning. Could we realistically expect books – or knowledge, information, skills – to be downloaded directly to our long-term memory via biological micro-chips implanted in the brain? (Think of the scene where someone learnt to fly a helicopter in the film *'The Matrix'*.)

Or maybe the future is the perfection of direct learning. It has already been proved that our non-conscious minds have tremendous capacity, far beyond anything we accept today. Work is already progressing on the ability of human thought to be passed to machines. But could it be that the next step is for our thoughts to pass directly from human mind to human mind? Maybe humans will be able to tune into any morphic field of knowledge and acquire skills implicitly without going through any conscious learning process. Maybe we can already do that and all that's holding us back is our beliefs. And just maybe the way to move towards that is to practise downloading and direct learning as described in this book.

As you develop your reading and learning skills and have greater successes with the techniques we offer here, please let us know. We would also like to hear of your struggles and perceived failures – they're part of the learning process, and our own learning about reading has grown just as much from understanding what people couldn't do as from working out what exceptional readers do naturally. And as you go on to discover new ways in which reading and learning can be enhanced, please do get in touch. We'd love to work with you.

©Susan Norman and Jan Cisek 2012

(532 words; total 3664)

MORE ABOUT READING

Reading and writing are a brilliant human invention – a simple way of passing huge amounts of knowledge to others across time and space. You don't have to travel across the world to meet experts. Millions of people can read their words and understand their ideas in the comfort of their own homes. For less than the price of a restaurant meal, you can buy a lifetime of wisdom and knowledge in the form of a book. All you need to do is read it.

Information overload

The challenge in modern times, though, is that there's so much to read. New material is being churned out every day. In 1992 an education conference keynote speaker said that the total amount of human knowledge was doubling every four years. That rate is now increasing exponentially and what we know collectively is doubling within months. Additionally, something like 25% of that information is going out of date within five years. How on earth can we keep on top of it all?

The answer, of course, is to use technology for efficient data storage and retrieval, and to use the human brain for what it does better than computers – make value judgments, make decisions, choose. What we most need to develop are our thinking skills. But we still need to read.

Learning to read and write

Reading and writing are unnatural! Animals don't do it. They are something humans have invented for themselves – which is why they need to be taught. Not everyone gets the best teaching in their early years, and even if they do, reading skills need to change and develop over time. The reading we do in primary school is very different from the reading we do as adults – and rarely does anyone help us make the transition. Once we know how to decipher words and sentences, we're on our own. Some of us work out our own systems, others of us need to be taught. And all of us can benefit from thinking about different ways of reading.
(338 words)

What is reading?

So what exactly is 'reading'? It's the transfer of information through the medium of the written word from one person to others. Reading involves the use of your eyes and your brain (or, in the case of Braille, your fingers and your brain). In fact it's about 10% eyes (or fingers) and 90% brain. It's the quality of your thinking that makes the difference. So it's worth considering what kinds of thinking you need to do in addition to taking in information in order for your reading to be of value.

What reading isn't

The first important thinking skill connected with reading is **comprehension**. Reading has little value if you don't understand what you're reading. It's therefore worth choosing material which suits your current level of understanding. As you understand more, you will be able to move towards more challenging material.

Reading per se isn't **remembering**. If you want to remember what you read you need first to notice (choose) what you want to remember, then do something to fix that in your mind (eg talk to yourself about what you're reading, make links between new information and things you already know), write it down (take notes with mindmaps or rhizomaps), and then review it.

Reading on its own doesn't guarantee **learning**. In order to learn most effectively, you need to alternate between taking in new information (reading) and putting it into practice, doing something with your new learning. Until you use your learning, you only know 'about' something, you don't necessarily 'know' it. You need to build your practical **experience**.

It's also worth mentioning that reading isn't **writing**. Although the two skills are often taught together, there is a significant difference between producing writing, which has to be done one letter and word at a time, and taking in the meaning of written material from chunks of written text (reading).

Higher level thinking and reading skills

You will need other thinking skills for higher level reading. The ability to 'read between the lines' is to **infer** what the writer is talking about even when it is not stated directly. This is much easier to do when you are reading chunks of information for meaning rather than focusing on individual words. The twin skills of **analysing** and **synthesising** involve separating a proposition into its component parts (analysing) and bringing together the essence of those ideas, possibly from different sources (synthesising). Syntopic processing allows you to do this working with four books at one time. Use your critical faculties to **evaluate** everything you read and judge its validity. Previewing helps you evaluate which material is worth reading in the first place. Read uncritically (suspend your disbelief) to allow you to take in the information more quickly, and then bring your critical faculties to bear once you have understood the writer's argument. This both saves you time and improves your ability to evaluate the information rather than being swayed by your own preconceptions and prejudices. Reading faster does not impair your ability to do any of these, and indeed should make them easier since you have access to more information more quickly. If appropriate, you might consider incorporating these higher level reading skills into your purpose. *(537 words)*

Reading for pleasure

Most of this book is focused on reading for information, particularly in situations where the reading gives you no intrinsic pleasure. However it is perfectly possible to use various of the techniques for improving your pleasure in reading.

Firstly, you can read more quickly if you so choose. Susan likes to read action stories quickly, and the pleasure comes from finding out what happened. But when the pleasure comes from the way in which the book is written, then she will often slow down to enjoy the words. Similarly, if she wants to get lost in the story she slows down so that she can imagine it more strongly. And with a really good book, she sometimes slows down towards the end because she doesn't want it to finish too quickly. Conversely, if she discovers that the writing is really not good, or the story is not completely gripping, she will speed up just to find out what happens, or speed up at bits she finds dull.

Susan's sister is one of the fastest readers we know and she will frequently read a novel two or three times (in the time it takes most of us to read it once). She says she gets different levels of understanding on each read, and because of the repetition she really knows and can remember the stories well.

If you don't want to read three times, but you want to remember the story, then you need either to jot down key points and review them as you would any other information – or you can do the same thing, but hold it in your head. Consciously note each thing you want to remember and make a strong visual image for it. Link the images together sequentially to form a visual summary. Then review it from time to time to keep the memory strong.

One word of caution. People often say that there are many books where they both enjoy the writing style and want the information. The temptation then is to read more slowly – which is fine for the pleasure part, but is unlikely to help you retain the information. We suggest that you use the spd rdng techniques to get the information, and then read the book separately in your leisure time – probably more quickly than you would have done previously because you've already been through it a couple of times.

Remember that it's OK to read slowly if you want to. There's a part of most of us which enjoys reading slowly, and it's perfectly acceptable to read for pleasure at whatever speed gives you pleasure. It's just that it isn't sensible to always read slowly.

Since the biggest factor in becoming a better reader is to read more, the important thing with your pleasure reading is that you enjoy it because you're likely to do more of it. *(482 words)*

Factors affecting reading

Every reading experience will be different from any other. Books are different from one another. People are different. We read different things for different reasons and purposes. We ourselves are different every time we start reading in that we've changed slightly since we last read. And all these things can have an effect on our reading.

You might like to consider the following factors which will can affect how efficiently we can read or process information on any given occasion.

Familiarity with the subject and terminology

The biggest impact on your reading ability will be your experience and how much you already know – your 'schema'. The more you know about something, the easier it is to absorb new information about it. The bigger your vocabulary, the more words you know, the easier it is to understand written material.

If you are approaching a new subject, the most important thing is to start by getting an overview of what it is about and what is involved, eg by previewing and downloading a lot of books on the subject, choosing the right books (for beginners), and doing a syntopic processing session with four books to produce a mindmap or rhizomap of the subject areas.

In order to build your vocabulary, read a lot. Read lots of different material. Start with easy material that you enjoy, and as your experience and vocabulary grow, you'll find new subjects less daunting. Downloading dictionaries and subject-related glossaries can also prime your brain to be more receptive to new vocabulary.

Perception, preconception and prejudice

Prejudice means 'pre-judging', and if you have made up your mind before you start reading, you are unlikely to benefit or learn from the new information. The most difficult thing about prejudice is that we very often don't recognise it in ourselves. There are some things which we just take for granted and it doesn't occur to us to question them.

We tend to see what we are looking for – which is why we have a purpose. One strategy is to consciously look for 'difference', things which do not conform with our current understanding, and it is also important to keep an open mind in order to be able to take in new ideas which we are less familiar with – which is what leads to learning! *(386 words)*

Clarity of purpose / lack of purpose

Most spd rdrs say that the technique which makes the biggest difference to their reading is to have a good purpose. If you begin to feel that you're not doing as well as you'd like with your new reading skills, the first thing to check is your purpose. Go back to read the relevant sections in the book again and really make sure that you've got a good purpose before you start reading.

The difficulty and quality of the text

Sometimes texts are badly written. The ideas might be very complex, and/or be written in an unclear, confusing or ambiguous way. Sometimes the font is too small or the material is badly designed or laid out. Identify these problems at the previewing stage and, if you have the choice, find other material where it is easier to access the content. If you don't have a choice about the source material, try to find something else to read about either the book or the subject which will help you get into it. Follow the usual spd rdng steps when working with this material, but be aware that – for reasons beyond your control – it might not be as quick or easy as usual.

Also be aware that certain books (eg books of philosophy, religion or scientific understandings of the universe) may represent a level of deep thinking which has challenged some of the world's greatest minds for years. You would not expect to reach this level of thinking after a 20-minute introductory read. But this is to do with thinking and understanding, not the skill of reading.

Urgency, stress, your state and physical conditions

There are numerous physical and mental conditions which will affect your ability to concentrate and read. Most of them are common sense. Check out the section on physical conditions, and remember always to get into a good state before you start reading: focus on your point of concentration to open your peripheral vision, pause and plan what you're about to do, take a deep breath in, smile and relax as you breathe out. The more you get used to being in a good state, the easier it is to do, and also the more effective it is when you really need it, for example in a job interview, or even for something as everyday as driving.

There is an added bonus when it comes to taking exams. The easiest conditions in which to remember information are those in which you learnt it, so if you are used to being in a good state for your work sessions, then getting into that same good state as you sit down in an exam will not only calm you and make it easier to concentrate, it will also make it easier to recall the information you need. And sorry, teenagers, but by the same token, it makes sense to study and revise sitting up at a table rather than lying on the floor since there are few exams in which you're allowed to lie on the floor. However lying on the floor for leisure reading is good

> **"** *To attain knowledge, add things every day. To attain wisdom, remove things every day."*
> *Lao Tzu*

because it strengthens your neck muscles (which has been shown to have a positive effect on reading ability in young people).

Motivation

Motivation and attitude are key factors in our ability to read well, and sometimes certain things we're obliged to read just don't motivate us. This is where the spd rdng techniques are particularly valuable. Once you know how much information you can get in one 20-minute session, or how quick and easy it is to gather all the information you need to write an essay or an article, or get on top of a subject, it can be really satisfying to sit down and get your reading done successfully so you are free to do all the other things which can seem more appealing. And spd rdrs often report that they actually get pleasure – even when working with intrinsically boring material – just from being able to read effectively and efficiently. As one so succinctly put it – 'spd rdng turned me from a book hater into a bookworm'. *(692 words)*

Problems and solutions

It is worth focusing specifically on a few of the factors which can specifically slow down reading and which therefore might be viewed as 'reading problems'.

• Subvocalising and vocalising

It's difficult to speak in English faster than 240 wpm (words per minute) and the main reason the average reading rate is 150-240 wpm is because that is about the rate at which people speak – and many people tend to mouth the words to themselves (or hear the words in their minds) as they read. Both of these tendencies are called 'subvocalising', and actually saying the words aloud is 'vocalising'.

Many speed reading books make a big deal about subvocalising and tell you not to do it - without actually telling you how. We don't actually think it's too big a deal – almost all of us do it sometimes. You might need to subvocalise to make sense of a complex idea, or something which is written in a complex way, or to check the pronunciation of a word (either because it's new to you, or because you're learning a foreign language). But it's not an efficient way to read if you do it all the time.

The problem will actually sort itself out as you start reading faster, but to subvocalise less while you're learning, first of all make sure that you're doing all the things to help you process information more efficiently – get into a good state (focusing on the concentration point can help you get into visual instead of auditory mode), have a clear purpose and work in 20-minute blocks. Then there are four specific techniques you can try:

(a) As a first step, **say the key words** in a sentence to yourself

99 In training and coaching thousands of professionals, I have found that lack of time is not the major issue for them (though they themselves may think it is); the real problem is lack of clarity and definition about what a project really is, and what the associated next-action steps required are."

David Allen, 'Getting Things Done'

rather than reading whole sentences – this will speed you up because you're not saying every word and is also a starting point for using key words for note-taking.

(b) Talk about what you're reading rather than saying the actual words to yourself, ie say verbally to yourself the sorts of things you might write down if you were taking notes; or describe what you're reading ('this is an example', 'that's explaining why he did it', 'that's a table about rainfall in London', etc).

(c) Press your **tongue to the roof of your mouth** – you can't talk if you can't move your tongue (this works better when you're a bit more experienced at using the other spd rdng techniques).

(d) Focus on the upper part of letters as you read (practise with the example below) – the change of focus can help you stop the inner voice. It is easier to read serif fonts (typefaces with little strokes – serifs – added to some letters) than sans-serif fonts (without the little strokes).

> **Boats and helicopters**
> There was a flood and everyone was being evacuated from the village. As the water rose, one man went to the top storey of his house. He remained calm, because he knew that he was a good man and that God would save him.
> A rescue boat came by, but the man said 'Don't worry about me. God will save me.'
> The water rose higher and he climbed onto the roof.
> A rescue helicopter lowered a ladder to him but he said 'Don't worry about me. God will save me.'
> Shortly afterwards, the water rose above the level of his house and he drowned.
> However, he was a good man, so he went to heaven but furiously asked God why he hadn't been saved.
> God looked at him and she said 'I sent you a boat, I sent you a helicopter. What more did you want?'

But as we said, as you get used to using all the spd rdng techniques and you're reading and processing information more quickly, you'll find that you subvocalise less anyway – you won't have time!

• Regression and progression
One of the classic reading 'problems' is going back over and over the same piece of text because you feel you haven't understood it, or because you realise you've drifted off into your own thoughts and have no idea what you've just read. This is called regression. Some people also report that they leap forwards and skip large chunks of text (progression).

However if you preview the material, get into a good state and set a clear purpose before you start a work session, it is easy to maintain your concentration for 20 minutes, so regression is not a problem, and we actively encourage spd rdrs to skip over large chunks of text which are irrelevant or that contain information which is repeated or which they already know. (How do you do that? In exactly the same way you can skip large portions of a newspaper and know that you don't need to read it.) The only times we need to go back to read something earlier is if we spot something which indicates there was some important information a bit earlier on, or if we're working backwards through the material (start with the difficult bits and work back towards the easier material – try it, it's quite motivating).

• Perfectionism

It seems ironic that the desire to be perfect is likely to make you less efficient rather than more. However, spending time reading every word in a book is almost certainly not worth your time and therefore does not qualify as 'perfect'. Similarly, wanting to get 'everything' from a book is a sure-fire recipe for failure.

There is no single book on earth which has been written specifically for you, and even if it existed, it would go out of date after its first reading and you'd need something slightly different. Therefore there must be lots of stuff in most books which you don't need to read. A more productive mindset is to get 'enough'.

Make sure you have a clear purpose for working with this particular book at this particular time – a purpose you can complete in 20 minutes. And be delighted if you can achieve 80% of your purpose, because (according to the Pareto principle, or 80/20 rule) it will give you lots of additional time to get more information from other books.

• Inner critic

Many people have an inner voice which, for all kinds of psychological reasons, sabotages your learning. It may be the voice of a parental figure. It may be extremely pessimistic about your chances of success. It may tell you that you don't deserve to enjoy yourself or do well without paying for it, or without working extremely hard ('no pain, no gain'). It is suspicious of pleasure and anything that is gained easily. It can also surface as an impatient scientist who finds this approach illogical or too touchy-feely, or an academic who feels that this not 'reading properly'. The inner critic also expects things to work perfectly the first time and all the time. However your inner critic appears, it can stop you from noticing what is working.

Firstly, be sympathetic to your inner critic. It's trying to look out for you. But stay detached from it and keep your sense of balance

– and your sense of humour. You can neutralize the voice to some extent by repeating its negative comments in a silly voice (Mickey Mouse, a robot, sexy seducer, cowboy drawl, etc) so that you don't take it seriously. And then you can remind yourself that mistakes are an essential part of learning. Note that - essential! People learn more from their mistakes than they do from getting things right all the time. So after every reading and learning experience, ask yourself, 'What did I learn about reading from this experience?' 'What will I do differently next time?' And then ask yourself how long it would have taken you to get this level of success using your traditional reading habits – and celebrate how much more you get with your new spd rdng habits.

● Dyslexia

Dyslexia is a catch-all term used to describe any number of 'reading difficulties'. For many people, dyslexia (whether diagnosed or not) is more a problem of writing (spelling) than reading, and many work out their own strategies for coping. For these, the techniques in this book will probably be a relief and should certainly help them read more effectively as they focus on getting the big picture rather than details and understanding the meaning of chunks of text rather than individual words. (See 'Resources' for recommended reading.)

● Content v process

Another factor that can affect your reading (particularly while you're learning spd rdng) is worrying too much about using or practising different spd rdng techniques. When you're learning anything new, part of your brain will be focusing on how to actually do each technique, but the emphasis in spd rdng is always on what information you want to get from your reading and what you're going to do with it. We don't mind how you do that. The techniques we offer in this book will shift you from reading in a traditional slow way all the time, but as soon as you have made the breakthrough and know that you are a confident spd rdr, you don't have to slavishly follow any of the techniques. If you are using an effective approach to different kinds of material, then you no longer need to do the techniques explained in this book. However, if you find yourself being less efficient or effective and slipping back into old slow habits, then following the techniques precisely will get you achieving more and more spd rdng successes.

If you're still not getting it

If you think are following all the spd rdng strategies as described but still feel you're not making progress, check through this list of the most common blocks:

● **Unclear purpose** Read the section on purpose (#4) again and check that you start each 20-minute session with a realistic purpose

- **Resistance to change** Most people resist change. They want different results but actually they don't want to change what they do. But 'if you always do what you've always done, you'll always get what you've always got'. Change may not always feel comfortable, but in this case the results are definitely worth it.

- **Unrealistic expectations** Most people secretly hope that there's a magic pill which will mean they can flick through a book in a few minutes and know everything that's in it. While we would like that too, we know that you need to do a bit more work than that. But once you focus on how much you have achieved by using the spd rdng strategies compared to how much you would have achieved with traditional reading, you will be amazed at how much you can achieve in short time. (Look back at 'Yes But … this isn't proper reading' p 80)

- **Waiting for the green dot** We once had a Spd Rdng course participant whose friend had improved his reading speed by using a system which involved focusing on a green dot. She wouldn't try any of the techniques and strategies we suggested because she was convinced that in order to improve her reading she needed this green dot – even though we told her we weren't going to use a green dot. She's the only person who hasn't improved at all on a spd rdng course. The spd rdng techniques work if you use them, but oddly enough, they don't work if you won't try them.

- **Fear of failure** Some people are so unwilling to fail at something (often due to having a fixed rather than growth mindset – see #34) that they won't even try it. Trying, failing, trying again, making mistakes – and continuing to try again is the normal pattern of successful learning. The only failure is in not trying at all.

- **Not seeing the wood for the trees** When people feel they need 'all the details' in a book, they tend to get lost in those details and end up going back to their old unhelpful habit of reading slowly and sequentially. For approximately 95% of people, their brains learn best if they get an overview of the subject matter before focusing on details. Read again the section on how to get an overview (#25).

- **Clinging to old reading habits** You've been reading with a degree of success in a particular way for years, so it is natural that it might take a bit of time to break old habits and learn new more effective habits. But it will be worth it. Keep going.

- **Not recognising boats and helicopters** Some people seem unable to recognise or accept successful results from spd rdng (see the story about Boats and Helicopters a couple of pages back), presumably because it doesn't feel the same as reading a book traditionally and they haven't got everything from a book after working with it for 20 minutes. It's true. It doesn't feel the same. But if you honestly focus on what you have achieved rather than what you think you should have achieved (see unrealistic expectations above), you will recognise that spd rdng strategies give you much more information in a great deal less time than reading slowly and sequentially (when, on average, you will forget 90% within two days).

- **Not giving it a fair trial** If they don't immediately succeed at something, most adults don't try anything more than twice before giving up. Keep going. You might not succeed at the first try, but the techniques are not difficult to learn. (Check again the section on expectations and habits #34.)

- **It feels too easy** Some people seem to think that suffering is a necessary part of learning (no pain, no gain) and therefore cannot accept that it really is this easy to read more efficiently and effectively. Keep going and trust that you are improving.

(2280 words)

Digital reading

Digital reading is a relatively new – and growing – phenomenon, and it merits specific consideration.

All 37 of the spd rdng techniques apply equally to paper-based texts and digital reading (including online reading). Some need slight modifications, some are easier digitally (such as scrolling quickly when downloading or previewing) and some of the things that we take for granted on our computers, reading devices and mobile phones (such as searching for information, not feeling obliged to read every word, stopping once we've found the information we need, etc) are strategies which can profitably feed back into our paper-based reading.

Kindle and ebooks

Hopefully you already know that a Kindle is a device (which you buy as an alternative to an iPad, for example), but whatever your device (including your computer and your phone), Kindle is also software which you can download for FREE, allowing you to read ebooks on any compatible device. (Systems similar to Kindle, eg iBooks, Kobo, work in a similar way.)

Clearly there are advantages when travelling to be able to carry one small device rather than a range of heavy books – train reading has been transformed by Kindle and the iPad. But just check that you're taking maximum advantage of all the features:

- **Most ebooks offer you free samples.** Many are so generous with the amount they offer, that you can get the information you need from the free sample alone so you don't need to read the rest of the book. It is always worth looking through the free sample as part of your online previewing.

- **The search function is a great way to find information** (thereby avoiding the need to use the speed-reading patterns to look for information 'manually' as it were). As soon as you've defined your purpose, identify the key words which you think will give you most information. As you find information, identify more key words to refine and extend your search.

By the way ...

Hard copy books ('normal' books) are now being referred to as 'pbooks' (print books) particularly by publishers to differentiate them from ebooks.

● **You can highlight important passages and take notes** (annotate) as you go along, and easily find them again. You can also save typing time, since both notes and highlighted passages can be exported directly to Twitter and Facebook (and from there to your computer). On an iPad with the relevant app you can also create a mindmap as you go – or later from your notes.

● **You can alter the format of the text** (font, type size, background colour, etc) to suit yourself. You might like to make it smaller for previewing and downloading, where you want to look through a lot of information quickly, and slightly larger for sequential reading or taking in information. However, have as much information as you can read comfortably on the screen at one time. Too big a font can slow down your reading just because there physically isn't as much information for you to take in.

● **When people (including you) highlight any key passages in the ebook,** Kindle knows it (because all the information is stored on the cloud), and by switching on the 'popular highlights' option in your preferences, you can see (as little dots underlining the text) what others have highlighted (and how many people have highlighted that bit). Thanks to 'crowd wisdom', as more and more people read a particular book, key passages are much more easily accessible. As a bonus, all popular highlights can be viewed online without even buying the book! (Find popular highlights on the Amazon website, near the bottom of the descriptive information about each book.)

● **Check out reviews on Amazon as part of your previewing.** Keep an open mind, but notice particularly the bad reviews (which won't have been written by the author's publisher, family and friends!)

Kindle - additional features

Ebooks are being published with all sorts of additional features (not all available with all ebooks). Look out for the following – and keep an eye out for new features as they are developed:

● **X-Ray** – as books are downloaded to your device, they are accompanied by a host of additional information items which you can look up without needing to be online. The sorts of things you can access are historical figures, places, ideas and topics of interest from Wikipedia, as well as information about the book itself.

● **Active links to other resources** – ebooks have links to external resources online that you can access with one click

● **Book extras** – You can read summaries, glossary items, memorable quotes, important places and people, and more.

● **Lending your ebook** – you can lend and borrow eligible ebooks just as you would a hard copy book. The lent ebook disappears from the owner's Kindle while it is accessed by the friend on their own device. How to do it: 1. visit Manage Your Kindle on your Amazon account. 2. in the Actions menu, select Loan this title. If Loan this title is not an option, lending is unavailable for the

Jan's experience

Jan was standing in a longish queue in a post office, and so as not to waste the time, he downloaded an ebook to his iPhone and in five minutes read all the popular highlights – and discovered that he had got all the key points from just this short read. When he got home he decided to check the value of the popular highlights, so he rapid read the book (from cover to cover) and realised that he hadn't missed anything of significance. He spotted a couple of additional anecdotes and quotes, but they didn't actually add anything to his understanding. Crowd wisdom rocks!

title. 3. add the recipient's email address. You can add a personal message. Note: make sure to use your friend's personal email address and not their Kindle email address. 4. click Send now.

• **Kindle is gathering and storing information on how readers read.** Since the book you are reading is actually stored on the cloud, Kindle is able to collect information about reading habits and styles. It knows when you start and stop reading a book, at what times you read, and for how long, etc. We hope in the future that we will have access to this information to help us build our spd rdng skills. *(923 words)*

Digitising books

Jan is so enamoured of the benefits of digital reading that he has digitised his whole library so he can access all his books on his iPhone, iPad, Mac computer and other devices. If you want to free up some space on your bookshelves go to www.spdrdng.com and read his blog about how to do it. (To keep in touch with the material world he kept one book – the paperback of this *Speed Reading Bible*.)

Jan's experience

Jan was able to gather and sort through almost a hundred scientific papers relevant to a project he was working on simply by using the search function to identify those containing the critical key words. This was in a fraction of the time it would have taken to look through every paper individually.

Online reading

There is no shortage of information in the world – what is missing are overviews and ways of finding relevant information. Once you've found it, you can use any relevant spd rdng technique or strategy to glean the information. So how do you find what you're looking for?

• One of the most effective aids to reading online is, once again, the search facility and it's worth learning how to search most effectively online. Go to Google and search for 'how to search on Google'. It will be one of the best five minutes you've ever spent and will save you tons of time.

• If you have particular interests, set up Google Alerts for relevant key words and Google will alert you to any new information that is published (you need to have an account with Google). In this way you don't have to look for information – information will find you. You can get these alerts in real time or every week etc, depending on what suits your needs. Similarly, ZITE is a brilliant app (Apple, Android) that learns what you're reading and finds relevant articles online for you.

• Find the best expert websites for your subject by subscribing to RSS feeds (Rich Site Summary) where you are effectively asking experts where they find key information. For example, probably the best and most comprehensive website on health and related issues is www.mercola.com, and www.TED.com is a brilliant website on technology, education and design.

• The future is mobile. Find the best app for your devices to read pdfs on the go. We use PDFAnnotate which is an excellent tool for organising documents.

(352 words)

Children's reading

We are frequently asked the questions: 'Do the spd rdng techniques apply to children? and 'At what age should they start?' The answers depend on the mental rather than chronological age of each child, but generally we recommend the following.

Start spd rdng techniques aged 15+ The spd rdng system explained in this book is designed for adults. We recommend that young people start using the techniques after they've had some experience of reading conventionally and when they need to be more efficient. This is probably aged about 15+, at a time when they need to read more for self-directed study rather than (or as well as) for pleasure.

Aged 5–15 Read a lot, for pleasure Before the age of 15, there is much to be gained from reading more slowly – you build up vocabulary, learn how sentences are structured, understand how stories develop. So the best thing children can do is to read as much as possible – of anything which interests them. It doesn't matter whether that's stories, football, factual information or comics. The parents' main job is to offer them books by authors they might not otherwise come across by themselves. But the worst thing you can do is turn children off reading by making it a boring chore. Foster a love of reading in any way you can – read yourself (this is especially important for boys: they need to see men – their father or other relatives – getting pleasure from reading), talk about books you've read, and keep books available for them to 'discover' by themselves.

For all children we also recommend that parents and teachers help children with 'learning to learn' techniques, which will lay the groundwork for improved reading skills. (See 'Resources' for recommended reading.)

Babies The biggest indicator of how good a reader someone is in later life is how much they were read to as a very young child – not how much they themselves read, although that too is a factor. Don't wait until children are 'old enough' to read. Even before they are one, they will enjoy sitting with you looking at the pictures in books, identifying things they know, learning colours, counting, listening to simple stories, singing nursery rhymes, etc. Board books help them learn to turn pages and hold the book the right way up, but interacting with you and the book engenders a love of reading.

Always be guided by what the child wants. If they want to interact and take an active role, let them. Sometimes though they will just want to sit back and enjoy the sound of your voice. And sometimes they will want to do something else entirely.

EXPERT TIP

Foster a love of reading. Have lots of books around. Let your children see that you love and value reading.

Learning to read The 'natural' age for learning to read is about 7 – in many countries with a high literacy rate children don't start school till they're 6 or 7. Many children will be ready to learn earlier than that (particularly if they're read to), but it should be because they want to, not because they're forced to.

When young children don't learn naturally for themselves, they are at the mercy of the school system and whatever reading system is in vogue. Many of the reading schemes work for many children, but children are different and different approaches work for different children. Unfortunately schools very often don't have the resources to cater for individuals who are not doing well in class.

99 *If we learnt to walk and talk in the way we are taught to read and write, we would all limp and stutter."*
Mark Twain

The normal sequence for understanding the reading process is:
- being read to – especially by a parent – while looking at the book
- making a connection between illustrations and real objects
- realising that the 'squiggles' on the page are somehow telling the story
- learning individual letters – usually starting with the initial letters of their name and the names of people and objects around them.
- recognising their own name
- being able to tell you the words on the page (even if it's from memory from constant repetition)
- suddenly realising that they can recognise what a word means from its letters – which may be the street sign in your road, one of their books, an advertising hoarding, a newspaper. This is the breakthrough point, children usually manage it by themselves, and from then on it is question of refinement and experience
- building up their reading skills through a combination of recognising individual letters and complete word shapes, linking words to meanings, writing letters and words, and then working out (often by being told) the link between the sounds of letters and how they can be built up to work out a complete word

Once children reach this stage, when they are functionally reading, apart from giving further practice, schools tend to leave children to their own devices – ignoring the fact that at a later stage, in secondary school, children would benefit hugely from additional spd rdng strategies. Some people work out a faster reading system for themselves – but many don't.

Ineffective reading strategies
There are also strategies for teaching reading which are not most effective for anyone:
- starting from letters (meaningless symbols to a young child) and building to words and sentences is much less effective than starting with stories and working back to words and letters
- asking children to read aloud is for the benefit of the teacher

so they can check the child's ability to decipher words – but it should be used in moderation. Reading aloud in front of the class is possibly the worst 'teaching' habit – the stress engendered in many children (of any age) can only inhibit both comprehension and the ability to read fluently, as well as (particularly in the case of boys) turning them off from reading at all. Reading is about getting meaning from the text, and you may remember from experience how difficult it can be to answer questions about a text when you've just been reading it aloud to someone else. It can also encourage children to move their lips while reading – which will slow them down later.

Children with reading problems

If your child is seven or older and unable to read:

- check whether they have sight problems or need glasses – they can't read if they can't see the words
- get them outside running around, twirling like helicopters, hanging upside down, doing somersaults and cartwheels, etc – all the things young children naturally like to do. This will help develop their vestibular system and neck muscles – both of which are essential before reading
- don't force the issue; offer to read with/to children things that they enjoy to build their trust and encourage them to work with you
- encourage children to read while lying on their tummies on the floor – it strengthens their neck muscles
- suggest older children read to younger siblings, relatives or friends – it gives them confidence to read something simpler while ostensibly it is for the benefit of the younger child

Remember, the best thing you can do to help your children's reading is to read with them and to them from an early age, and encourage them to read for pleasure – basically, make sure it's fun! *(1185 words)*

GLOSSARY / INDEX

The 'rule' states that 20% of the effort you expend in any enterprise gives you 80% of the result you want to achieve, while the remaining 80% of your effort generates only the remaining 20% of result. In reading, the implication is that if you are happy with achieving 80% of your **purpose**, you will read five times as much material in any given time. Also, in most books, more than 80% of the message is contained in less than 20% of the words – hence looking for the **hot spots** of key information (see **Stauffer**). Also named the **Pareto Principle** by **Joseph M Juran**, after the Italian economist, **Vilfredo Pareto**, who first noticed that 80% of peas in his garden were produced by 20% of peapods – and then that 80% of Italy's wealth was owned by 20% of its population.

Name given in the west to the adaptation of **Suggestopedia**, the teaching method developed by **Dr Georgi Lozanov** which drew on the amazing abilities of the **non-conscious mind**

One of the criteria of a **SMART purpose**. Your purpose needs to be realistic and achievable in a 20-minute **work session**. See also **Specific, Measurable, Real, Relevant, Timed, Timely**

A variety of **Spd Rdng** techniques (eg **downloading, previewing**) can be of value to actors, but it is particularly recommended to set your **purpose** to gather information on one specific role at a time

Term used in the **PhotoReading Whole Mind System** for all conscious techniques for working with a book (eg **rapid reading** from cover to cover, **skittering** or **super-reading** to look for **hot spots** of key information) with the intention of bringing to conscious awareness information which has been **downloaded** into the **non-conscious mind**. (We do not use the term in the spd rdng approach since it tends to set up false expectations.)

Author of 'How to Read a Book' in which he suggests 'syntopical reading', a precursor of **syntopic processing**

Analysing 141
A **higher level thinking and reading skill** which involves separating a proposition into its component parts, possibly prior to bringing together the essence of the ideas again (**synthesising**)

Babies 153
It is important to read to babies from a very young age (six months old) in order to engender a love of reading. The biggest indicator of future reading success is how much a child is read to when very young.

Background reading 22, 114
As well as focused, purposeful reading, it is also beneficial to read as much as possible of anything which interests you, since it isn't always possible to predict which information will be of use and it will add to your **schema**. This background or **unfocused reading** also helps create links between your subject and others, which is what leads to creativity.

Beginnings and endings 52, 84, 99, 115-6
(1) A way of reading a book to get an overview of its contents, where you start by reading the first chapter (and/or the introduction) and the last chapter. If necessary, you also read the beginning and ending of each chapter (keeping an eye out for **summaries**), the beginning and end of each section of each page or even of each paragraph. See also **First and last**
(2) You also remember more from the beginning and ending of a learning session. See also **Primacy and Recency effects**

Bennett, Dr Michael 50
US professor of reading who coined the term **skittering**

Berg, Howard Stephen 137
Self-styled 'fastest reader in the world', developer of the Maximum Power Reading system

Best comprehension speed 9, 12, 42, 46
Reading as fast as you can while still understanding what you read

Bibliography 17
The list of books recommended by an author in a book which is both a source of further reading in a subject and possibly helps you judge the credibility of the book and/or author when **previewing**

Blurb 17
When **previewing** a book, check out the information on the cover (the **cover blurb**) while being aware that it is written by the publishers to sell the book and isn't always accurate

Children's reading 153-5
The **Spd Rdng** system is designed for adults or children with a mental age of 15+ (the time when they need to read more for self-directed study). Before that children need to build other reading skills, so the important thing is to encourage them to read a lot for pleasure, to read with and to them, and for them to see adults reading a lot and enjoying reading. See also **Babies**

Chunking for meaning 30-1, 39, 66, 135, 141, 148
Reading small groups of words at one time according to their meaning rather than according to an arbitrary numerical division (eg three words at a time). Chunking for meaning helps you read faster; chunking numerically is a very slow way of trying to improve your reading speed.

Coaching 100-101, 145
A variety of **Spd Rdng** techniques (eg **downloading, previewing**) can be of value to coaches, but it is particularly recommended to set your **purpose** to gather information in relation to one specific client at a time

Collaborative learning 73, 104, 137
Studying together with others. See also **Study**, **Exams**

Comprehension 7, 9, 30, 42, 107, 141
Understanding what you read is essential if you are to **remember** and make use of the information. The more information you have (the larger your **schema**), the easier it is to understand it – so read more. The better your **vocabulary**, the easier it is to understand texts, and the best way to increase your vocabulary is to read more. See also **Understanding**

Comprehension questions 22
When you have to answer comprehension questions on a text, read the questions first and only read enough of the text to find the answers. The questions effectively become your **purpose** for reading.

Computer manuals 96, 100
After **downloading** computer manuals, alternate **working sessions** with putting the information into **practice** with specific projects

Concentration point 9, 36-7, 42, 71, 84, 105, 106, 137, 144, 145
Focusing on this point, about 30 cms above and behind the top of the head, can increase the ability to read (eg with **dyslexia**), the speed of reading, and the ability to take in information. It also automatically opens **peripheral vision**, allowing you to take in more information at one time.

Conscious mind 25, 78, 88, 89, 90, 91, 92, 93, 94, 95, 136, 139
While most of what we think we do to learn is done consciously, the part of the brain which learns most effectively is the hugely more powerful **non-conscious mind**. Two **Spd Rdng** techniques (**downloading, direct learning**) rely on the power of the non-conscious mind, and the system is designed to appeal to the non-conscious mind, although most of the techniques are directed at the **conscious mind**.

Content words 39
Words (usually **nouns and verbs**, such as 'vampires', 'biting') which carry the principal **meaning** of a text

Context 22, 23, 25, 100, 101
When writing a **SMART purpose** for a reading session, it is easier for your brain to recognise the information when you are clear about the context in which you will use it.

Continuous story line 78, 99
When books have a continuous story line (**novels**, biographies, historical material), read them sequentially using **rapid reading, super-duper-reading** and **speed-reading patterns**. (You can also **preview** and **download** them). We call such books **train reading.**

Conventional reading 79, 80, 153
With conventional reading you can take three or more days to read a book, you usually forget 90% of what you read within 48 hours, you read everything in the same way, it is easy for your attention to wander, the author determines how you get information whether you need it or not, and it implies that reading something is enough to make you an expert. Compare **Spd Rdng**

Cover blurb 17
When **previewing** a book, check out the information on the cover (the **blurb**) while being aware that it is written by the publishers to sell the book and isn't always accurate

Credibility 17, 130
While **previewing**, check things such as references, the **bibliography**, information about the author, reviews and recommendations to establish the credibility of the material and the author

Critical thinking 38, 39, 141
A **higher level thinking and reading skill** which involves passing judgement on an author's viewpoint; it is easier to do this if you initially keep an **open mind**

Crowd wisdom 62, 151
The phenomenon whereby the ideas and solutions generated consensually by a large group of people will tend to be as good as those generated by an expert (the majority override the oddities of the few) – so the sections highlighted in much-read **ebooks** are often a good **summary** of the important points.

Date of publication 17
Check the date of publication when **previewing**, particularly with subjects which quickly go out of date (eg computing)

Davis, Ron 37, 137, 195
Author of *'The Gift of Dyslexia'* (1997) who taught people diagnosed with **dyslexia** to read by focusing on their **concentration point** above and behind their heads

Deleuze, Gilles 59, 137
Philosopher who, together with Fleix Guattari, coined the term 'rhizomatic thinking' which led to the development of **rhizomapping**

Dennison, Paul and Gail 137
Developers of the **Brain Gym** exercises

Dense, information-heavy texts 50, 52, 83, 99
You might have to read complex or dense texts more slowly, so try to find well-written texts when **previewing**. If you have to read such texts, make them more accessible and memorable by adding your own examples

Detail 10, 16, 20, 28, 81-2, 97, 99, 115, 116, 148
Although speed reading is often seen as an excellent way to get the **overview** of a subject, it is possible to go into as much detail as you need by continually refining your **purpose**

Dictionary technique 15, 21, 93, 105
Using a book like a dictionary or book of reference to find specific information. Also called **scanning** – looking quickly through a text in order to find specific information you think it contains. (What you actually do is similar to **skimming** and **rapid reading**, but the **purpose** of finding specific information is what defines the activity as scanning).

Difference 40, 56, 57
Consciously looking for difference when reading, leads to learning about new things, (whereas **sameness** leads to greater understanding). It can also be beneficial to look for other **patterns**.To a large extent, the spd rdng approach is driven by difference: people are different and take in and process

information in different ways, books are different and need different approaches, purposes for reading are different, you need to read different books at different speeds, etc – which is why you need a variety of techniques which offer a flexible approach.

Digital reading 15, 16, 62, 92
Reading **online** and on digital devices such as **Ebook readers**

Dipping 45, 50, 78, 105, 119
Slowing down briefly to read more closely when you have found a **hot spot** of key information.

Direct learning 29, 89, 91, 95-6, 138, 139
One possible effect of **downloading**, where the downloaded information is spontaneously available, either to the conscious mind, or to the body where it manifests as a physical skill (eg better golf swing) or better health. Direct learning bypasses the normal **learning sequence**.

Dixon, Norman 136
Author of '*Preconscious programming*' (1981) which detailed his work on the **non-conscious mind** and **priming**

Downloading 78, 88-92, 93, 94-6, 99, 103, 105, 137, 139, 143, 150, 151
Looking very briefly (one second per page) at every page of a book, being confident that the information will be taken in by the **non-conscious mind** and taken into **long-term memory**, even when it is not seen consciously. Downloading is known as **mental photography** or **subliminal photography** in the system developed by **Dr Richard Welch**, and is one (key) step in the **PhotoReading Whole Mind System**, where it is known as '**photoreading**'. See also **Rapid reading**

Duns Scotus, John 37, 137
13th century monk who encouraged children to improve their reading by focusing on a **concentration point** above and behind their heads

Dweck, Carol 108
Author of '*Mindset: The New Psychology of Success*' in which she explains the difference between **Growth mindset** and **Fixed mindset**

Dyslexia 10, 30, 37, 136, 137, 148, 195
Term used to describe innate difficulties with reading and writing. The 'disability' can have any one of numerous causes. It can slow down the initial stages of learning to read (confusing one letter shape with another, for example), but once this has been overcome, it usually causes more problems with writing and

spelling than with reading. Most of the spd rdng techniques make reading easier for those diagnosed as dyslexic.

Ebook 62, 150-2

Books stored in electronic/digital formats which can be downloaded (and printed out), or read on a computer screen or on an **ebook reading device**; spd rdng techniques can be used with ebooks as well as hard copy **pbooks**

Ebook reader / reading device 150
An electronic device on which you can store and read **ebooks** and other texts in electronic or digital format. iPad, iPhone and Kindle are currently the most popular mobile ebook readers. You can read ebooks on your PC or Mac or mobile phones too - just download the **Kindle** software for free to your computer or mobile device.

Email 15, 16, 67
Messages sent electronically through cyberspace from one computer to another. Spd rdng techniques can also be used to read emails, and similarly the techniques many people have for dealing with emails (looking quickly through for the gist, prioritising, ignoring unimportant information, etc) can also be applied to hard-copy books (**pbooks**) and other texts.

Endorphins 32
The happy hormones which can be released simply by **smiling**. Being in a good **state** can enhance your ability to understand and take in information when reading.

Enough 27, 64, 76, 98
It is more productive to want to achieve 'enough' from your reading, rather than aspiring to **perfectionism** which is a recipe for failure

Evaluating 22, 63-4, 72, 73, 75, 105, 112, 141
(1) **Preview** material to evaluate how relevant it is to you and how much time it's worth spending on it. See also **Reading critically**
(2) After a **work session**, pause to evaluate how much of your purpose you have achieved and to learn from **failure** and **celebrate successes**

Exaggeration 41, 57, 75
While reading, keep your mind engaged by looking for **patterns**, such as what is exaggerated. Exaggeration can also make things more memorable

Examples 38, 39, 59, 99, 129, 146
Look out for words in a text which indicate the import of that

section, for example words such as 'in the case of', 'to illustrate this point' indicate that the author is offering examples, stories or case studies. Once you have understood the author's point, these are sections you do not need to read as you look for the next **hot spot** of key information. See also **Explanation, Importance, Lists, Opinion, Watch out words**

Exams 21, 24, 25, 37,43, 69, 82, 91, 96, 102, 103-4, 120, 128, 144
When **studying** for exams, look at past papers and use actual questions as the purpose for **work sessions** or **syntopic processing**. See also **Collaborative learning**

Expectations 108-10, 118, 149
Since actual performance rarely matches up to expectations, if you lower expectations, performance will also fall. It is therefore important to keep expectations high – read more, more quickly.

Experience 28, 75, 109, 141, 143, 154
(1) How easy you find reading is partly to do with your current level of knowledge and experience (your **schema**). The more of an expert you are, the easier it is to take in new information on your subject.
(2) Reading is not enough to build learning, you also need to put the information into **practice** and gain experience.

Expert 7, 28, 56, 80, 82, 95, 100
It takes 10,000 hours to become an outstandingly world-class expert in something worthwhile, according to **Malcolm Gladwell** in his book 'Outliers'. With spd rdng techniques (including **downloading**), you can achieve a normal level of expertise much more quickly, but you do need to apply your chosen skill.

Explanation 38, 39, 129
Look out for words in a text which indicate the import of that section, for example words such as 'in other words', 'to put it another way' indicate that the author is offering an explanation. Once you have understood the author's point, these are sections you do not need to read as you look for the next **hot spot** of key information. See also **Examples, Importance, Lists, Opinion, Watch out words**

Eye exercises 84, 85, 106
Exercise the eyes (palming, focusing alternately on objects near and far, etc) to keep them in optimum condition for reading.

Eyes 29, 31, 71, 84, 85, 135, 140
While it is important to take care of your eyes, reading is actually only 10% to do with the eyes and 90% to do with the thinking and planning done by the **brain**. See also **Eye exercises**

Factual books 15, 16, 19, 20, 97
The **Spd Rdng** system was primarily designed to help you extract
information from factual books (and **reports**, **journals**, etc),
although it can be adapted for any kind of written material. See
also **Emails, Novels, Poems**

Failure 56, 64, 109, 139, 147, 149
The **brain** is programmed to notice **failure** because it can learn
from it, but in addition it is important to **celebrate successes**
with your reading in order to build **motivation**

Familiarity 78, 143
How familiar you are with the text or the subject matter will have
a great influence on how quickly you are able to read.

Faster reading / Reading faster 7, 8, 13, 23, 34, 46, 47,
55, 93, 108, 135, 136, 141, 145, 154
There are several **Spd Rdng** techniques (**super-duper-reading,
underlining** and other **speed-reading patterns**, etc) which are
designed simply to speed up your reading, however the system
offers many more techniques which allow you to process much
more information, and help you **remember** and apply what you
read to enhance your **learning**

Feeling of missing something 78, 79
Novice spd rdrs often complain that they feel they're missing
something by not **reading from cover to cover**. This is partly
just a feeling, which can be overcome with practice, success and
using the **rapid reading** technique. It is actually not a big problem
when spd rdng because your **purpose** makes it easier to focus on
what you need. Also people tend to forget how much more they
are likely to miss (and forget) with **conventional reading**

Finance / Investment 101
A variety of **Spd Rdng** techniques (eg **downloading,
previewing**) can be of value to financiers, but it is particularly
recommended to set your **purpose** to gather information in
relation to one specific client or type of investment at a time

Finding information 20
Changing your **mindset** from **reading faster** or more (**quantity**)
to finding information (**quality**) is the key to making many of the
Spd Rdng techniques work more effectively. See also **Search**

First and last 45, 46, 52-3, 81, 115-6
One of the **speed-reading patterns** used to find out what a
text is about or to look for **hot spots** of key information. In
this case people read just the beginnings and endings of pages,
sections, columns or paragraphs. If no information is found in the

beginnings and endings, then look for information in the **middles** of these sections. Other patterns are **underlining, super-reading, capital-I shape, skittering (zigzag, random).** See also **F-pattern** and **Beginnings and endings**

Firsts 51, 52, 53
A subdivision of **first and last**, one of the **speed-reading patterns** where you only read the beginnings of chapters, pages, sections or paragraphs

Fixation 33, 135
The eyes do not move smoothly and evenly along a line of text when reading. They jump from one point to the next. Each 'jump' is called a **saccade**. Each point where it stops is a fixation. The point of fixation is in focus (in **foveal** or **macular vision**), but words to either side will be slightly out of focus (in **peripheral vision**). Opening your peripheral vision and taking fewer fixations per line will help you read more quickly.

Fixed mindset 108
Research (reported in **Carol Dweck**'s book *'Mindset: The New Psychology of Success'*) has shown that people who believe that intelligence is fixed are less effective learners than those with a **growth mindset** who believe that intelligence develops with experience and practice.

Flexibility 41, 93, 138
Effective readers are flexible about the speed at which they read and in the techniques they employ – the more techniques and approaches you know, the more flexible you can be. Spd Rdng is a flexible, not fixed, system because you need to use different approaches and different **purposes** with different materials.

Fonts 17, 144, 146, 151
Typefaces, scripts used for print in texts; **'serif' fonts** have a small addition or stroke (serif) to the basic form of many letters (eg Times New Roman), and are thought to be easier to read, however **'sans-serif' fonts** (without the serif such as Verdana, Arial, Helvetica) fonts are much more common online, so people are getting more used to reading them.

Forgetting 57-8, 68, 80
Forgetting is healthy and natural. If you want to **remember** something, you need to take active steps to do so.

Formulae 96
Downloading can be a useful technique to help you take in mathematical formulae, but you will need to apply them in order to understand them fully

Forwards and backwards 46-7, 53
A subdivision of **underlining**, one of the **speed-reading patterns**, where you read alternate lines forwards and backwards

Foveal vision 33
Only a small part of what you look at is in clear focus at any one time, and that part is said to be in foveal vision or **macular vision**. Everything else, which is to a greater or lesser degree out of focus, is in **peripheral vision**. See also **Fixation, Saccades**

F-pattern / Online F-pattern 54
Research has shown that when people read text online, eg on websites, they typically tend to read in the shape of the letter F: the first two or three lines, then the words down the left hand side, then a couple more lines, and then a few more words on the left before stopping. This may also be typical of how people look selectively at pages of off-line text.

Gladwell, Malcolm 19, 95
Author of numerous popular books, including 'Blink', in which he uses the term **thin-slicing** to mean taking the smallest slice of cake vertically in order to find out what the cake is like. Similarly the spd rdng techniques are designed to allow you to focus on the smallest amount of information possible to understand a subject or text.

Goal / Life goal 21, 24, 27
Ultimately you may be reading in order to fulfil a life goal such as passing an exam or getting a promotion, but this is not to be confused with your **purpose** for reading a particular book, which may be to answer a specific exam question, or gather the information you need to give a presentation, etc.

Grammar words 38, 130
Words such as 'to, it, is, a, the' etc which facilitate the flow of language but can usually be ignored when reading fast because they do not add much **meaning**. See also **Content words, Nouns and verbs, Watch out words**

Growth mindset 108
Research (reported in **Carol Dweck**'s book 'Mindset: The New Psychology of Success') has shown that people with a growth mindset who believe that intelligence develops with experience and practice are more effective learners than those with a **fixed mindset** who believe that intelligence is fixed and cannot be changed.

Headings and titles 17, 38, 46, 105
Whichever **speed-reading patterns** you use to look for **hot spots** of information, always remember to look at titles, headings, bold text, etc

Higher level thinking and reading skills 141
These include **inference** (understanding what an author means even when it is not directly stated), **evaluating** (judging the value and **credibility** of an author's viewpoint), **critical thinking** (passing judgement on an author's viewpoint), **analysing** (separating a proposition into its component parts – possibly prior to bring together the essence of the ideas again: **synthesising**)

Highlighting 7, 10, 11, 62, 99, 151
Highlighting important text (or making margin notes or notes on post-its) can be an effective way of keeping your attention while reading away from your desk, eg on a train, and makes it easier to check back on those parts later. See also **Popular highlights**

Horn, Robert E 138
Developer of **visual language**, the combination of images and words which he describes in his book of the same name

Hot spots 28, 38-40, 45, 50, 63, 71, 78, 93, 99, 105, 115, 118, 129
Words, phrases or sections of text which contain key meaningful information; although initially readers tend to notice words and phrases, the most efficient readers focus on the key **message**.

Importance 39, 116
Look out for words in a text which indicate the import of that section, for example words such as 'crucially, 'a key factor' indicate that the author is saying that something is important so it may be a **hot spot** (as long as the author's view of importance coincides with your purpose for reading). See also **Examples, Explanation, Lists, Opinion, Watch out words**

Incubation 137
Time (ideally during sleep) needed by the **non-conscious mind** to 'sort out' textual material which has been **downloaded**.

Index 15, 17, 22, 39, 55, 63, 99, 105
When **previewing** a book, check the index (list of all important terms in the book) for key terms of interest to you and to see which items have the most entries (which is what the book is likely to be about); when reading, as you identify new key terms, you can use the index to **search** for further references

Information overload 140
We urgently need strategies and systems such as **Spd Rdng** to deal with the huge amounts of information currently being generated at an exponential rate

Inner critic 147-8
The inner voice which can sabotage your learning

Interest / Motivation 40, 145, 147, 153
How interested you are in the subject of the text will influence how quickly you are able to read it; the more you can (even artificially) stimulate your interest and motivation, the easier it will be to assimilate the information.

Intuition 98, 99
The more you use the spd rdng techniques, the more you will **trust** both the process and your own intuition – and the more effective the techniques will be.

IT / Information technology 100
To build IT skills, computer manuals can be **downloaded**, and then alternate **working sessions** with putting the information into **practice** with specific projects

Javel, Emil 135
French ophthalmologist who established that while reading the eye does a series of jumps (**saccades**) along the line and takes in information when it makes a stop (**fixation**)

Joker 73-5, 76, 102, 105, 137
Additional book on a non-related topic read during **syntopic processing** to help you approach the task more creatively. (The term was coined by Jan Cisek and Susan Norman and is currently unique to **Spd Rdng**.)

Journals 5, 15, 16, 19, 114
The **Spd Rdng** system was primarily designed to help you extract information from factual books (and **reports**, journals, etc), although it can be adapted for any kind of written material. See also **Emails, Novels, Poems**

Juran, Joseph M 28, 137
Management consultant who gave the name the '**Pareto principle**' to the **80/20 rule**

Key terms (words/phrases/ideas) 17, 18, 38, 39, 59, 61, 62, 67, 78, 145, 150, 152
Words, phrases or sections of text that are essential to understanding (**hot spots**); these are likely to be **nouns and**

verbs, although it is important to look out for words and phrases such as 'however, not, although, on the other hand' (**watch out words**), which indicate that alternative views are being expressed. However, it is more important to read the **message** than it is to focus on specific words. Key words and phrases are also important when formulating one's own notes. See also **Note-taking**

Kindle 150-2, 194
Free software which can be downloaded onto any suitable device (eg computer, phone) which allows you to download and read **ebooks**; also the name of a device on which you can read ebooks

Koch, Richard 27
Author of '*Living the 80/20 way*' which is about the application of the **80/20 rule**

Kurzweil, Ray 138
Author of '*The Singularity is Near*' which describes **technological singularity**, a combination of technology and the human brain which will have greater-than-human intelligence

Language learning 89, 96, 195
Numerous **Spd Rdng** techniques (especially **downloading**) can be used to enhance language learning, but be sure also to listen to the pronunciation as well as reading.

Layout and design 17, 74
The layout and design (**font**, illustrations, etc) of a book can have a significant impact on how easy and quick it is to get the information from it, so take this into account when **previewing**. Whenever possible, choose books which are easy to read.

Learning 25, 28, 41, 43, 56, 73, 81, 91, 94-5, 112, 137, 138, 139, 140, 141, 147, 148, 149, 154
Reading is just one step in the learning process. It is important to put information into practice if you want to learn it. See also **Learning sequence**

Learning sequence 94, 95
The usual sequence for learning (acquiring a new skill or becoming expert in a subject), is 'unconscious incompetence' (you don't know that you don't know), 'conscious incompetence' (you know you don't know and start doing something about it), 'conscious competence' (the long period of practice, where you still have to concentrate on what you're doing, or make a conscious effort to remember), leading to 'unconscious competence' (you can do it without thinking, you are an expert who really knows the subject).

The sequence is bypassed when learning skills with **direct learning**.

Leisure reading 16, 20, 21, 26, 79, 114, 142
When reading is a leisure activity, read in whatever way and at whatever speed gives you pleasure. **Spd rdng** is about reading at different speeds appropriate to the task. See also **Slow reading**, **Reading for pleasure**

Life goal / goal 21, 24, 27
Ultimately you may be reading in order to fulfil a life goal such as passing an exam or getting a promotion, but this is not to be confused with your **purpose** for reading a particular book, which may be to answer a specific exam question, or gather the information you need to give a presentation, etc.

Lighting 106
One of the **physical factors** which can affect reading ability – it is important to have adequate ambient lighting (preferably daylight, and preferably not neon lights) as well as good direct/task lighting on the reading material.

Lists 39
Look out for words in a text which indicate the import of that section, for example words such as 'firstly', 'in the first place' indicate that the author is offering a list of different points. This may indicate that you have to read all the items, if they are important, or that you can overlook the remaining items and move onto the next **hot spot** of key information if you have understood the author's point. See also **Examples, Explanation, Importance, Opinion, Watch out words**

Long-term memory 19, 88, 90, 92, 139
Traditional reading involves **short-term memory**, which is programmed to forget. Using techniques for **remembering** ensures that information is retained in long-term memory – you know it and don't have to make further efforts to remember.

Lozanov, Georgi 136
Bulgarian doctor, psychotherapist and educationist who developed **Suggestopedia**, the precursor to **Accelerated Learning**

Macular vision 33
Only a small part of what you look at is in clear focus at any one time, and that part is said to be in macular vision or **foveal vision**. Everything else, which is to a greater or lesser degree out of focus, is in **peripheral vision**. See **Fixation, Saccades**

Margin notes 62, 99
Making notes in the margin, as well as **highlighting** text, can be an effective way of keeping your attention while reading away from your desk, eg on a train, and makes it easier to check back on those parts later.

McClean, Paul 43
McClean was given a Nobel Prize in the 1950s for his **triune brain theory** which proposed that the brain cannot concentrate on higher thinking if you are physically uncomfortable or emotionally unbalanced

Meaning 27, 28, 29-31, 38, 46, 57, 58, 89, 99, 136, 137, 138, 148, 155
(1) Although initially when looking for **hot spots** of key information you will tend to notice individual **content words**, the aim is to absorb the meaning or **message** of chunks of text
(2) It is important that material you **download** is meaningful to your **conscious mind** in order for the **non-conscious mind** to be able to absorb it

Measurable 22, 23, 105
One of the criteria of a **SMART purpose**. You will get more information when it is possible to measure how much of your **purpose** you have achieved. It can be useful to state a number of ideas you wish to find (eg 6 items in a 20-minute work session). See also **Specific, Achievable, Real, Relevant, Timed, Timely**

Medicine 100
A variety of **Spd Rdng** techniques (eg **downloading, previewing**) can be of value to medics, but it is particularly recommended to set your **purpose** to gather information in relation to one specific patient or disease at a time

Memory 56-8, 61, 68-9, 84
Conventional reading involves **short-term memory**, which forgets over time. Using techniques for **remembering** ensures that information is retained in **long-term memory** – you know it and don't have to make further efforts to remember.

Mental photography / Subliminal photography 92, 136
Term used in the system originally developed by **Dr Richard Welch** to mean looking very briefly (one second per page) at every page of a book, being confident that the information will be taken in by the **non-conscious mind** and taken into **long-term memory**, even when it is not seen consciously. Called **downloading** in the **Spd Rdng** approach, it is one (key) step in the **PhotoReading Whole Mind System**, where it is known as 'photoreading'. See also **Rapid reading**

Mentor 20, 81
When you change your **mindset** from 'reading' (**quantity**) to 'getting information' (**quality**), you can look at other sources for information, including getting an expert mentor to advise you.

Message 6, 15, 21, 28, 29, 30, 33, 38, 39, 64, 83, 93, 98, 105, 115
(1) Although it can be important to notice specific key words and phrases which are essential to understanding a text (**hot spots**), it is more important to read the message or **meaning** they convey than it is to focus on individual words. See also **Watch out words**
(2) Your **purpose** for reading will either be to get a book's message (use the **newspaper technique, skimming**) or to look for **specific information**, in which case you'll use the **dictionary technique** (**scanning**).

Metaphor 58
One thing representing another. It is important to have a good metaphor for your memory (eg like an elephant, a memory bank, rather than like a sieve), and for your approach to reading and learning in general.

Middles 52, 105
One of the **speed-reading patterns** used to find out what a text is about or to look for **hot spots** of key information. In this case people read around the middle of pages, sections, columns or paragraphs. If no information is found in the middles, then look for information in the **first and last** lines of these sections. See also **Beginnings and endings**

Mindmapping 6, 24, 57, 59-62, 63, 72, 73, 82, 83, 99, 102, 103, 104, 105, 136, 141, 143, 151, 194
Technique for **note-taking** and **note-making** devised by **Tony Buzan**: key ideas radiate on 'branches' from the central subject of the mindmap, and secondary ideas are written on lesser branches radiating from the key idea branches. The technique is preferable to linear note-taking, since it leads to greater creativity and memorability, and it is particularly useful when the structure of the subject is known in advance. See also **Rhizomapping**

Mindset 20, 108, 137, 147
Changing one's mindset from 'how many books have I read?' (**quantity**) to 'how much relevant information have I got?' (**quality**) is an important element in accepting the import of other spd rdng techniques, and for speeding up reading generally. See also **Fixed** and **Growth mindset**

Morphic fields / Morphic resonance 120, 121, 127-8, 129, 131
Theory proposed by **Rupert Sheldrake**: Morphic fields are fields

of energy around living organisms which contain a sort of blueprint of the organism which helps their growth and development to be like others of their kind. The ability of morphic fields to evolve and communicate he calls 'morphic resonance'.

Most frequent words 39
The words which appear most frequently in a language are usually '**grammar words**' such as 'a, the, some, he, it, is', etc, rather than '**content words**' (usually nouns and verbs such as 'dolphin, swimming') which carry the **meaning** or **message**

Motivation / Interest 40, 145, 147, 153
How interested you are in the subject of a text will influence both your motivation and how quickly you are able to read it; the more you can (even artificially) stimulate your interest, the easier it will be to assimilate the information

Newspaper technique 15, 21, 93, 105
Looking quickly through a text in order to discover its message, also called **skimming**. (The technique is similar to **scanning** and **rapid reading**, but your purpose of getting a general understanding of what the text is about is what defines it as skimming).

Non-conscious mind 19, 25, 26, 78, 88-92, 93, 94-6, 97, 99, 136, 137, 139
Everything perceived by the senses (sight, touch, hearing, taste, smell) is processed by the non-conscious mind which directs certain things to the attention of the **conscious mind**. The non-conscious mind has much greater capacity than the conscious and many of the spd rdng techniques are designed to harness its power to help you read and learn more efficiently and effectively. While most of what we think we do to learn is done consciously, the part of the brain which learns most effectively is the hugely more powerful non-conscious mind. Only two **Spd Rdng** techniques (**downloading, direct learning**) rely totally on the power of the non-conscious mind, everything else is done consciously. See also **Priming**

Note-making 59-62
Generating your own ideas in note form rather than taking notes from other people, books, lectures, etc (**note-taking**); we recommend **rhizomapping** and **mindmapping** rather than making linear notes.

Note-taking 57, 59-62, 75, 83, 99, 104, 105, 106, 137, 146, 151
Taking notes from other people, books, lectures, etc, rather than

generating your own ideas in note form (**note-making**); we recommend **rhizomapping** and **mindmapping** rather than taking linear notes. Note-taking is an important step in helping you remember what it is you've read. Whether or not you refer back to the notes, the activity itself involves making decisions about what is important, and rephrasing the ideas into a shorter form – which helps the ideas crystallise. These 'crystals' stick in the brain much more than ideas you understand receptively without making any effort to remember them.

Nouns and verbs 38, 39, 46
Content words which carry the principal **meaning** of a text are usually nouns and verbs (such as 'pirates', 'burying')

Novels 15, 16, 97, 99, 142
When novels are **leisure reading**, read them in whatever way gives you pleasure. If you wish to **read faster**, use the techniques prescribed for texts with a **continuous story line.** For **study** purposes, use all the other techniques in this book as if they were **factual books**

O'Brien, John Anthony 135
Author of '*Silent Reading*' which made the point in 1921 that it was possible to read groups of words without **vocalising**

Omissions 18, 41, 56, 75
While reading, keep your mind engaged by looking for **patterns**, such as what is omitted as well as what is included.

Online reading 15, 18, 54, 83, 151, 152, 194
Many of the techniques people already use for reading online or **digitally** are included in the spd rdng approach because they are effective and efficient – similarly almost all the techniques in this book apply to online reading. See also **F-pattern**

Open mind 39, 73, 129, 136, 143, 151
Keeping an open mind, suspending your disbelief, when you are reading something challenging helps you read it more quickly to get an unbiased view before you bring your **critical** faculties to bear

Opinion 39, 41
Look out for words in a text which indicate the import of that section, for example words such as 'I think', 'in my view' indicate that the author is offering a personal opinion. Take this into account if you are reading critically. See also **Examples, Explanation, Importance, Lists, Watch out words**

Overview 18, 28, 61, 72, 75, 78, 81-2, 83, 97, 99, 101, 102, 103, 104, 115, 116, 143, 149
All the key areas encompassed by a subject (or a text), the big picture. The brain learns best by understanding generally what is involved in the subject before going into the details. The activity of **previewing** a book gives an overview of its contents. See also **Detail**

Pacer 45-6, 118, 136
Tool (finger, pen, computer cursor) to help establish a rhythm for your eyes to follow when looking through text, eg when using a **speed-reading pattern**

Palming 85
An **eye exercise** where you cover your eyes with your palms and gently massage around the eyes.

Pareto principle 27-8, 137, 147
The **80/20 rule**, which states that 20% of the effort you expend in any enterprise gives you 80% of the result you want to achieve, while the remaining 80% of your effort generates only the remaining 20% of the result. In reading, the implication is that if you are happy with achieving 80% of your **purpose**, you will gather five times as much information in the same time. Also, in most books, more than 80% of the message is contained in less than 20% of the words – hence looking for the **hot spots** of key information (see **Stauffer**). Named by **Joseph M Juran** after the Italian economist, **Vilfredo Pareto**, who first noticed that 80% of peas in his garden were produced by 20% of peapods, and that 80% of Italy's wealth was owned by 20% of its population.

Pareto, Vilfredo 28, 137
Italian economist after whom the **Pareto principle** (or **80/20 rule**) was named by **Joseph M Juran**

Parkinson's Law 64, 76
Parkinson's Law states that 'work expands to fill the time available'. Conversely, setting **time frames** for **work sessions** can speed up the reading process, since you do not allow yourself excess time 'to be filled'. See **thin slicing, 80-20 rule**

Patterns 40, 41
The **brain** is designed to notice patterns, so while reading, keep your mind engaged by looking for patterns such as **omissions, change, exaggeration, repetition, sameness, difference**. See also **Speed-reading patterns**

Pause 35, 36, 42, 84, 103, 105, 106, 112, 144
As part of getting into an optimal **state** for reading, pause to **plan** what you are about to do. You also pause after reading to **evaluate** how much you have achieved and **celebrate successes**

Pbook 150
A print book (what has always been called a 'book') - used to distinguish it from an **ebook**

Perfectionism 27-8, 147
The desire for perfection (eg wanting to know everything in a book, or **reading from cover to cover**) can significantly slow down your reading. Overcoming this desire by applying the **80/20 rule** can lead you to get **enough** ('perfect' is too much for most things) which will speed up your **learning**

Peripheral vision 9, 33, 34, 35, 36, 37, 42, 43, 46, 47, 49, 54, 70, 84, 88, 103, 105, 106, 144
Only a small part of what you look at is in clear focus at any one time, and that part is said to be in **foveal** or **macular vision**. Everything else, which is to a greater or lesser degree out of focus, is in peripheral vision. See also **Fixation**, **Saccades**, and for opening the peripheral vision see **Concentration point**

Perkins, David 112
Harvard University professor who proposes that **Reflective Intelligence** (RI) is key to learning

Personal development 100
When setting your **purpose** for some aspect of personal development, make sure you identify techniques which you can (and will) put into **practice**

Photographic memory 57
It is a misconception that **photoreading** involves developing a photographic memory. If you could 'take a mental photograph' of the page, you would still need to spend time 'reading it in your head'. Consciously sorting the information before you use techniques to help you remember it is more efficient, while **downloading** the book into your **non-conscious mind** allows your brain to sort out the information for itself.

Photoreading 92, 93, 137, 138
Looking very briefly (one second per page) at every page of a book, being confident that the information will be taken in by the **non-conscious mind** and taken into **long-term memory**, even when it is not seen consciously. Called **downloading** in the

"Cut doors and windows for a room; It is the holes which make it useful. Therefore profit comes from what is there; Usefulness from what is not there."
Lao Tzu

Spd Rdng approach, and **mental photography** or **subliminal photography** in the system developed by **Dr Richard Welch**, it is one (key) step in the **PhotoReading Whole Mind System**, where it is known as 'photoreading'. See also **Rapid reading**

PhotoReading Whole Mind System 37, 92, 137
A speed-reading system developed by **Paul Scheele** which involves **previewing**, setting a **purpose**, getting into a good **state** for reading, and **photoreading** (**downloading**), followed by a range of other **activation** techniques designed to bring the information to conscious awareness.

Physical exercises 84, 86-7
Physical exercise can enhance your optimal **state** for reading and taking in information. See also **Brain Gym**, **Eye exercises**

Physical factors 106-7, 144
The physical factors as you read, eg lighting, being comfortable, crossing your ankles, where you hold the book, etc, can greatly affect your ability to understand and take in information.

Plan 35, 36, 42, 43, 64, 84, 103, 105, 106, 144
As part of getting into an optimal **state** for reading, **pause** to plan what you are about to do.

Poems / Poetry 15, 16, 70
When poems are **leisure reading**, read them in whatever way gives you pleasure – including slowly and aloud if you wish. For **study** purposes, use all the other techniques in this book as if they were **factual books**. See also **Slow reading**

Popular highlights 62, 151
A feature on **Kindle** where anyone reading an **ebook** can highlight anything they think is important. When a few people have highlighted the same section, you can see those sections (dotted underlining) by switching on the popular highlights feature. Thanks to **crowd wisdom**, the highlights of a much-read ebook are often a good **summary** of the important points.

Practice 6, 23, 28, 55, 82, 93, 94, 95, 101, 111, 141
Reading alone is not enough to ensure **learning** or expertise – you also need to put what you read into practice

Prediction 29, 31, 134
Guessing/predicting in advance what you expect to read can speed up your reading (even if you're wrong, your brain becomes alert, purposeful, **questioning** – part of the optimal **state** for taking in information). See also **Comprehension questions**

Having a clear purpose (reason) for reading a book (eg in order to fulfil a task, or improve an aspect of your life) is one of the key techniques for identifying what information is important; a good purpose should be **SMART** (**Specific, Measurable, Achievable, Real, Timed**). Purpose is not to be confused with your **life goals** (eg passing an exam, getting a job).

Quality of information
Change your **mindset** from the **quantity of reading** to the quality of the information you have found

Quantity of reading
Change your **mindset** from the quantity of reading to the **quality of the information** you have found

Questioning
Having an alert, purposeful, questioning mind is part of the optimal **state** for taking in information when reading, so ask yourself questions about what you expect to read in advance of reading, and about the ideas as you read. See also **Comprehension questions, Prediction**

Random
One of the **skittering** techniques (a **speed-reading pattern**) used to look for **hot spots** of key information when (consciously) reading more quickly. As the name implies, in this case there is no clear pattern as such. Other patterns are **underlining, super-reading, capital-I shape, first and last, middles.** See also **F-pattern**

Rapid reading
Looking briefly at every page of a book (from cover to cover), frequently after having worked with it, as a means of consciously picking up bits of information one might have missed, while being confident that the **non-conscious mind** is taking in all of the information. See also **Downloading**

Reading
Deciphering symbols (letters) in order to understand the words and sentences which express the author's thoughts or message. Whereas writing demands that thoughts are expressed letter by letter, effective reading is a much faster process since it is possible to move onto the next word, sentence or idea as soon as one has understood the previous one. Unfortunately, reading and writing are frequently taught together as if they are similar

skills and many people do not progress beyond the basic ability to read words one at a time, possibly **vocalising** or **subvocalising** (saying the individual words to themselves) as they read.

Reading aloud 16, 155
Reading aloud is useful for teachers to judge whether learners are able to decipher words and sentences, but it is a very inefficient strategy for the reader to comprehend or remember the information. See also **Vocalising**

Reading critically 38-9, 141
Criticising challenging material as you read for the first time tends to slow you down and confirm your prejudices, whereas reading with an **open mind** allows you to absorb and understand the author's view more quickly; it also gives you a more unbiased view so that you are able to employ your **critical thinking** in a more balanced way.

Reading faster / Faster reading 6, 7, 9, 13, 34, 48, 55, 93, 108, 135, 136, 141, 145
There are several **Spd Rdng** techniques (**super-duper-reading**, **underlining** and other **speed-reading patterns**, etc) which are designed simply to speed up your reading, however the system offers many more techniques which allow you to process much more information, and help you **remember** and apply what you read to enhance your **learning**

Reading for pleasure 16, 21, 114, 142
When reading is a leisure activity, read in whatever way and at whatever speed gives you pleasure. **Spd Rdng** is about reading at different speeds appropriate to the task. However, remember that there is a great deal of pleasure and satisfaction to be derived from reading quickly, effectively and efficiently too. See also **Leisure reading, Slow reading**

Reading from cover to cover 10, 28, 40, 64, 78-9, 88, 92, 93, 97, 99
People are used to reading from cover to cover and when they don't they can have a **feeling of missing something**. This is partly just a feeling, which can be overcome with practice, success and using the **rapid reading** technique. It is actually not a big problem when spd rdng because your **purpose** makes it easier to focus on what you need. Also people tend to forget how much more they are likely to miss (and forget) with **conventional reading**

Reading problems 136, 143, 144, 145-50, 155
The spd rdng techniques automatically overcome many so-called reading problems (eg **regression, progression**) and can help with problems such as **dyslexia** and **subvocalising** or **vocalising**

being aware of your habitual ways of thinking and learning so that you can improve them.

Regression 136, 146-7
When your eyes jump back to text that has already been read – which can significantly slow down reading. See also **Progression**

Relax 32, 35, 36, 43, 63, 79, 88, 91, 96, 144
A relaxed, purposeful, **questioning** mind is an optimal **state** for taking in new information when reading

Relevant 20, 22, 25, 26, 57, 72, 73, 80, 99, 102, 152
It is important to look for information which is relevant to you and to use the appropriate or relevant techniques to do so. When setting your **SMART purpose** for reading, ask yourself, 'In what **context** will I use this information?'

Remembering 7, 10, 20, 25, 37, 43, 56-8, 59, 62, 66, 67, 68-9, 78, 83, 84, 91, 95, 97, 115, 141, 142, 144
Understanding what you read (**comprehension**) is just the first step of the process. It is also important to have strategies such as **note-taking**, **talking**, etc, in order to remember and be able to **recognise** or **recall** important information when it is needed. See also **Forgetting**

Repetition 38, 41, 56-7, 68, 90, 97, 129, 142
(1) There is a lot of repetition in most texts. You only need to read something once to understand it, particularly if you keep an **open mind**
(2) While reading, keep your mind engaged by looking for **patterns**, such as what is repeated.
(3) Repetition is also helpful for strengthening **memory**.

Reports 15, 16, 99
The **Spd Rdng** system was primarily designed to help you extract information from **factual books** (and reports, **journals**, etc), although it can be adapted for any kind of written material. See also **Emails, Novels, Poems**

Review 56, 57, 68-9, 75, 97, 105, 136, 141, 142
In order to fix new information in memory, it is helpful to review it at fixed intervals: after 1 day, 1 week, 1 month.

Rewards 112-3
Encourage yourself to **evaluate** your **work sessions**, and notice and **celebrate success** by giving yourself rewards

Rhizomapping 6, 57, 59-62, 63, 72, 73, 82, 83, 104, 105, 137, 141, 143
Procedure devised by Jan Cisek and Susan Norman, term coined

by Hugh L'Estrange, for **note-making** and **note-taking** in a random way. A rhizome is a complex root system. (The internet works in a kind of rhizomatic way.) The concept of rhizomatic thinking was originally developed by a French philosopher, **Gilles Deleuze**. To make a rhizomap, you make or take notes haphazardly on the page. Afterwards, look back at the notes and make links between them, by circling or underlining things in different colours, or drawing lines between them. It is often easier to make a rhizomap when you are not sure in advance what the key ideas are going to be. It can later be beneficial to reorganise notes into a more coherent **mindmap**. (This technique is currently unique to **Spd Rdng**.)

Saccades 33, 135
The eyes do not move smoothly and evenly along a line of text when reading. They jump from one point to the next. Each 'jump' is called a saccade. Each point where it stops is a **fixation**. The point of fixation is in focus (in **foveal** or **macular vision**), but words to either side will be slightly out of focus (in **peripheral vision**).

Sameness 40, 41
It is beneficial to look consciously for sameness and **difference** when reading. Sameness leads to greater understanding, while difference leads to new learning. It can also be beneficial to look for other **patterns**.

Sans-serif font 146
A typeface (or **font** such as Verdana, Arial, Helvetica) without the little strokes (serifs) added to some letters. These are commonly used online. See also **Serif font**

Scanning 21, 22, 93
Looking quickly through a text in order to find specific information you think it contains (what you actually do is similar to **skimming** and **rapid reading**, but the **purpose** of finding specific information is what defines the activity as scanning). We sometimes call this the **dictionary technique** (because you're using the book like a dictionary or book of reference to find specific information).

Scheele, Paul 37, 92, 136-7
Developer of the **PhotoReading Whole Mind System** which focused particularly on the **photoreading** step (known as **downloading** in **Spd Rdng**)

Schema 22, 84, 143
What you know, the amount of information you already have. The

more you know about something (the bigger your schema), the easier it is to take in information as you read.

Search 17, 18, 39, 62, 78, 102, 150, 152, 194
When you change your **mindset** from reading (**quantity**) to searching for information (**quality**) you will **read faster** and more effectively. When reading **online** or **digital** material, using the search facility will speed up your ability to find relevant information

Serif font 146
A typeface (or **font** such as Times) with little strokes (serifs) added to some letters. These are thought to be easier to read than **sans-serif fonts** (fonts without the serif).

Sheldrake, Rupert 120, 121, 128, 129, 130-2
Scientist and author of numerous books including '*The Sense of Being Stared At*' and '*Dogs That Know When Their Owners Are Coming Home*', who proposed the theory of **morphic fields**

Short-term memory 61
Conventional reading involves short-term memory, which forgets with time. Using techniques for **remembering** ensures that information is retained in **long-term memory**.

Skimming 21, 22, 93
Looking quickly through a text in order to discover its message (the technique is similar to **scanning** and **rapid reading**, but your purpose of getting a general understanding of what the text is about is what defines it as skimming). We sometimes refer to skimming as the **newspaper technique**, because most people already have the skill of looking quickly through newspapers to find out what they contain.

Skittering 45, 46, 50, 54, 71, 93, 99, 105
Term coined by **Dr Michael Bennett** for some of the more random **speed-reading patterns** such as any pattern of your choice (including **zigzag**) or completely **random** used to look for **hot spots** of key information when consciously reading more quickly. Other patterns are **underlining, super-reading, capital-I shape, first and last, middles.** See also **F-pattern**

Sleep 21, 57, 88, 90, 103, 105, 107
The brain processes new information during sleep which is therefore essential for **learning**

Slow reading 10, 12, 16, 23, 24, 30, 33, 39, 40, 45, 50, 51, 53, 63, 66, 70, 71, 78, 83, 89, 93, 97, 107, 108, 112, 115, 142, 148, 149, 150, 153, 155
It is good sometimes to satisfy the part of us which likes to read

slowly, and to recognise that it is important at times to read more slowly, for example when **proof-reading**, when concentrating on the sound of words, learning vocabulary, when grappling with complicated writing or concepts, or when you want to enjoy the way the author writes or immerse yourself in the atmosphere of a story. **Spd rdng** is about reading at different speeds appropriate to the task. See also **Dipping** and **Leisure reading** or **Reading for pleasure**

SMART 22, 105
A way of evaluating an effective **purpose** for reading.
The acronym stands for: **Specific, Measurable, Achievable, Real, Timed (Timely)**.

Smiling 9, 32, 43, 105
One element of getting into an optimal **state** for reading; smiling has been proven to help people take in information.

Spd Rdng (History of Spd Rdng 135-8, Spd Rdng System 105)
Name (suggested by Holly Craigs and coined by Susan Norman and Jan Cisek) for the flexible approach to reading described in this book which not only involves reading more quickly (**speed reading**), but also includes strategies for absorbing very much more information in the time available, and being able to apply and recall information as needed to incorporate reading into the learning process. It appeals particularly to the **non-conscious mind**, although only two techniques (**downloading** and **direct learning**) rely on it totally.

Specific 22, 23, 25, 72, 90, 94, 99, 101, 105
One of the criteria of a **SMART purpose**. You will get more information with a tightly defined **purpose** where you know the specific **context** in which the information will be used. See also **Measurable, Achievable, Real, Relevant, Timed, Timely**

Specific information 15, 16, 21, 45, 63, 119
Your purpose for reading will either be to get a book's message (use the **newspaper technique, skimming**) or to look for specific information, in which case you'll use the **dictionary technique (scanning)**. See also **Reference books**

Speed reading 1, 13, 30-1, 39, 71, 78, 93, 118, 135-8
Speed reading involves taking fewer **fixations** and/or using **speed-reading patterns** in order to read more quickly. It is basically a speedier version of **conventional reading** (whereas the whole **Spd Rdng** approach described in this book also involves strategies for identifying, **remembering** and applying the information).

Speed-reading patterns 13, 40, 45-55, 63, 71, 78, 99, 105, 115, 118-9
Patterns such as **super-reading, skittering (random, zigzag), capital-I shape, underlining, first and last, middles** used to look for **hot spots** of key information when consciously reading more quickly. See also **F-pattern**

State 6, 9, 32, 35-7, 43-4, 56, 63, 70, 71, 72, 73, 74, 75, 79, 84, 85, 99, 103, 106, 112, 118, 119, 132, 134, 137, 144-5, 147
Being in the right state while you are reading can enhance your ability to take in and retain information; the ideal state is to be relaxed, focused and **questioning**. Before you start reading, focus on the **concentration point** to open your **peripheral vision, pause** and **plan** what you're about to do, take a deep **breath, relax**, and **smile**. See also **Eye exercises, Brain gym, Breaks**

Stauffer, Dr Russell 38, 137
Author of 'Teaching Reading as a Thinking Process' (1969), in which he notes that in most books the **meaning** is carried by 4-11% of the words

Stops 33-4
When reading the eye moves in a series of jerks (**saccades**) and takes in information each time it makes a stop (a **fixation**). Taking fewer stops can speed up your reading.

Stress 43, 56, 91, 144, 155
It is thought that about 80% of learning and reading problems are caused by stress, which is why it is important to get into an optimal relaxed **state** before reading

Study / Students 16, 18, 56, 68, 79, 92, 100, 102-4, 106, 133, 138, 144
Spd Rdng skills are ideal for helping students to get on top of their studies, often allowing them to read up to 30 books a week. See also **Exams, Collaborative learning**

Subliminal Dynamics 136
Reading system developed by **Dr Richard Welch** which included **mental photography** or **subliminal photography**

Subliminal photography / Mental photography 92, 136
Term used in the system originally developed by **Dr Richard Welch** to mean looking very briefly (one second per page) at every page of a book, being confident that the information will be taken in by the **non-conscious mind** and go straight to **long-term memory**, even when it is not seen consciously. Called **downloading** in the **Spd Rdng** approach, it is one (key) step in

the **PhotoReading Whole Mind System**, where it is known as **photoreading**. See also **Rapid reading**

Subvocalising 34, 66, 70, 136, 137, 145-6
Saying words (silently) to yourself as you read, which may also involve moving your lips. Most people subvocalise to some extent, and when used appropriately, subvocalising is useful when the pronunciation of the word is important, and it can help with processing complex information, or information written in a complex way; however, it is also likely to slow down the reading process since it is only possible to speak (in English) at between about 70-240 **wpm**. Strategies to reduce word-for-word subvocalising include saying key words to yourself rather than whole sentences word for word, and/or mentally talking to yourself about what you're reading by questioning or summarising. A key benefit of reading faster is that you don't have time to subvocalise. See also **Vocalising**

Suggestopedia 90, 136
Accelerated learning teaching method developed by **Dr Georgi Lozanov** which drew on the amazing abilities of the **non-conscious mind**

Suffix effect 84
Although you remember more from the beginnings of sessions (**primacy effect**) and the end of sessions (**Recency effect**), if at the end of your work session you do something other than concentrate on your subject (eg ring a friend, look at your shopping list), that is what you will remember rather than the subject matter. This is know as the suffix effect.

Summaries 18, 83, 105
Short version of a text containing the **key ideas.** Research shows that people remember more for longer from reading summaries than from reading the original text.

Super-duper-reading 9, 42, 46, 47, 55, 71, 93, 99, 105, 118
Term coined by Jan Cisek and Susan Norman for looking quickly down the centre of pages or columns of text more quickly than you can consciously take in information in order to speed up the brain so that subsequent reading is quicker (this is essentially the same process as **super-reading**, but the purpose is different).

Super-reading 33, 34, 45, 46, 47-9, 52, 54, 71, 93, 99, 105, 118, 119
Looking quickly down the centre of a page or column to understand the meaning of the text or look for **hot spots** of key

information; one of the **speed-reading patterns** used for looking sequentially through a text (this is essentially the same process as **super-duper-reading**, but the purpose is different and super-duper-reading is done more quickly than you can consciously take in information). Other patterns are **underlining, skittering (zigzag, random), capital-I shape, first and last, middles.** See also **F-pattern**

Synthesising 141
A **higher level thinking and reading skill** which brings together ideas from different sources, possibly after they have been separated into their component parts (**analysing**)

Syntopic processing 22, 24, 60, 72-5, 76, 79, 81, 82, 101, 102, 104, 105, 108, 135, 137, 141, 143
Working with several books at one time in order to fulfil one purpose ('syntopical reading' was briefly described by **Mortimer Adler** in his book '*How to Read a Book*'); the procedure gives an unprecedented opportunity for comparing and contrasting the ideas of different authors, or for getting an **overview** of a new subject.

Tachistoscope 135
Device, first described by **A W Volkman** in 1859, which showed experimental subjects visual stimuli for controlled durations

Talking 56, 57, 61, 63, 67, 78, 105, 146
Talking about what you read is an effective technique (a) while you're reading for reducing **subvocalisation** and (b) after you're read for increasing retention.

Technological singularity 138
Term coined by **Vernor Vinge** and described in **Ray Kurzweil's** book '*The Singularity is Near*' which describes this combination of technology and the human brain which will have greater-than-human intelligence

Text messaging 29
Since the advent of text messaging, people are more used to making sense of incomplete or incorrect words and phrases

Thin-slicing 10, 19
Term used by **Malcolm Gladwell** in his book '*Blink*', which means taking the smallest slice of cake vertically in order to find out what the cake is like. Similarly the spd rdng techniques are designed to allow you to focus on the smallest amount of information possible to understand a subject or text.

first and last, middles. See also **F-pattern, Forwards and backwards**

Understanding 7, 12, 22, 24, 30, 38-9, 41, 42, 43, 48, 66, 81, 93, 97, 106, 108, 115, 136, 138, 139, 141, 142, 143, 144, 148, 151, 154
Understanding what you read (**comprehension**) is essential if you are to **remember** and make use of the information. The more information you have (the larger your **schema**), the easier it is to understand – so read more. The better your **vocabulary**, the easier it is to understand texts, and the best way to increase your vocabulary is to read more.

Unfocused reading 114
As well as focused, purposeful reading, it is also beneficial to read as much as possible of anything which interests you, since it isn't always possible to predict which information will be of use and it will add to your **schema**. This unfocused or **background reading** also helps create links between your subject and others, which is what leads to creativity.

Vinge, Vernor 138
Science fiction writer who coined the term **technological singularity**, a combination of technology and the human brain which will have greater-than-human intelligence described in **Ray Kurzweil**'s book '*The Singularity is Near*'

Visual language 138
Combination of images and words described in **Robert E Horn**'s book of the same name

Vocabulary 7, 70, 89, 114, 125, 136, 143, 153
One of the factors influencing **reading rate**: the larger your vocabulary, the quicker you will be able to read. Reading more will also help you enlarge your vocabulary.

Vocalising 34, 66, 145
Mouthing/saying words to yourself (aloud) while reading them one by one. This is often a remnant from when one learnt to read in childhood and is an extremely inefficient way of taking in information when reading. See **subvocalising** (saying the words silently) for strategies to stop vocalising.

Volkman, A W 135
German psychologist who, in 1859, first described a **tachistoscope**

Watch out words 39
Words such as 'not, however, although, on the other hand', which indicate that an alternative viewpoint is being expressed

Welch, Dr Richard 136
Self-styled 'father of **mental photography**', developer of '**Subliminal Dynamics**' and originator of **mental photography** or **subliminal photography** (which in **Spd Rdng** became **downloading**)

WIIFM 22, 105
Acronym standing for: What's In It For Me? Ask WIIFM when formulating your purpose for reading to help make sure you have a real **purpose**.

Wood, Evelyn Nielsen 136
Author of '*Reading Skills*' (1959) and founder of 'Evelyn Wood Speed Reading Dynamics' who coined the term '**speed reading**'

Work session 6, 26, 43, 55, 63-5, 72, 76, 78, 84, 93, 98, 99, 101, 105, 108, 112, 147
Working with texts for a fixed amount of time using a variety of techniques (eg **super-reading** or **skittering** to identify **hot spots** of key information) in order to fulfil one **purpose**. Recommended **time frames** for a work session are 20 minutes for one book or 75 minutes for a **syntopic processing** session with several books.

Wpm (words per minute) 8, 66, 136, 145
The measure of **reading rate** (speed); an average reading speed is 170-250 wpm.

Writing 30, 52, 59-62, 70, 79, 102, 138, 140-2, 148, 151, 154
(1) Writing for **note-taking** is very helpful for helping you remember what you read. (2) Although reading and writing share many characteristics, it is not helpful to teach them as if they are two sides of the same skill. You always need to write letter by letter and word by word, but it is usually more effective to read chunks of words for their **meaning**.

Zigzag 45, 50, 53, 99, 105, 119
One of the **skittering** techniques (a **speed-reading pattern**) used to look for **hot spots** of key information when (consciously) reading more quickly, which includes looking sequentially in a (wide or narrow) zigzag pattern down the page or column of text. Other patterns are **underlining, super-reading, capital-I shape, first and last, middles.** See also **F-pattern**

About the authors

Susan Norman is an expert photoreader, Spd Rdr and speed reading teacher. She has been running courses with Jan since 2004. She is an international presenter, a former Director of SEAL (Society For Effective Affective Learning), and author of more than 45 books on accelerated learning, language teaching and NLP (Neuro-Linguistic Programming) – see Resources.
susan@spdrdng.com

Jan Cisek was the first PhotoReading Instructor to be licensed in the UK in 2001 and since then he has taught the skills to thousands of people worldwide, as well as presenting at numerous conferences internationally. He is also an environmental psychologist interested in how learning is affected by the environment. *Spd Rdng – The Speed Reading Bible* is his first book.
jan@spdrdng.com

Acknowledgments

We would like to thank all the participants on our spd rdng and photoreading courses, whose learning experiences have helped us refine the approach. Thanks too to Hugh L'Estrange and Zoe Simone for their proof-reading, and to Holly Craigs for giving this system a name. Thanks to Jacek Utko and Anna Skowrońska who helped with the design of the book.

Translations

Many thanks to our translators. The following are (or will soon be) available online (check for the latest updates on our website www.spdrdng.com):
'Lctra Rpda – La Biblia de la Lectura Rápida' translated into Spanish by Peter Hearn
'Lttra Vlce – La Bibbia della Lettura Veloce' translated into Italian by Marisa Carrara
'SchnlLsn – die Schnelllesebibel' translated into German by Christiane White
'La Lctr Rpd – la bible de la lecture rapide' translated into French by Nadine Chadier
'Biblia Szybkiego Czytania' translated into Polish by Bożena Latek
'Ltr Dnm – A Bíblia de Leitura Dinâmica' translated into Portuguese by Inês Teles
'Spd Rdng – Bibeln för Snabbläsning' translated into Swedish by John Wannerot

Resources

www.spdrdng.com – our site is regulsrly updated with resources (FAQ, Glossary, Tips, Videos, etc) Our blog has the latest info and research on speed reading, reading, etc. The Links page is in the footer of our website.

Free Kindle for smartphones, mobile devices and PC/Mac
You don't need to own a Kindle device to read Kindle ebooks. Download a FREE Kindle app to start reading Kindle books on your computer and mobile devices. www.amazon.co.uk

Ebooks
www.amazon.co.uk – Kindle
iTunes www.apple.com/itunes
www.books.google.com
All classics which are out of copyright can be downloaded for free. Just google the title, for example, "Sherlock Holmes free".

Learn how to search on Google
Google 'Basic search help' for tips to save you time and frustration when searching for information online.

Summaries – go to Amazon and search for:
Passing Time in the Loo: Volume 1, 2, 3 and Shakespeare
Most classics have been summarised on Wikipedia.

Mindmapping software
Always try the trial version to see if it's what you need.
http://freemind.sourceforge.net – FREE software
www.inspiration.com
www.mind-mapping.co.uk
SimpleMindX – iPhone app – on iTunes
MindNode – FREE for Mac – on iTunes

TED – inspirational talks on almost everything from technology, education and design www.ted.com

Top online courses (free)
Khan Academy – www.khanacademy.org
Udacity – www.udacity.com
Open Learn – http://openlearn.open.ac.uk
TED – ed – http://ed.ted.com
iTunes University – download the app: https://itunes.apple.com

BrainGym
www.braingym.com

EFT (Emotional Freedom Technique) – a simple technique for managing stress – www.eftuniverse.com

Learning languages
Michel Thomas tapes: Spanish, German, Italian and French - the best introduction to these languages (no memorising, no books approach) www.michelthomas.com
Accelerated Learning (Spanish, German, Italian and French) by Colin Rose www.acceleratedlearning.com

Get Things Done – The Efficiency Guru – www.davidco.com

Children's Reading
Recommended books for children's learning are: *'The Great Little Book of Learning'* and *'The Great Little Book of Revision'* both by John O'Brien, and *'Accelerated Learning Pocketbook'* by Brin Best. See also numerous books by Eva Hoffmann: *'The Learning Adventure'*, *'Introducing Children to...: Mind Mapping in 12 Easy Steps'*, *'Introducing Children to...: Their Intelligences'*, *'Introducing Children to...: Their Senses'*

Dyslexia
For parents or teachers who want to help young people who may have dyslexia, we recommend *'Dyslexia Pocketbook'* by Julie Bennett. Two other books of interest are: *'Unicorns Are Real'* by Barbara Meister-Vitale and *'The Gift of Dyslexia'* by Ronald Davis

Other books by Susan Norman
Susan Norman, one of the authors of this book and the spd rdng approach, has written more than 45 books, many on teaching and learning. A couple which might interest spd rdrs are:
'In Your Hands – NLP for teaching and learning' (with Jane Revell)
'Handing Over – NLP-based activities for language learning'
'Transforming Learning – an introduction to SEAL approaches' – a compendium of information about accelerated learning
'Stepping Stones – First Lessons in Accelerated Learning for use with children aged 7-11' (with Eva Hoffman)

Notes

Notes

Notes